Agile, DevOps and Cloud Computing with Microsoft Azure

Hands-on DevOps practices implementation using Azure DevOps

by

Mitesh Soni

FIRST EDITION 2019

Copyright © BPB Publications, India

ISBN: 978-93-88511-902

Distributors:

BPB PUBLICATIONS
20, Ansari Road, Darya Ganj
New Delhi-110002
Ph: 23254990/23254991

DECCAN AGENCIES
4-3-329, Bank Street,
Hyderabad-500195
Ph: 24756967/24756400

MICRO MEDIA
Shop No. 5, Mahendra Chambers,
150 DN Rd. Next to Capital Cinema,
V.T. (C.S.T.) Station, MUMBAI-400 001
Ph: 22078296/22078297

BPB BOOK CENTRE
376 Old Lajpat Rai Market,
Delhi-110006
Ph: 23861747

Published by Manish Jain for BPB Publications, 20 Ansari Road, Darya Ganj, New Delhi-110002 and Printed by him at Repro India Ltd, Mumbai

Dedicated to

Dada, Dadi, Shreyu, My Parents, Jigi, Priyanka, Ruby, Mayur and Vinay Kher

About the Author

Mitesh Soni is a DevOps engineer. He is in love with the DevOps culture and concept. Continuous improvement is his motto in life with existing imperfection.

Mitesh Soni has worked on multiple DevOps practices implementation initiatives. His primary focus is on improvement of the existing culture of an organization or a project using Continuous Integration and Continuous Delivery. He believes that attitude and dedication are one of the biggest virtues that can improve professional as well as personal life!

He has good experience on DevOps consulting and he enjoys talking about DevOps and *culture* transformation using existing practices and improving them with open source or commercial tools.

Mitesh Soni always believes that DevOps is a cultural transformation and it is facilitated by People, Processes and Tools. DevOps transformation is a tool's agnostic approach.

He loves to give training and share his knowledge with the community. He has keen knowledge of programming and is aware about different languages/frameworks/platforms such as Java, Android, iOS, NodeJS, Angular. His main objective is to get enough information related to projects in a way that it is helpful in creating end to end automation pipeline.

His favorite tool / services for DevOps Practices implementation is Azure DevOps and Jenkins in commercial and open sources categories respectively.

In his leisure time, he likes to walk in the garden, do photography and go for cycling. He prefers to spend time in peaceful places.

About the Reviewer

Rohit Anand is an Azure Consultant who has exposure to Microsoft Azure / Azure Stack and DevOps technologies. He is very passionate about technologies like Azure Identity Solution, DevOps, Hybrid Cloud deployment and other services like Machine Learning & AI. He shares his knowledge with the community by writing technical articles, blog posts and frequently speaking at multiple technology community.

Acknowledgement

I wish to thank Ruby, without her this book would not have seen it's dawn. She has been with me in the thick and thins, I thank her for inspiring me to take on challenges and helping me to make the right decisions. Her presence itself has made my life easier in tough times. I thank her for being an indifferent part of the story of my life, the world is a better place with her. Her patience and understanding along with her commitment towards our relationship has helped me grow into a better human being, I thank her for everything she has done for me.

With this opportunity I would like to thank Nitesh, my family members, Akkusss, Nalini and her Family, Varsha and Mantola, Radhika and her Parents, Mukund, Ramya-Srivats, Radhika's all cousins, Prajakta – Keep Singing, Priyanka S, Gauri, Aishwarya (Hitler), Avanti, Mitul, Kanak, Bapu, Vimal, Ashish, Navrang, Dharmesh, Anupama-Mihir and Priyanka-Hemant, Rohini, Yohan, Bhavna, Amit, Vijay, Priya G, Harshal, Sharvil, Apoorva S, Rinka, Vishakha S, Pradnya B, Viral I, Chaitali, Parinda, Hetal, Sonal, Kesar, Aruna, Arpita, Jinesh, Vihan, Kim and Yaashi, Kirti, Bindiya, Jai, Nitesh, Munal, Deepika, Pragya, Jyotiben, Khushboo, Beena, Ragni, Rohan C, Chintan, Vijay, Nikul, Paresh, Raju, Yogendra, Ajay, Nikunj and Masi, Saputara Group, Jayesh & his family, Ramesh and his Family, Munni Bhabhi and her Family, Jyoti N, Vishwajit, Shrini, Bharti, Chitra Madam, Kittu and Family, N.D.Patel, Oracle Team, Siddharth, My Village, School and College Friends, and Teachers for always being there for me.

Special Thanks to Gowri-Arya, Sourabh Mishra, Sid, Rita, and Sudeep for always supporting me.

Last but not the least I would like to express my gratitude towards the DevOps team and the BPB Publications' production team without whom my thoughts could not have been shaped into this beautiful book.

– *Mitesh Soni*

Preface

In the last few years, DevOps has been very popular and has become the point of discussion at the time of project kick-off meetings. The main aim to adapt to the DevOps culture is quality and offer faster time to market. Quality matters and hence DevOps implementation matters too. It is about changing the existing culture and transforming the mindset to understand that quality is an essential part of routine. Continuous improvement with continuous practices such as Continuous Integration, Continuous Delivery, Continuous Testing, Continuous Planning, Continuous Monitoring, and Continuous Innovation helps to create a unique culture based on the existing best practices.

The DevOps practices implementation is a tools-agnostic approach and any tool whether it is open source or commercial can be used to serve the purpose.

This book will be helpful to learn the basic and advance concepts of DevOps and the DevOps practices implementation. This book is divided into nine chapters and it provides a detailed description of the core concepts of DevOps with the use of Microsoft Azure DevOps and Microsoft Azure Cloud.

Chapter 1, introduces the concepts of Agile principles and Scrum. It explainsthe waterfall model, Agile values and principles and provides details on how Agile has changed the game for organizations in their approaches.

Chapter 2, covers the DevOps Practices implementation that helps organizations and individuals experience faster time to market by achieving transformation culture using people, process, and tools.

Chapter 3, introduces the concept of Cloud computing, its different models and benefits. It is important to understand how Cloud can play a game changer in DevOps adoption.

Chapter 4, addresses details regarding different Agile-based frameworks. It helps gain an understanding of Azure DevOps Boards service to manage planning of multiple processes such as Basic, CMMI, Agile, and Scrum.

Chapter 5, addresses details about code repositories. It helps gain an understanding of Azure repos and best practices for branch management. It also covers topics such as Hosted Git Azure Repo, Clone Repository in Azure DevOps, fork repository in Azure DevOps, branches, and tags, and code management in Azure DevOps Dashboard.

Chapter 6, provides a brief description about Microsoft Azure Services and other important details about Microsoft Azure Cloud. It covers topics such as Microsoft Azure, resource groups, role-based access, and Microsoft Azure Services.

Chapter 7, provides a brief description about Microsoft Azure Services and other important details about Microsoft Azure Cloud. It covers topics such as Infrastructure as a Service -VMs, Platform as a Service - Azure App Services, Monitoring of resources, and high availability and fault tolerance.

Chapter 8, includes an overview of build definitions available in Microsoft Azure DevOps. It helps understand how continuous integration is configured in Azure DevOps. It covers topics such asbuild pipeline implementation, Java application - pipeline YAML, unit tests, and hosted agent - Continuous Code Inspection.

Chapter 9, includesan overview of release definitions available in Microsoft Azure DevOps. It covers topics such as Azure Resource Manager Service Connection and Continuous Delivery - release pipeline.

Chapter 10, covers hands-on lab in a stepbystep manner to implement a multi-stage pipeline that is a preview feature in Azure DevOps. This chaptercontains the automation pipeline in the form of YAML script. The script consists of stages and jobs for Continuous Integration and Continuous Delivery. It explains Code Coverage and Build Quality Checks.

Errata

We take immense pride in our work at BPB Publications and follow best practices to ensure the accuracy of our content to provide with an indulging reading experience to our subscribers. Our readers are our mirrors, and we use their inputs to reflect and improve upon human errors if any, occurred during the publishing processes involved. To let us maintain the quality and help us reach out to any readers who might be having difficulties due to any unforeseen errors, please write to us at :

errata@bpbonline.com

Your support, suggestions and feedbacks are highly appreciated by the BPB Publications' Family.

Table of Contents

CHAPTER 1
Overview of Agile and Scrum Framework

Agile is an idea or a philosophy. Every organization want to become *Agile*. They want to adopt Agile principles to achieve better quality and faster time to market. However, for Agile to make sense, it is important to understand the traditional waterfall model approach, and understand its challenges. I will share my experiences whenever it is relevant. The important thing to consider here is that I have tried to map a lot of concepts with Azure DevOps dashboard mapping for better visualization. In this book, I am focusing on Azure DevOps, however, the book will also cover Agile, Scrum, cloud computing, DevOps, and the continuous practices of DevOps.

Structure

In this chapter, we will cover the following topics:

- Waterfall model
- Agile way of software development
- Scrum
- The Scrum Team
- Product Backlog
- Scrum events

- **Certified Scrum Master (CSM)** Certification
- How Agile/Scrum Framework brings culture change?

Objective

The aim of this chapter is to explain the details of the Waterfall model, Agile values, and principles, and provide details on how Agile has changed the game for organizations in their approaches.

Waterfall model

The Waterfall model was one of the most popular models to develop software before Agile arrived. It is simple and easy to understand. Waterfall model is a linear and sequential model where each phase in **Software Development Life Cycle (SDLC)** starts when the previous one is completed. There are different phases in the Waterfall model as described in the following diagram:

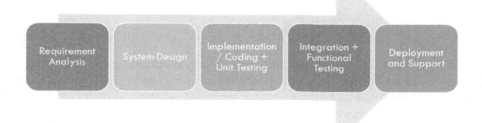

Figure 1.1: Waterfall model

The Waterfall model is extremely useful when all the requirements are clear and well defined. Organizations know exactly what needs to be implemented. Technology and market are not dynamic; all skilled resources are available to implement all the features.

However, we know that reality is different. *Tom Clancy* has rightly said, *The difference between fiction and reality? Fiction has to make sense.* At times, based on market situation, technology evaluation, and competition, the reality is far different than what Waterfall model can cope up with. Let's understand what are the challenges in the Waterfall approach. The following are the challenges faced by the Waterfall model:

- Product or application is available only after entire lifecycle is completed.
- It results into surprises or a shock if requirements are not understood correctly.

Figure 1.2: Expectations vs. Reality

- Customers or end users have no say once a phase starts.
- No mechanism to integrate and adopt continuous feedback from the customers.
- Very difficult to accommodate changes even if market scenario requires them.

The above-mentioned challenges of waterfall model made way for Agile values and principles, as well as frameworks that implement those values and principles.

Agile way of software development

Agile is an idea or a philosophy. First time ever, *Divide and Rule* policy is helping businesses never like before. Divide the feature implementation in different phases, take continuous feedback from the customer, and rule over customer's heart and mind. Agile brings pace to development and delivery, while DevOps practices make sure that the pace is maintained, and hence it complements Agile. Consider Agile as an engine of a train while DevOps practices or continuous practices or automation as a smooth track.

The Agile Manifesto was created in 2001 to find better approaches to build software or application. The Agile Manifesto includes four values and twelve principles. It helps to integrate new cultures in application development process. The main objective is to have a high quality package with faster time to market.

Values

There are four values according to Agile Manifesto:

1. Individuals and Interactions
2. Working Software
3. Customer Collaboration
4. Responding to Change

1. Processes and Tools
2. Comprehensive Documentation
3. Contract Negotiation
4. Following a Plan

Figure 1.3: Agile values

Let's understand the most important of all values, which is explained as follows:

- **Individuals and interactions over processes and tools:** People or professionals are more important in the process of transforming existing cultures. Processes and Tools are important but not more than people. People across the level drive the organizations and hence they are more important to bring the change. With respect to culture change, interaction within project teams, across different locations in the same business unit, and within different business units of an organization are important.

- **Working software over comprehensive documentation:** Traditionally, software development process includes many types of documentation such as requirements documentation, UI design documentation, architecture design documentation, technical documentation, quality assurance documentation, user documentation, and so on. Effective documentation with development process is an additional work. Agile inspires a change where it manages documentation in the form of epics, user stories, tasks, and so on. Agile supports minimum yet sufficient documentation, and hence the focus remains on working software.

- **Customer collaboration over contract negotiation:** Customer collaboration at every stage of application development not only helps to gain customer confidence, but also helps to build a high-quality application according to customer expectations. Continuous feedback helps in faster time to market. It avoids unnecessary delays.

- **Responding to change over following a plan:** Change is constant. Improvement is impossible without change. In the Waterfall model, it is very difficult to inject change due to its nature. All the planning and priorities are fixed in the beginning, and stakeholders are stuck in case of any change. Iterative approach of agile makes it easier to integrate any change or reset priorities. In Agile, plan is flexible and due to its sheer nature of short delivery time, it is easy to integrate change.

Principles

There are 12 principles according to Agile Manifesto, as shown in the following diagram:

| 1. Our highest priority is to satisfy the customer through early and continuous delivery of valuable software. | 2. Welcome changing requirements, even late in development. Agile processes harness change for the customer's competitive advantage. | 3. Deliver working software frequently, from a couple of weeks to a couple of months, with a preference to the shorter timescale. |

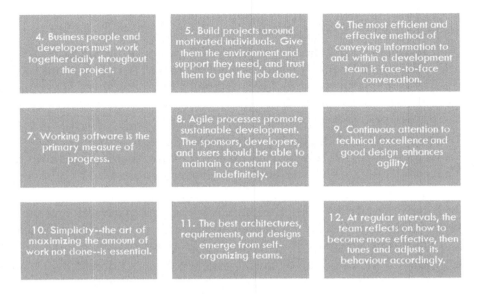

Figure 1.4: Agile principles

Let's understand the most important of all principles, which is explained as follows:

- Our highest priority is to satisfy the customer through early and continuous delivery of valuable software: The *show and tell* or *iteration review* is a meeting where all stakeholders review the work and give their feedback. It is better to give a product with minimal feature to customer, take feedback, and integrate it to gain confidence and customer satisfaction.

- Welcome changing requirements, even late in development. Agile processes harness change for the customer's competitive advantage: Culture to accommodate feasible changes throughout the development process helps customers gain competitive advantage. It also encourages the Development Team to implement a feature or fix a bug without resistance.

- Deliver working software frequently, from a couple of weeks to a couple of months, with a preference to the shorter timescale: Shorter delivery cycles or Sprints mean continuous delivery of application or software to customers. It helps gather feedback, which it integrates in the development process to meet customer requirements.

- Business people and developers must work together daily throughout the project: Communication and collaboration are main pillars of Agile and DevOps culture. It is easier to implement features which fulfill acceptance criteria when all the stakeholders are aligned.

- Build projects around motivated individuals. Give them the environment and support they need, and trust them to get the job done: People, processes, and tools are important part of this initiative of culture transformation with people as the center. Happy, inspired, and dedicated professionals meet customer requirements more often than not.

- The most efficient and effective method of conveying information to and within a Development Team is face-to-face conversation: Direct communication is most effective with co-located Development Team members. It is important to enable it, instead of wasting time in long discussions, by working within the frameworks that implement Agile principles.

- Working software is the primary measure of progress: It is always good to deliver software that functions as expected by the customer or the end user. That is the ultimate measurement of satisfaction, success, and improvements.

- Agile processes promote sustainable development. The sponsors, developers, and users should be able to maintain a constant pace indefinitely: Agile frameworks enforce continuous development by nature. It allows learning from past mistakes to estimate better and work efficiently.

- Continuous attention to technical excellence and good design enhance agility: Apt technical and behavioral skills, minimum yet required team size, efficient implementation of Agile principles, and efficient design help to maintain speed for faster time to market and adopt change.

- Simplicity-- Understand requirements and implement what meets acceptance criteria. Follows **KISS (Keep It Simple Stupid)** principle.

- The best architectures, requirements, and designs emerge from self-organizing teams: Self-organizing teams take responsibility and bring transparency with regular communication and collaboration. Technical competency, behavioral aspects, trust, transparency, continuous improvement, and continuous innovation are some of the important traits of a good team.

- At regular intervals, the team reflects on how to become more effective, then tunes and adjusts its behavior accordingly: Retrospective reflection plays an important part in Agile development as it drives the team to continuously improve itself by discussing past actions and learning from them. Learning can be in the form of improvements, such as communication, collaboration, process, technical skills, and so on.

Following are some of the benefits of Agile:

- Fixed and clear goals
- Visibility
- Known deadlines – incremental product development
- Continuous feedback from customer
- Productivity gains for Dev's team
- Faster time to market
- Self-organized and cross-functional team

Frameworks

Agile is a philosophy. There are frameworks which implement this philosophy for quick and qualitative software product. Let's have a look at some of the frameworks:

Frameworks	History	Description	Details
Scrum	*Hirotaka Takeuchi* and *Ikujiro Nonaka* introduced the term scrum for product development in their 1986 Harvard Business Review article. In 2002, *Schwaber* with others founded the Scrum Alliance. *Ken Schwaber* and *Jeff Sutherland* created The Scrum Guide.	Work is completed in multiple time box iteration with each iteration or Sprint having a potentially releasable product in form of product Increment.	It is composed into roles, Scrum events, and Scrum artifacts.
Kanban	Toyota engineer *Taiichi Ohno* invented the Kanban framework.	It keeps focus on capacity and demands and balances them out.	Pull mechanism is used to fetch the work based on capacity.
Scrumban	Objective of Scrumban to make it relatively easier for Scrum Teams to explore Kanban.	Management framework that provides hybrid approach of Scrum and Kanban.	Important role of management and it allows specialized teams while Scrum doesn't.
Extreme programming	*Kent Beck* created Extreme programming during his work on the **Chrysler Comprehensive Compensation(C3)** system payroll project.	Use best practices to the extreme level.	Programming in pairs or doing extensive code review. Unit Test Coverage of all code.

Table 1.1: Agile based Frameworks

We will understand Scrum in detail in the following sections. In this book, we will use Scrum only in Azure DevOps.

Scrum

According to the Scrum Guide, *Scrum is a process framework that is lightweight and simple to understand within which people can address complex adaptive problems, while productively and creatively delivering products of the highest possible value.* Scrum is widely used for application development where time to market is quick. It is used synonymously with Agile, which says a lot about its popularity. It is a part of the strategy in many organizations to become Agile within a specified duration. In a highly competitive market, technology innovations and ease of using innovations have helped in recognizing the true value of Agile and Scrum over the time.

As DevOps is a culture and not a tool, technology or methodology; similarly, Scrum is a framework and not a process, technique, or a definitive method. We will discuss DevOps and Scrum in detail in the coming chapters.

To understand the SCRUM framework, let's understand how it is different from the Waterfall approach:

Figure 1.5: Scrum Framework

Let's see more details of each iteration in a diagrammatic manner:

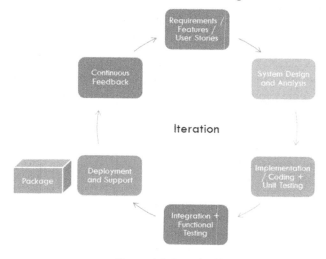

Figure 1.6: Iteration/Sprint in Scrum

Attributes of Scrum

The attributes of Scrum is as follows:

- Incremental
- Iterative
- Provides high priority features in product increments
- Continuous feedback
- Effective communication and collaboration
- Cross functional teams
- Suitable for product development, web, and mobile app development
- Checks and balances

Scrum Framework consists of events, artifacts, roles, rules, agreement, and so on, as shown in the following diagram:

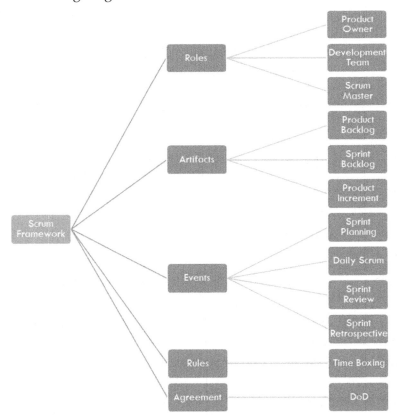

***Figure 1.7:** Scrum Events, Artifacts, Roles, Rules, Agreement*

Now let's see everything in one diagram, which is as follows:

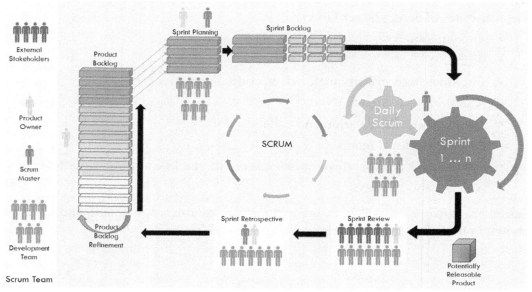

Figure 1.8: *How Scrum Framework works*

In the following sections, we will try to understand all the components of the Scrum Framework.

The Scrum Team

There are three important roles in the Scrum Team:

- A product owner
- The development team
- A Scrum master

Scrum team is a self-driven team, and the main objectives of the Scrum team are as follows:

- To deliver high quality product incrementally with every iteration
- To get continuous feedback from customer
- To improve processes based on the feedback

Product Owner

The **Product Owner (PO)** is responsible for shaping the product or application based on her understanding of needs of an end user. It is PO's responsibility to make sure that every member of the Scrum Team is on board and that they understand the vision. The PO comes to the rescue whenever there is any confusion regarding any feature. Let's meet the PO:

Figure 1.9: Product Owner

PO's job is similar to the job of DevOps lead or architect with respect to what is expected. It is a full-time job:

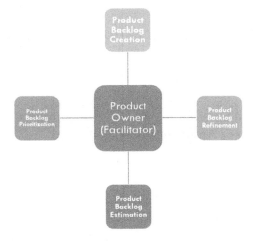

Figure 1.10: Product Owner's Work

There is a popular phrase in cricket: *Little bit of this and little bit of that* player (a batsman who can bowl a bit or a bowler who can bat a bit) can't win you matches. Specialists are required to do the Job and hence Full time PO is a must.

Following are some important things to know about the PO:

- PO is a guide, leader, takes ownership, and is accountable for:
  - o Collaborating with business-side stakeholders.
  - o Collaborating with Scrum Master.
  - o Collaborating with Development Team to explain user stories or **Product Backlog Items(PBIs)** clearly.
- Knowledgeable and empowered decision maker to facilitate product/ application implementation process, such as:

- o   PO has complete understanding of product/application and business priorities.
- PO is a person, and not a group of individuals, who is responsible to achieve product vision by:
  - o   Understanding the problems faced by an end user, who then maps it with solutions.
- Primary responsibility of a PO is to set priorities for the features/PBIs Product Backlog in Backlog.
- PO re-prioritizes the Product Backlog as per requirements to achieve product vision, and enhances the value of the end product. PO plays an important part in refining the Product Backlog.
- PO controls whether a product can be released or not, considering the developed features and effectiveness of the product Increment,
  - o   Review the work of Development Team, and provide feedback considering the definition of done.
- PO keeps transparency and visibility with respect to Scrum framework components.
- Represents business side of product development activities, however, can work as a **Business Analyst(BA)** as well
  - o   PO has complete understanding of what is required, and hence PO has the best seat to write high level test cases for verification of features
- PO can attend all the Scrum events described in the upcoming section.
- PO can be a part of a development or other technical activity as well.
- PO makes a product or an application relevant, considering the market scenario, technology evaluation, and other factors.

PO needs to make sure that effective product Increment, which satisfies **Definition of Done (DoD),** is released. PO can accept user stories that are implemented within the boundaries of DoD, and can also reject those that are not implemented within the boundaries of DoD. Refer to the following table:

Scrum event	Activities/Contribution
Sprint Planning	Explains PBIs to The Scrum Team
Sprint	To help in development, to clarify any doubt, give feedback on user story completion and whether it meets DoD
Daily scrum	Observer

| Sprint review | Verifies all the Sprint backlog items against DoD |
| Sprint retrospective | Participant cum observer |

Table 1.2: Product Owner's role in Scrum Events

My experience

There was a UK-based project in around 2013-2014, where it was my first encounter with Scrum. One of the solution architects from the customer side was our PO. He used to be available for all the discussions. In our case, Business Analysts from our side at customer location used to set priorities to PBIs after discussing them with the PO. He used to come once in a while in daily Scrum but never used to interfere. The PO used to provide us all the documents, architecture diagram, sometimes even tell us how to document. He used to clarify each and every doubt on priority. He was just a ping or a mail away, and that was a fascinating experience. One of the challenging parts was a PO who was a solution architect. Being a solution architect, we often had technical discussions, and not just business-side discussion with him. It was challenging, but it helped us as a Development Team to achieve product Increment more efficiently. In one line, the PO was everywhere as a facilitator from the business side.

Scrum Master

The Scrum Master is an Agile coach and a leader in an organization or a business unit. The main responsibility of a Scrum Master is as a facilitator. The Scrum Master makes sure that Scrum values, Scrum principles, and Scrum practices are followed with discipline, and everyone in the Scrum Team is aware of Agile, Scrum framework, Scrum artifacts, Scrum events, Scrum roles, and so on. The Scrum Master's role is to create effective and efficient work environment and maximize the quality of a product or an application by facilitating Scrum Team and an organization as well. Let's meet the Scrum Master.

Figure 1.11: Scrum Master

Essentially, the Scrum Master serves as a bridge between the PO and the Development Team by keeping Scrum Framework at a focal point. Take a look at the following points:

- Scrum Master is not a Project Manager but a change agent, Agile practitioner, and a brand ambassador of Scrum
- Facilitates scrum adoption across the organization
- Helps the team to be self-reliant, self-organized, and self-managed
- Protects the team from external interferences
- Encourages the team to follow best practices in specific phases of application lifecycle management
- Focus on impediments to resolve them as early as possible to facilitate the Scrum Team
- Facilitates in Scrum events
- Mentoring the Development Team if Scrum is new for the team and the organization
- Facilitates the scrum team for productivity gains
- Facilitates the scrum team to understand vision, scope, PBIs Product Backlog, and the importance of effective communication and collaboration
- Helps the Development Team to excel in their way of implementation, based on her/his experience in the past Scrum-based projects
- Motivates team members to go the extra yard in implementation of the best practices in different technical areas
- Scrum Mater helps the team to realize their potential to increase the efficiency
- Facilitates the PO so that the PO can execute his role effectively

Essentially, the Scrum Master is a servant leader whose prime role is as a coach or a leader to serve the Scrum team. Scrum Master is not needed to have specialization in any technology but some technical know-how serves as a game changer. Let's see the contribution of Scrum Master in some of the Scrum events:

Scrum event	Activities/Contribution
Sprint Planning	Facilitator
Sprint	Facilitator
Daily scrum	Facilitator
Sprint review	Facilitator
Sprint retrospective	Facilitator

Table 1.3: Scrum Master's Role in Scrum events

Another important question that we came across during multiple projects was the role of a Manager. Yes, traditionally, a Manager is found in the culture of all organizations. Often, the Scrum Master's role is considered as a Manager's, which is an incorrect interpretation. Managers have a say in the implementation, and they are authorized in traditional approaches, while Scrum Master is a servant leader and a facilitator. Development Team decides and authorizes work on a Sprint backlog and not the Scrum Master.

However, the role of Managers is not completely irrelevant even though it is a defined one in Scrum. In my experience, Managers play an important role in selecting team members, changing teams based on requirements or on performance criteria, taking decisions in cases of major changes in architecture or upgradation, empowering teams to take decisions in cases of conflicts, implementing best practices for development, testing, cloud, and DevOps, guiding the team for efficient product Increment.

My experience

In one of my projects, the Scrum Master had higher level of technical know-how, knowledge of best practices in development, some knowledge about test automation, and how it helps in Sprints for faster time to market. It helped us a lot to bring automation to our business unit's culture. Scrum Master used to share past experiences in projects, the best practices they used, and what we could learn from them. He not only made sure that we adopted test automation, but he motivated team members to implement PoCs that could help the team when not receiving data from the backend. He managed the team members well as a Scrum Master. He made the team members realize that they are good for the role even when they were not sure about their own capabilities. After a while, with constant motivation from the Scrum Master, team members gained confidence, which helped the team. His idea was of improving all the time, using new technology, using collective technical knowledge, and seeing what is not feasible at first glance. One of the good qualities he had was using Agile values and principles for even real-life situations. Once, I asked him the reason, and he replied, *Practice makes a Scrum Master Perfect!* The more he used Scrum values, principles, and practices in real life situations, the easier it became for him to apply Scrum values, principles, and practices in the project seamlessly. I asked, how? He replied, "Once you start doing it frequently, it becomes a habit, and your habits form your routine for which you don't need to go the extra yard." One of his qualities which I observed was his honesty towards the role and transparency. He was very clear and straightforward in his communication, and he never had any hidden agendas. He made sure that team members are recognized for their efforts.

His role was not limited to one project as a Scrum Master, considering his initiatives and actions. He tried to bring in the Agile / Scrum culture in all the teams across locations by trainings and facilitating them for using Scrum effectively. To our surprise, his relations and communication with the PO was fascinating to all of us. The PO used to discuss a lot of PBIs Product Backlog with him and he participated in many Product Backlog grooming activities.

In another project, we had two Scrum Masters, namely, Onsite and Offshore. Earlier we had only one Scrum Master from Onsite, and hence we had communication or availability issues due to different time zones. This issue was addressed when we had offshore Scrum Master later on.

Scrum Master's job is based on the need of a Development Team. If the team is new to Scrum, then full-time job is essential from the SM's perspective. If Development Team is well aware of Scrum practices, then it is possible for the Scrum Master to take up a combination of roles. I worked as a Scrum Master as well as a DevOps lead for four months, as the team was self-organized and didn't require my fulltime attention. A Scrum Master can manage two teams based on her availability, and considering how self-organized both teams are! However, a Scrum Master and a PO cannot be the same as it creates conflicts and confusion, considering that the Scrum Master's roles and responsibilities for the Scrum Team.

Development Team

Let's discuss the Development Team and its contribution. The role of the Development Team is to implement product Increments in a Sprint with high priority feature list at a given point of time according to the vision:

Figure 1.12: Development team

Following are some of the important details about Development Team:

- Cross-functional team with *size > 3 and < 9 or 7 +/- 2*: Larger the team, it is difficult to communicate and collaborate effectively, while smaller the team, it is difficult to implement product Increment in a timely manner
- Skills include development, testing, cloud computing, automation, UX designers, BAs, and so on, based on the requirement of expertise in the project (One project I worked had Two Scrum teams 1) Onsite 2) Offshore; each having a Scrum Master, however, development was done offshore. In another project, it was a team of 15 members due to priority of the project (3 iOS developers + 3 Android developers + 2 Middleware developers +

3 Sitecore developers + 2 Testers + 1 UX designer + 1 Cloud and DevOps expert)

- Responsible for implementing solution according to best practices in specific domains, implementing design patterns, and using object-oriented concepts
- Self-organizing/self-managing team is the ultimate success factor of Scrum. The Development Team decides the amount of work it can manage in a Sprint, learn from it, and improve the estimation in future Sprints based on the velocity of the team
- Takes ownership to contribute effectively for product Increment
- Communicate and collaborate with face to face conversation or in other ways that are faster and feasible
- Development Team is like a team which is playing a team sport, such as cricket or football; individual achievements are not important; Product Increment/Win is important
- Co-located team is more efficient but no longer a limitation
- Represents technical side of product development activities

Let's see what are the contributions of a Development Team in different Scrum events, through the following table:

Scrum event	Activities / Contribution
Sprint Planning	Collaborate with PO
	Estimation of PBIs in Product Backlog Grooming
	Selection of PBIs in Sprint backlog for Product Increment
	Creating plan/tasks on how to implement PBIs
Sprint	Implementation of PBIs selected from Product Backlog to Sprint backlog
	Continuous code inspection and code fixes
	Continuous Integration
	Build execution
	Unit tests
	Package creation
	Continuous delivery
	Automated deployment
	Continuous testing
	Continuous deployment

Daily scrum	Attend daily scrum meeting without fail and on time
	Provides feedback for betterment of product Increment
	Track progress of the product Increment
Sprint review	Contribute in the review of product Increment
	Future implementation based on learning and experience
Sprint retrospective	Provide constructive feedback on what went well? What went wrong? How to improve in future Sprints?

Table 1.4: Development Team's Role in Scrum events

My experience

In all the projects within my experience that followed Scrum, every team member was selected based on their skills that were required to deliver an application. Some roles were naturally cross functional and hence could be merged. However, in my experience **Subject Matter Experts (SMEs)** are selected in the team as per requirement:

- Java developer(s)
- iOS developer(s)
- Android developer(s)
- QA engineer
- Sitecore engineer
- Cloud specialist

Over time, Cloud architecture becomes stable. Automation or **CICD** implementation **(Continuous Integration and Continuous Delivery)** or DevOps practices implementation become stable, and hence specialists are no longer required to perform specific duties, except troubleshooting. In such cases, knowledge transfer takes place and Developers take care of the cloud resources and the automation part.

In one of my projects, a Java developer took care of sitecore, cloud, as well as managed automation. It was efficiently managed for 2 years after I left the team.

In another project, we had team members from specific technical areas, such as development in Sharepoint, database, infrastructure, UI, testing, automation, cloud, and so on. There were two teams, considering the size of the team and two Scrum Masters were assigned at onsite and offshore.

Product Backlog

Product Backlog is a collection/set of desired and prioritized features that the customer wants to see as a final outcome.

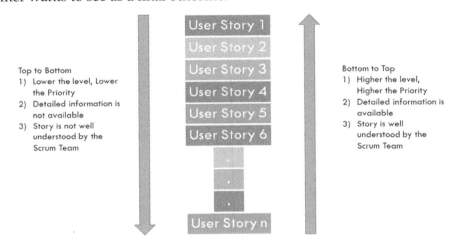

Top to Bottom
1) Lower the level, Lower the Priority
2) Detailed information is not available
3) Story is not well understood by the Scrum Team

Bottom to Top
1) Higher the level, Higher the Priority
2) Detailed information is available
3) Story is well understood by the Scrum Team

Figure 1.13: User stories and priorities

Product Backlog contains functional requirements, non-functional requirements, enhancements, proof of concepts for technology innovations, defects, and enhancements after continuous feedback.

Following are some of the important details about Product Backlog:

- Continuously evolved, based on understanding and changes with respect to market scenario, technology innovation, and so on.
- Continuously refined by the Scrum Team.
- Takes form of product Increment.
- Contains features, functionality, requirements, bug fixes that are prioritized for multiple product Increments.
- With time, Product Backlog becomes exhaustive, based on experience, innovations, and understanding, and that is Product Backlog refinement.
- Top priority items in Product Backlog are defined in detail.
- Lower priority items are initially not clear, or not well thought out so they are described in detail as and when the understanding is gained.

PBI describes features in detail, generally in a form of user story. The following figures show the relationships between epic, user story, and tasks:

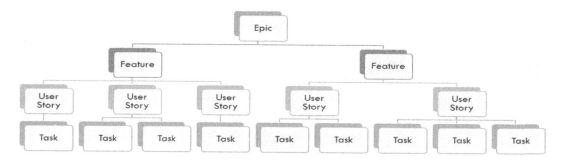

Figure 1.14: Epics, User Stories, and Tasks

In Azure DevOps, Product Backlog looks like the following screenshot:

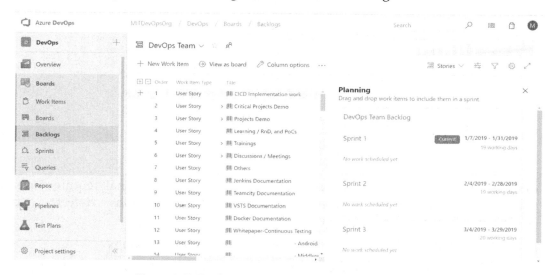

Figure 1.15: Product Backlog in Azure DevOps Dashboard

Product Backlog can contain multiple things, as shown in Azure DevOps Product Backlog. You can also create **New Work Item**, such as bug, epic, feature, issue, task, and so on, as shown in the following screenshot:

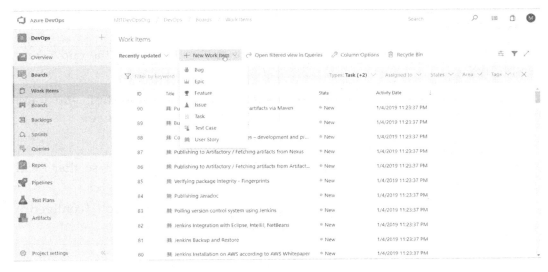

Figure 1.16: Product Backlog Items in Azure DevOps Dashboard

Epic

Epics are large. It can be broken into meaningful and shippable yet small user stories. Epics define the vision broadly. Unlike user stories, epics can span across different Sprints.

In Azure DevOps, epics look like the following screenshot:

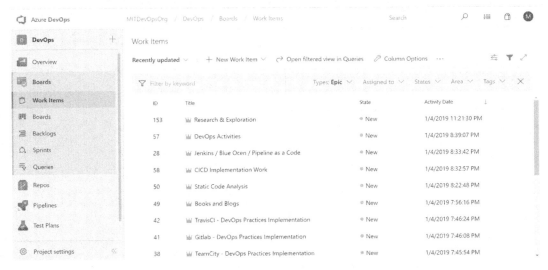

Figure 1.17: Epics in Azure DevOps Dashboard

User story

A user story provides simplified description of any feature from the end user's perspective.

User story format: As a `<role/type of user>`, I want `<feature/what you want to be implemented>` so that `<reason/why you want this feature>`.

Examples of user stories are:

- As a user, I want to book a meeting room/conference room so that I can conduct a daily Scum meeting.
- As an administrator, I want to approve booking of meeting room/conference room so that I can avoid the conflicts in booking.

A good user story should follow the following checklist:

- "I" ndependent
- "N" egotiable (PO and Development Team should be able to negotiate)
- "V" aluable
- "E" stimable (Estimation of user story should be possible)
- "S" mall (so as to fit within a Sprint)
- "T" estable

In Azure DevOps user story format looks like the following screenshot:

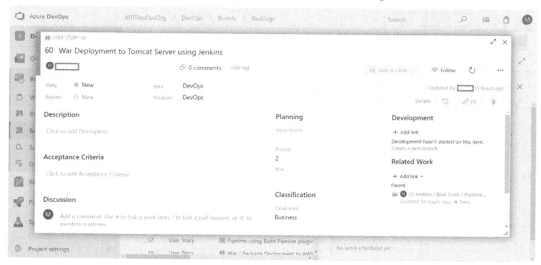

Figure 1.18: User Stories in Azure DevOps Dashboard

Task

User story can be broken into a number of tasks that will achieve implementation of user story. It is the fastest way to implement and deliver.

In Azure DevOps, a task format looks like the following screenshot:

Figure 1.19: Task in Azure DevOps Dashboard

Estimation

PBI has DoD and acceptance criteria attached with it. Efforts for PBI are estimated by Development Team in a relative manner, by playing poker using story points. All the estimation is done by the Development Team only. PO comes into the picture to help the Development Team understand PBI clearly.

Planning poker is one of the most popular techniques for estimation and planning used by organizations. Consensus is at the core of planning poker activity. The Scrum team uses planning poker activity to estimate Product Backlogs.

Figure 1.20: Story Points

In my very first Scrum project, we started with a reference story. We picked up a reasonably complex story for which the team had the best understanding. Considering all the factors, we all agreed to give it 5 story points. In our case, it was a special session so that the Development Team understood what needs to be done.

> Story points are not number of days or hours. It is an estimation of relative efforts at its best.

Usually, the PO reads the story and explains it so that the Development Team can estimate it.

Once all the team members understand the story properly, they try to compare it with the reference story, and discuss if this story is more complex or less complex than the reference story, and then each team member comes up with the size of the story based on his or her understanding of it. The Development team asks questions to PO whenever any clarification is needed.

Each member of the Development Team shows the card to everyone at the same time to avoid bias in estimation. There are multiple scenarios here:

- All members of the Development Team select the same size (not possible most of the times due to different understanding of members): Assign the size as a story point to the story and move on to the next one
- Difference in the estimation size is less: assign the size as a story point to the story, and move on to the next story
- Difference in the estimation size is too big:
  - o Each member explains the rationale behind his or her estimation
  - o PO clarifies any doubt on the story and explains it again if required
  - o Development Team continues to estimate until difference in the estimation size is zero or less than THREE rounds
  - o If even after THREE rounds, consensus is not achieved then the story can be put on hold until more information is available

Hence, the story point is a relative measure of the Development Team's understanding of complexity of the story with -certainty. Estimation gets better only with experience and understanding of the Scrum framework, as well as product and technology involved in the development process.

Definition of Done (DoD)

Definition of Done (DoD) is an EXIT criterion or a checklist defined for transparency and clear understanding between Scrum team members. It guides the Scrum team to achieve successful story implementation when it is considered complete with respect to functionality as well as quality. DoD helps team members in the following manner:

- Scrum team to have clear understanding of outcome
- Development Team to implement user stories in correct way
- PO verifies implementation against DoD
- Examples:
  - o Analyzed using static code analysis tool, so that all high priority (critical, major, blocker) bugs and vulnerabilities are fixed before application goes live
  - o 80% code coverage – Unit Tests
  - o CICD has to be configured
  - o Architecture document needs to be updated as required
  - o Minimal but sufficient documentation of critical features
  - o Automated testing for all critical features
  - o Infrastructure as a code should be utilized for cloud resources

At different stages of application lifecycle management, DoD may differ based on its relevance. In Azure DevOps **Acceptance Criteria** looks like the following screenshot:

Figure 1.21: Acceptance Criteria in Azure DevOps Dashboard

My Experience

In one of the projects, Product Backlog was created by PO in Visual Studio Team Services that is now known as Azure DevOps. All user stories were prioritized in VSTS. In that project, we had two teams working on the product, one from offshore and one from onsite. The PO used to create main Product Backlog and two Sprint backlogs were managed. In Sprint Planning meeting, all prioritized user stories were discussed and included in Sprint backlog under the guidance of the PO and Business

Analysts. The PO used to consult the BAs and Development Team well before setting the final priorities. Hence, we effectively improved both communication and collaboration. It helped in making Product Backlog crisp and clear, which helped the Development Team at the time of Sprint Planning.

Scrum events

There are pre-defined events for specific purposes in the Scrum Framework. One of the important aspects of all Scrum events is the time box attached to it.

But what is a timebox? In a wider context of Scrum, timebox is nothing but fixed span of time or Sprint. Each Sprint has its goal, length (1-4 weeks), and product Increment at the end of each Sprint.

The following diagram represents Scrum events:

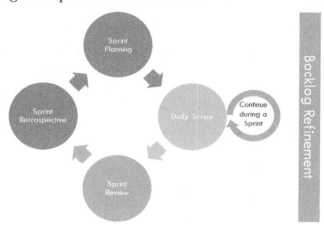

Figure 1.22: Scrum events

All events are timeboxed events. Timeboxing helps the Scrum team to focus on the vision and achieve it without delay. Hence, it helps to ensure that product Increment is available after a Sprint. The following table provides details of specific event and their timebox:

Event	Timebox
Sprint	One to four weeks (usually 2-3 weeks)
Sprint Planning	Maximum of eight hours for a one-month Sprint
Daily Scrum	15 Minutes
Sprint Review	At most a four-hour meeting for one-month Sprints
Sprint Retrospective	At most a three-hour meeting for one-month Sprints

Table 1.5: Scrum Events and Timebox

All these events are designed to adopt changes, enable transparency and visibility. Let's discuss all scrum events.

Sprint

Sprint is a Scrum event that ends with potentially releasable product Increment. It provides a working product with implemented features/PBIs as decided in the Sprint Planning. Usually, Sprints have a constant duration across the product development life cycle. Sprint **n+1** starts immediately when Sprint n is over. Sprint contains many events such as Sprint Planning, Daily Scrums, implementation, the Sprint Review, and the Sprint Retrospective.

Following are some important details of Sprint:

- Each Sprint has a defined goal
- The Scrum team focuses on the Sprint goal and try to achieve it
- Scope of the Sprint can be adjusted between the Scrum team, based on new learning and knowledge
- PO can cancel a Sprint before its completion if Sprint goal can't be achieved by keeping all stakeholders in confidence;
  - o   Cancellations are rare
  - o   In one of my projects, we had to cancel a Sprint as major technology components were changed due to introduction of cloud resources

Any work that is completed according to DoD during cancelled Sprint is considered for a review. All incomplete work items go to Product Backlog again. Following image shows the relation between user stories and Sprints is as shown in below figure:

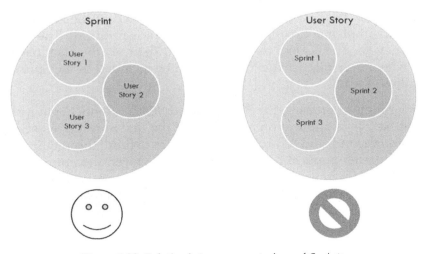

Figure 1.23: *Relation between user stories and Sprints*

Each Sprint is planned with specific amount of work based on the Development Team's capacity. Multiple user stories can be part of one Sprint but one user story can't span across multiple Sprints as it kills the idea of increment delivery. Each Sprint starts with Sprint Planning.

Sprint Planning

Prioritized Product Backlog contains n number of features or PBIs that may not be completed in one Sprint. All the PBIs can be completed across multiple Sprints based on the capacity of the team. Hence, the Scrum team participates in one of the most important Scrum events for the next product Increment, where the team selects High priority features that will be implemented in Sprint duration. The Scrum Team defines a Sprint goal and creates a Sprint plan to achieve a product Increment. The following image shows input, Sprint Planning, and output in diagrammatic form:

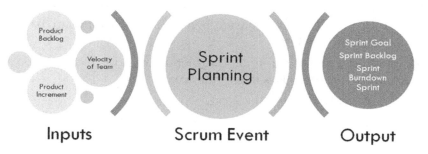

Figure 1.24: Input, Sprint Planning and Output

Every Sprint starts with Sprint Planning.

Sprint Planning is the process to plan the work that will be completed in the upcoming Sprint. The PO has the best idea about what is required at the end of a Sprint in terms of feature implementation, considering business priorities. The Scum Master facilitates the event. The PO and the Development Team are the main participants in this event, where they discuss the PBIs that can be included in the Sprint based on the capabilities of team.

In one of my previous projects, the PO described that he wants Login feature ready for a cloud-based Java application at the end of the first Sprint. We used Microsoft Azure as a public cloud, and Azure Active Directory to fulfill this requirement, along with Java-based web application development. However, the entire goal was not feasible as some PBIs required analytics-related tool and its expertise, which was not available at the time of Sprint Planning. As a Development Team, we decided not to take those stories until we have resources and skills to protect the goal and product Increment.

Following is the diagram that shows participants in Sprint Planning:

Figure 1.25: Participants in Sprint Planning

In the first part/half of the meeting, the Scrum team decides what can be implemented in the upcoming Sprint and in next part/half, the team discusses how to implement PBIs in the upcoming Sprint, and break down PBIs/user stories into tasks. PBIs are adjusted accordingly, if the Development Team feels that PBIs are too many or too less after this planning.

The Development Team selects PBIs from Product Backlog to Sprint backlog based on the available capability of the team. It is the Scrum master's responsibility to ensure that Sprint Planning takes place, and each member of the team understands its objective. Scrum Master also works as a time keeper to manage time.

The Development Team selects the work for a Sprint. Though the Scrum Master and the PO can facilitate the selection of the work for an upcoming Sprint, but the final decision rests on the Development Team. However, the Scrum Master and the PO can cross question PBIs' commitment for a Sprint to get the best outcome from the Development Team. Based on experience, the selection criteria of work to be performed in the Sprint might change. It works on estimation, and hence it improves over time.

It is very important to select PBIs that have DoD associated with it. In case it's absent, it creates confusion on when the User story will be considered as complete.

It is important to consider the three pillars of Scrum, as shown in the following figure:

Figure 1.26: Three Pillars of Scrum

Continuous visibility and monitoring, with respect to processes, and continuous improvement based on the feedback given in Sprint Review helps the Scrum Team to manage their work effectively in Sprint.

At the end of every Sprint Planning meeting, the Sprint goal and the Sprint backlog are decided and agreed upon; Development Team need to implement the Sprint backlog Items in a Sprint for a desired product Increment.

One important part of the Sprint Planning is the team capacity. Recently, I created a Product Backlog for all the tasks that I wanted a team to implement for DevOps practices implementation.

Yes, I divided all those activities that compliment Agile principles in implementing a part of the Scrum development. Following are the details:

Parameters	Numbers	Calculations
Development team members	5	5
Sprint duration	3 weeks	5 * (3)
Effective days in Sprint	5 (15 Days)	5 * (3 * 5)
No of working hours per day	9	5 * 3 * 5 * 9 = 675
Total hours		675

No one is going to work 9 hours a day for Sprint backlog implementation. Don't get me wrong, it is not about the Development Team's unwillingness to work. It is because they are engaged in many activities as well. Let's try to find effective work hours.

Effective capacity hours per day:

Total hours – (Time spent in Scrum events + Time spent in other activities + Buffer + Personal time)

Time spent in Scrum events	Sprint Planning – 8 hours	8 + 4 hours almost + 4 + 3 + 5 hours = 24 hours * No. of team members (5)
	Daily Scrum 15 minutes daily 15 * 15 = 225 minutes	120 hours
	Sprint Review – 4 hours	
	Sprint Retrospective – 3 hours	
	Backlog Grooming – 5 hours	

Time spent in other activities (emails, other meetings, support to other projects in case of issues)	1 hour daily	1 * 15 = 15 * No. of team members (5) 75 hours
Personal time (tea, breakfast, lunch)	2 hours daily	2 * 15 = 30 * No. of team members (5)
There are external factors that affect this personal time such as seats are not available in canteen and food at work place is not allowed hence this time is around 2 hours daily		150 hours
Total hours in other activities		120 hours + 75 hours + 150 hours 345 hours
Effective productive hours to implement Sprint backlog Items are: Total hours - Total hours in other activities		675 – 345 hours = 330 hours
Per person effective productive hours to implement Sprint backlog Items in a Sprint are		330 hours / 5 team members 66 hours in a Sprint of 15 days
Per person effective productive hours to implement Sprint backlog Items in a day for a Sprint are		66 hours / 15 days 4.4 hours a day

Table 1.6: Calculation of productive hours

We haven't considered any leaves here for any of the Development Team members. In case we consider leaves then time will reduce further but that will be calculated person wise.

In Azure DevOps, we will see how this capacity is considered and leaves are considered into overall efforts. In Azure DevOps, capacity is calculated team member wise. We can configure team capacity in Microsoft Azure DevOps in the following way:

Figure 1.27: *Capacity in Azure DevOps Dashboard*

Sprint goal should be adjusted after the second half of the Sprint Planning, based on following:

- Tasks
- Estimated hours
- Availability of Development Team's members

Let's see Sprint goal and Sprint backlog in detail:

- **Sprint goal:** Sprint goal is an identification of outcome of the Sprint in the form of product Increment. It works as a lighthouse in guiding the Development Team for the product Increment. Sprint goal is decided in the Sprint Planning meeting only. To be successful and effective, the Development Team needs to develop product Increment by keeping Sprint goal in the center. It is possible to re-negotiate the goal within a Sprint if the need arises.

- **Sprint backlog:** Sprint backlog is a subset of Product Backlog in simple words. Sprint backlog contains PBIs that are selected by the Scrum Team for development in the coming Sprint. The following diagram represents Sprint backlog:

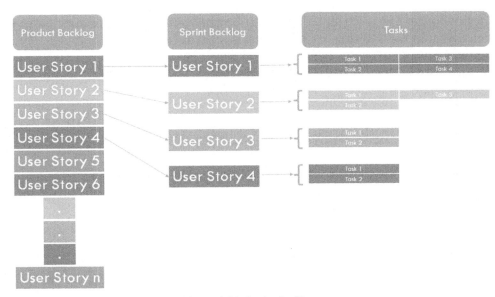

Figure 1.28: Sprint backlog

It also includes a development plan on how to implement the features to satisfy the Spring Goal. Sprint backlog continuously evolves as the Development Team follows the plan and implements features to achieve the Sprint goal. As and when tasks are completed, the Development Team updates the Sprint backlog. In case of any further clarification, the Development Team collaborates with the PO and the Scrum Master. The remaining work is also updated by the Development Team. Tasks can be added or removed based on the understanding of the team.

Sprint backlog is real-time monitoring of the work that the Development Team is doing in the Sprint duration. Only the Development Team can update the Sprint backlog. The Development Team finalizes tasks that need to be implemented initially.

Based on improved understanding, the Development Team can decide to take up additional user stories to achieve the Sprint goal and utilize existing capabilities effectively.

The following table shows some difference between Product backlog and Sprint backlog:

Product Backlog	Sprint backlog
Superset of Sprint backlog	Subset of Sprint backlog
Dynamic	More stable compared to Product Backlog
Focus is on entire product	Focus is on product Increment
PO is the in charge	Development Team is in charge

Table 1.7: Product Backlog vs. Sprint Backlog

The following is the representation when Sprint backlog items or user stories are broken down in tasks and task execution has already started:

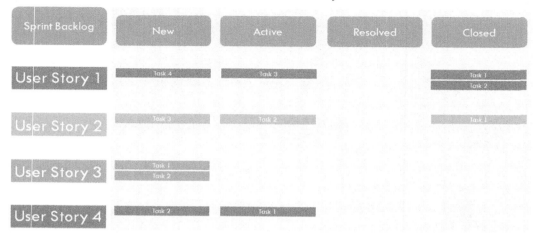

Figure 1.29: Task Status

At the end of the Sprint Planning meeting, we have a Sprint goal, Sprint backlog, and commitment from the Development Team that the Sprint backlog items will be converted in the form of product Increment.

My Experience

In one of the projects, we used to do continuous conversations with the PO and the BAs. The BAs were our first level of people to whom we could reach out to solve any kind of query. Based on the conversations and conclusions, Sprint backlog or Product Backlog was edited.

In a Sprint meeting, we realized that the Development Team does not have a clear understanding of PBIs, hence we requested a pre-meeting where we could only clear our doubts. Once clear, we used to conduct Sprint Planning meeting. The Scrum Master has to keep an eye on story conversations as many times it is hijacked by a specific team member. It happens often, and results into a waste of time as the entire team is available in Sprint Planning or Product Backlog grooming.

Daily Scrum

The Daily Scrum is an entity of Scrum Framework and by far the most popular event among the Development Teams.

Figure 1.30: Input, Daily Scrum and Output

The following figure shows participants in Daily Scrum:

Figure 1.31: Ideal Participants in Daily Scrum

The Scrum Master has to ensure that Daily Scrum happens every day. Following are some important details related to Daily Scrum:

- It takes place at the same time and the same location every day to avoid any delay, miscommunication about time, and place.
- Team doesn't wait for team members who are not on time.
- Usually, each member answers the following questions:
  - o What did I do yesterday?
  - o What will I do today?
  - o Impediments, if any?
- One team member at a time.
- All team members need to attend it physically, virtually, or by sending status via another team member.
- Team members give status in no particular order but it can be in group or team wise:
  - o Group wise
    - ▪ Web Development Team

- Testing team
- Mobile Development Team
- CMS team
- Cloud team

o Using ball – team members throw it to another team member randomly

- No detailed discussions regarding Impediments are encouraged - detailed discussions are held only after the Daily Scrum with required stakeholders.

- Scrum Master makes sure that a 15minute time limit is respected, and no discussion takes place in between Daily Scrum.

- It is the responsibility of the Development Team to conduct a meeting, which is however, always facilitated by the Scrum Master.

- No external stake holder is allowed in the Daily Scrum, and if they are present then they can't disrupt the Daily Scrum.

- Helpful to avoid lengthy meetings where all team members are not required – to gain productivity.

- It promotes transparency, visibility, accountability, and effective decision making in a quick manner.

- Essentially, it is a way to monitor progress towards Sprint goal achievement and solve impediments, if any.

What doesn't work?

Latecomers
Reporting
External interference
It is a Standup Meeting: No chairs are allowed.
All team members need to concentrate while status is given by another member
Mobiles, other communication
Speeches and Confrontations

What Works?

Punctuality - only 15 Minutes Timebox event
Transparency
No External interference
No Chairs are allowed so members try to finish meeting fast to avoid discomfort caused by standing long time
All members participate in the event - Collaboration
No Electronic devices
Appropriate details in 1-2 statements; preferred if team members keep notes on 1)What did s(he) do yesterday? 2) What will s(he) accomplish today? 3) Impediments, if any?

Figure 1.32: What works and what doesn't work in Daily Scrum

Sprint Execution

The development Team implements all the committed PBIs in the Sprint backlog. The PO, the Scrum Master, and the Development Team participate in the Sprint Execution. Let's see the inputs and the outputs for Sprint Execution in the following diagram:

Figure 1.33: *Input, Sprint Execution, and Output*

The PO facilitates the Development Team if any clarification is needed to understand a Product Backlog Item or provide feedback. The Scrum Master's role is also that of a facilitator, for both the Development Team and the PO. The SM makes sure that impediments are resolved quickly, and communication between the PO and the Development Team is smooth.

Sprint execution planning is done in the second half of a Sprint Planning where PBIs/user stories are broken into tasks. Task planning can be done across the Sprint duration. Let's understand Sprint Burndown in next section.

- **Sprint burndown:** In a Sprint, the Development Team members update the tasks regarding remaining hours as soon as they complete it or spend time on it. It is helpful in tracking the overall progress. In Azure DevOps, at the start of the Sprint, the Burndown chart looks like the following screenshot:

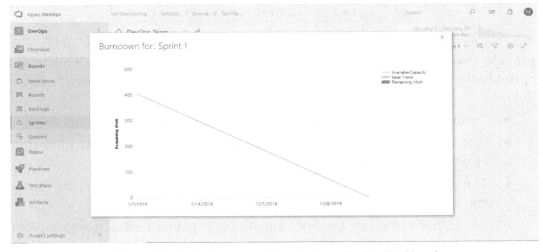

Figure 1.34: *Sprint Burndown Chart in Azure DevOps Dashboard*

Sprint Review

A Sprint Review is an informal Scrum event that takes places at the end of the Sprint. Let's see inputs and outputs for a Sprint Review in the following diagram:

Figure 1.35: Input, Sprint Review and Output

In a Sprint Review, product Increment is verified and Product Backlog is refined based on requirements. The following are some of the members who attend the Sprint Review meeting:

Figure 1.36: Participants in Sprint Review

The Scrum Team and other stakeholders, such as customers, end users, and others, provide feedback during the Sprint Review by keeping product Increment and Sprint backlog in context. Let's understand some important points related to Sprint Review:

- Product Increment is the focal point of Sprint Review.
- Sprint Review takes place immediately after Sprint execution and just before Sprint Retrospective.
- The Scrum Master should ensure that the Sprint Review takes place at the end of Sprint for gathering feedback from all stockholders.
    - o Sprint Review provides a platform to gather feedback and improve based on this feedback in future events.

- The PO starts with the explanation of the Sprint goal, what has been Done and what has not been *Done* or what is pending; *Not Done* or pending PBIs are sent back to Product Backlog with revised priorities decided by the PO.
- Development Team members share their experience and learning during the Sprint duration
- The Development Team gives demo of all the PBIs implemented and Done in the Sprint.
- Stakeholders provide feedback that Scrum team should consider as a part of learning for continuous improvement for next the Sprints.
- The Scrum Team and external stakeholders discuss the next Sprint's goal, and provide feedback for the next Sprint Planning based on market scenario or any other innovation or observation.
- The feedback is converted into PBIs and included in Product Backlog; The PO decides priorities for such PBIs.

The outcome of the Sprint Review meeting is following:

- Updated Product Backlog
- Revised priorities based on the feedback
- Revised Scope of the Product Backlog according to change in priorities

In one of my projects, we used to do following things:

- To make sure PO has already seen the demo of completed user stories and they satisfy DoD – Continuous feedback from PO regarding Completed user stories is important to avoid any confrontation in Sprint review
- Create a list of user stories such as *Completed* and *Not Completed – Reasons*
- Create a presentation to explain what we are going to cover with specific highlights
- Selection of team members who will present multiple team members based on who will present what?
- Making list of stakeholders to whom we need to send invite
- Creating a video demo of product Increment along with live demo
- Backup processes in case of live demo doesn't work
- Scheduling Sprint review for 4-hour timebox
- Booking a meeting room where audio and video conferencing facilities are available
- To make sure that everyone from the Scrum Team is available at the time of Sprint Review

Let see product Increment in detail:

- **Product Increment:** Each Sprint ends with a product Increment or potentially releasable product with desired features implemented by the Development Team and approved by product owner. Stakeholders or customers give continuous feedback on product Increment, which is integrated in the next Sprint for improving existing processes or practices. Product Increment is a cumulative outcome of a completed Sprint until features of the current Sprint are approved by the PO. At the end of each Sprint, there should be product Increment that is releasable, and that the features or PBIs are implemented according to DoD. Increment is one step closer to the overall vision of the product.

Sprint Retrospective

Sprint Retrospective marks an end of the Sprint. It is the time of constructive feedback after identifying improvement areas rather than a blaming other team members for issues. Let's see inputs and output for Sprint Retrospective in the following diagram:

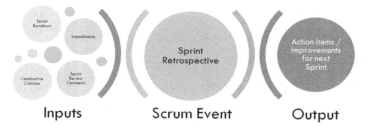

Figure 1.37: Input, Sprint Retrospective and Output

The Scrum Team collaborates and introspects on what went well and what did not in the Sprint; what kind of actions can be taken to improve the things that went wrong to avoid it in future Sprints. Following are some of the members who attend the Sprint Retrospective meeting:

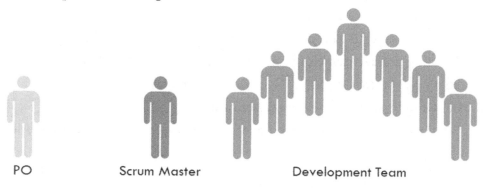

Figure 1.38: Participants in Sprint Retrospective

Following are some important points related to Sprint Retrospective:

- Scrum Masters helps the Development Team in Sprint Retrospective to introspect and come with action items for future improvements.
- The entire Scrum Team must be present at the time of Sprint Retrospective; Scrum Team can invite others who are not part of the Team if required but the Scrum Team is essential to decide improvement areas and action items.
- Sprint Retrospective has to be finished after Sprint review and before next Sprint Planning with improvement areas and action items.
- Positive and constructive feedback and introspection is a key for improvement planning for the next Sprint.
- Sprint Retrospective plan of improvements to be considered in the upcoming Sprints.

Hence, it is a formal opportunity for the Development Team's Self inspection, Introspection, and Improvement.

Initially, Sprint Retrospectives often becomes battle ground. Blame game starts and that is where the Scrum Master comes into the picture to explain the real meaning and purpose of a Sprint Retrospective meeting.

My Experience

It was painful to attend the very first Sprint Retrospective meeting. There were many members from different technologies in the meeting, and hence it created a chaos. Everyone wanted to share their issues only, and at times it resulted into a blame game. Some people from the senior management tried to impose their thoughts and it was all a chaos. Then the Scrum Master took charge and explained what Sprint Retrospective is for. From the next meeting onwards, only the Scrum Team was present for Sprint Retrospective and it went well from then on.

Since then, I loved these meetings always as I have always believed in disagreeing with respect and if proper processes are not followed. It is just to improve the existing practices. Practices can be technical, with respect to communication, or infrastructure, or automation.

We need to understand the fact that Sprint Retrospective initiates the engine of continuous improvement. It is not only a place to find what went wrong. It is also a place to find what went well and appreciate things which are good.

In my last project, we entered into a meeting room with whiteboard having three partitions as follows:

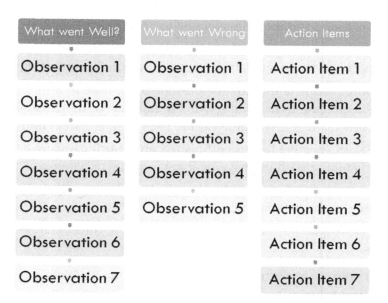

Figure 1.39: *Chart for Sprint Retrospective*

- Each of the 5 Members of the Development Team wrote their observations during the Sprint, and stuck those sticky notes in the specified section.

- Observation and Action Items are clarified by the team members while sticking it on a whiteboard.

- Often, few observations are same in all three categories so one of the team members grouped them.

- All the items, after grouping, are discussed in detail to list out action items. Action item section also contains best practices that need to be adopted by the team.

- After all the action items were listed; we used to give priorities to the actions items, and based on priorities and feasibilities these action items used to be integrated in the next Sprint.

- It is important to improve on how to do Sprint Retrospective and hence Retrospective of Sprint Retrospective is very important.

Product Backlog refinement

Let's see inputs and outputs for Product Backlog refinement in the following diagram:

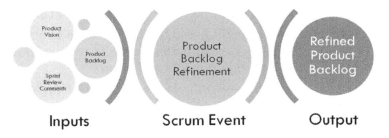

Figure 1.40: Input, Product Backlog Refinement and Output

Backlog grooming or Product Backlog refinement is one of the most important activities in Scrum framework as it improves estimation based on past learning. Estimation is the focal point of Sprint Planning. Overall, PBIs are estimated based on the current understanding. However, understanding regarding features/PBIs evolve, Development Team gains knowledge and finds better ways to implement features or technology changes, and through them, situational changes. A change in market scenario also brings a new dimension for a product that is coming out in the market incrementally.

Following are some of the members who attend Product Backlog refinement meeting:

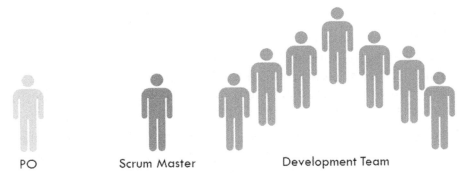

Figure 1.41: Participants in Product Backlog Refinement

Hence, based on the Scrum Team's understanding as well as of stakeholders, PBIs evolve. It is always helpful in achieving Sprint goal as well, to achieve overall vision with effectiveness, considering external factors such as market scenario. This is the activity that keeps Product Backlog up to date. Let's understand some important points related to Product Backlog:

- Ongoing activity
- PO and Development Team along with internal and external stakeholders participate in Product Backlog refinement
- PBIs are broken in a way so that it is easily manageable and understandable
- PO explains PBIs

- Development Team asks questions in case of queries or confusion
- Scrum Team adds more details based on improved understanding over time in form of business rules, design patterns that fit in, workflow, automation required, testing-related requirements and so on
- Development Team estimates PBI after gaining clear understanding about PBI
- Revised PBIs are prioritized by the PO based on business requirements and added in next the Sprint if it fits in

My Experience

In my project, we used to do Product Backlog grooming after Sprint Retrospective is over. It can be scheduled by the PO any time between a Sprint.

In another project, the PO used to keep user story, description, and DoD ready. All technical and solution architects were invited for backlog grooming along with the Scrum Team to discuss specific stories where inputs from architects were required.

BAs used to explain each story, and based on it we all used to re-picturize it and change its story points if required.

Velocity

Velocity is one of the crucial metrics in Scrum. It is a number that shows how efficient the estimation of the Development Team was with respect to capacity and capabilities of the team. One important thing to remember is how to measure capacity of the team, through story points or through hours.

It is better to measure capacity in terms of story points rather than hours as the latter is too complicated and may not depict the proper picture. However, it can be considered based on experience. In my previous projects, story points were considered as the measure of the team's capacity or velocity. Let's take a look at them.

Scrum Team:

Role	Number of skilled team members
Scrum Master / DevOps Lead	1
Java developer	1
Mobile developers	2
Tester	1
PO (customer representative)	1

Table 1.8: Scrum Team

Sprint duration: 3 weeks

The team is available for the entire Sprint. Productive hours, excluding Scrum events, are 4.4 hours per day (we calculated it earlier).

Total productive hours in a Sprint are: 5 days * 4.4 hours * 3 weeks * 5 (# of members in Development Team) = 330 hours

Sprint 1:

Total productive hours in a Sprint are: 5 days * 4.4 hours * 3 weeks * 5 (# of members in Development Team) = 330 hours

Sprint backlog:

Story #	Story point (estimated)
1	1
2	1
3	2
4	3
5	3
6	3
7	8
8	13
9	3
10	3
Total	40

Table 1.9: Sprint backlog with story points

The Development Team was able to complete only 30 story points in the Sprint.

Sprint Review:

Story #	Story point (estimated)	Status (velocity)
1	1	Done
2	1	Done
3	2	Not Done
4	3	Done
5	3	Done
6	3	Done
7	8	Not Done

8	13	Done
9	3	Done
10	3	Done
Total	**40**	**30**

Table 1.10: Sprint backlog with story points and status

Sprint 2:

Total productive hours in a Sprint are: 5 days * 4.4 hours * 3 weeks * 5 (# of members in Development Team) = 330 hours

Sprint backlog:

Story #	Story point (velocity)
1	3
2	3
3	5
4	8
5	8
6	2
7	5
8	1
Total	**35**

Table 1.11: Sprint backlog with story points

Number of story points is 35 but the Development Team finished work earlier and added new stories as time was available, and completed them in **Sprint 2**.

Sprint Review:

Story #	Story point (estimated)	Status (velocity)
1	3	Done
2	3	Done
3	5	Done
4	8	Done
5	8	Done
6	2	Done
7	5	Done
8	1	Done

9	5	Done
Total	**35**	**40**

Table 1.12: Sprint backlog with story points and status

Sprint 3:

Total productive hours in a Sprint are: 5 days * 4.4 hours * 3 weeks * 5 (# of members in Development Team) = 330 hours

Sprint backlog:

Story #	Story point (estimated)
1	2
2	2
3	2
4	3
5	5
6	3
7	8
8	13
9	1
10	1
Total	**40**

Table 1.13: Sprint backlog with story points

Number of story points are 40, but the Development Team couldn't finish all the work on time in **Sprint 3**.

Sprint Review:

Story #	Story point (estimated)	Status (velocity)
1	2	Done
2	2	Done
3	2	Not Done
4	3	Done
5	5	Done
6	3	Done
7	8	Done
8	13	Done

9	1	Done
10	1	Done
Total	**40**	**38**

Table 1.14: Sprint backlog with story points and status

Sprint 4:

Total productive hours in a Sprint are: 5 days * 4.4 hours * 3 weeks * 5 (# of members in Development Team) = 330 hours

Sprint backlog:

Story #	Story point (estimated)
1	2
2	3
3	1
4	2
5	3
6	3
7	8
8	8
9	5
10	5
Total	**40**

Table 1.15: Sprint backlog with story points

Number of story points is 40, but the Development Team finished work earlier and added new stories as time was available, and completed them in **Sprint 4**.

Sprint Review:

Story #	Story point (estimated)	Status (velocity)
1	2	Done
2	3	Done
3	1	Done
4	2	Done
5	3	Done
6	3	Done
7	8	Done

8	8	Done
9	5	Done
10	5	Done
11	5	Done
Total	**40**	**45**

Table 1.16: Sprint backlog with story points and status

The following image will help us understand the velocity history:

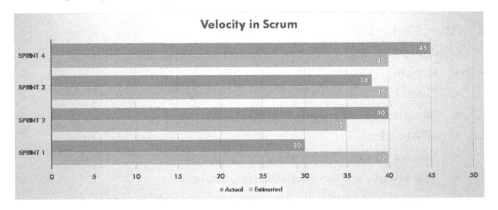

Figure 1.42: Velocity History

Hence, after 4 Sprints, following is the situation:

	Estimated	Actual
Sprint 1	40	30
Sprint 2	35	40
Sprint 3	40	38
Sprint 4	40	45

Table 1.17: Velocity History

Average velocity is *(30 + 40 + 38 + 45) / 4 = 38* approximately.

So, it is good enough to estimate that with the same team size and productive hours, the Development Team can achieve an average velocity of 38 in the next Sprint.

In case the productive hours are less due to leaves of some of team members during a specific time, then based on the productive hours, velocity of that Sprint can be calculated. For example:

If *330* productive hours ->velocity is *38*. So, for *300* productive hours ->velocity is?

It is all about relative estimation, learn from the past estimation and reality; and improve the estimation based on improved knowledge and understanding. Velocity indicates what PBIs have been implemented into the product Increment. It helps to guide the Scrum Team on estimating future Sprint activities.

Certified Scrum Master (CSM) Certification

There are multiple steps involved in getting **Certified Scrum Master (CSM)** Certification:

1. Familiarity with Scrum Framework.
2. Attend 2-day workshop conducted by Certified Scrum Trainer.
3. CSM test:
    *   Online
    *   Open book
    *   50 multiple-choice questions
    *   60 Minutes
    *   Passing Score – 74%
    *   Test results will be available immediately
4. If you pass, go to **https://www.scrumalliance.org** dashboard.
5. Accept the license agreement.
6. Complete Scrum Alliance membership profile.
7. The certificate is valid for two years.
8. You can renew the certificate by paying 100 USD from Scrum Alliance dashboard but no re-test is required.

How Agile/Scrum Framework brings culture change?

Agile principles are based on faster delivery of the Product. In Scrum, product Increments, or potentially releasable products are available for deployment at the end of Sprint. If there is a three weeks' Sprint, then all the activities performed for Software life cycle management has to be completed in three weeks. It results into multiple cycles of development, testing, and deployment into different environments, and so on.

Traditionally, manual activities are involved in SDLC, which works as a speed breaker in case of Scrum Framework.

Hence, it is important to utilize automation in existing practices. DevOps Practices, such as continuous integration, continuous testing, and continuous delivery help in speeding up the process. We will see DevOps and DevOps practices related details in the next chapter.

Conclusion

In this chapter, we have covered challenges in waterfall approach, emergence of Agile, Scrum methodologies, and different aspects of Scrum methodologies.

In the next chapter, we will cover DevOps in details.

CHAPTER 2
DevOps Culture and Continuous Practices

Application/product/software development is a fragile process, and many challenges affect it, such as:

- Faster time to market to gain market advantage
- High quality – to detect failures to fix them early
- To adopt changes based on business demands
- To adopt changes based on technology evolution
- Effective collaboration
- Effective communication
- To integrate feedback effectively in existing development processes to get better
- To adopt improvements and innovations
- To avoid error-prone manual processes in application lifecycle phases – utilize automation
- Employee satisfaction and productivity gains – to allow employees to enjoy their weekends

How to overcome this roadblock of fragility? Answer to this is in the use of Agile Development Frameworks.

Great! But nothing comes free in this world. Agile brings its own challenges, for betterment of course.

Agile development and implementation of Scrum methodologies require quick delivery of application. Manual activities to manage application lifecycle are no longer sufficient. Automation helps to achieve faster time to market in Agile development approach.

Structure

In this chapter, we are going to cover the following topics:
- Definition of DevOps
- DevOps practices/continuous practices
- Benefits
- Strategy
- Maturity model
- Roadmap
- Nudge theory

Objective

Objective is cover DevOps practices implementation that helps to achieve speed for faster time to market, using transformation in culture, people, process, and tools.

Definition of DevOps

DevOps (Development and Operations) or **DevSecOps (Development, Security and Operations)** practices or continuous practices are focal point of any discussions related to software/application/product development. The question should be, why?

Every organization is looking for the following:
- Faster time to market
- Better quality

But what is DevOps?

I know quite well what comes to my mind when I try to define DevOps. Picture of a wall with development team and operations team on different sides of it is what comes into Google image search. There are a few other things that come to my mind immediately after reading lots of books and blogs, which are as follows:

- DevOps is not a methodology
- DevOps is not a process
- DevOps is not a tool or technology
- DevOps is not a framework
- DevOps is not a set of design patterns where problems and solutions are well defined
- DevOps is not scripting
- DevOps is not automation only

Ok, then what is DevOps?

My first memory of DevOps is development team and operations team sitting on either sides of the wall and trying to deliver a product with no effective communication and collaboration even though the end goal is one: To deliver high quality product.

DevOps is a culture that focuses on people, process, and tools to automate application lifecycle phases for delivering high-quality software with faster time to market to gain a sustainable, competitive business advantage. It is a mindset/culture/routine to utilize best practices to achieve faster time to market and to achieve better quality with effective communication and collaboration.

Interesting! Yes, it is a culture that evolves over time and adapts according to the situation. Essentially, when I try to implement continuous practices in any project or unit, my goal is to find out existing practices, find bottlenecks and use continuous practices to remove those bottlenecks, and make processes or daily work more effective.

I have worked in six organizations until now, in small, medium, and large businesses. Each organization had different kinds of culture, and it included not only different tools, technologies, processes, and policies, but even Ides. Yes, IDEs were different based on the organization, and hence best practices were obviously different.

One organization started working on Cloud and Big Data extensively in 2008, while the other big name in the market started it around 2009-2010. Automation with respect to application lifecycle management started in one organization in 2014, while it started in 2016 in another one of the organizations.

All these also change based on the business unit, as well as on the few people who are ready to accept the change. Leadership makes a huge contribution with respect to change. Change is not easy, and when it is specifically related to cultural change, which affects people, processes, and tools, it becomes extremely difficult due to resistance from people. Following are some important attributes of culture:

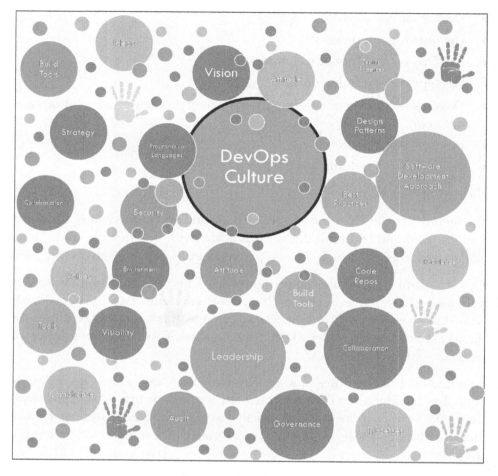

Figure 2.1: *DevOps culture*

In traditional or AS-IS environment, many manual activities are involved in application lifecycle management. DevOps brings about a change in culture with automation in application lifecycle management, along with the above attributes. The idea is faster time to market with high quality of product by making existing practices more effective using automation, with the help of people, processes, and tools.

In every organization, culture varies, and various sets of practices exist, and hence it is very difficult to change things until people change their attitude and mindset. In such situations, there will be 4 set of people:

- People who welcome change
- People who takes charge of change
- People who resist change
- People who are fence sitter

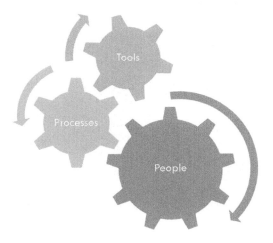

Figure 2.2: *People, processes, and tools*

For people who resist and are fence sitters, we need to put in processes, organize training, and perform pilot execution using tools that are already utilized in an organization or with any open source tools. This trinity helps to form a firm base to develop a culture of automation to achieve faster time to market with quality.

Out of my six organizations, only one organization had visualized the benefits, prepared a vision, set processes, and utilize different tools as per project requirements. Most of the time, organizations try to bring automation for application lifecycle management in a parachute style, which fails more often than not until people are convinced about the benefits of it.

Visualization and training make huge impact on the mindset of people who resist change. It is the best way to convince them of the benefits of DevOps culture and practices.

Overview of continuous practices

In this section, we will discuss the different continuous practices that makes DevOps culture effective, as represented in the following diagram:

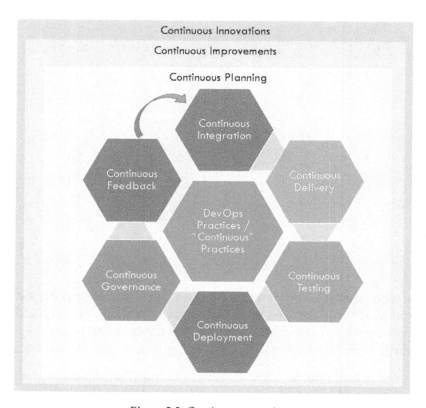

Figure 2.3: Continuous practices

Continuous planning

We have discussed planning in *Chapter 1: Overview of Agile and Scrum Framework.* Yes, indeed. Let me remind you.

Agile is an idea or a philosophy. First time ever, *Divide and Rule* policy is helping the business like never before. Divide the feature implementation in different phases, take continuous feedback from the customer, and rule over the customer's heart and mind. Agile brings pace to development and delivery, while DevOps practices make sure that pace is maintained, and hence it complements Agile. Consider Agile as an engine of a train, while DevOps practices or continuous practices or automation as a smooth track.

There are many frameworks that come under the Agile umbrella. Scrum is one of the most popular frameworks in the market. Scrum is a process framework that is lightweight and simple to understand, within which people can address complex adaptive problems, while productively and creatively delivering products of the highest possible value.

Have some patience; I am coming to the planning part. Let's understand how and who are involved in planning part.

- **Product Owner (PO)** is continuously planning on what to include in Product Increment by using Product Backlog. Product Backlog is a collection/set of desired and prioritized features the customer wants to see as a final outcome. Product Backlog contains functional requirements, non-functional requirements, enhancements, proof of concepts for technology innovations, defects, and enhancements post continuous feedback.

- Once Product Backlog is ready, it is considered as a superset and divided into different categories based on priorities, and implemented with each Sprint. Sprint is a Scrum event that ends with potentially releasable product Increment. It provides a working product with specified features as decided in the Sprint planning. Each Sprint is planned with specific amount of work based on the Development Team's capacity.

  o Each Sprint starts with Sprint Planning.

  o Sprint Planning is the process of planning the work that will be completed in the Sprint. The Product Owner and the Development Team are the main participants in this event, who discuss PBIs that can be included in the Sprint, based on the capabilities of the team. Let us see the diagrammatic representation of continuous planning:

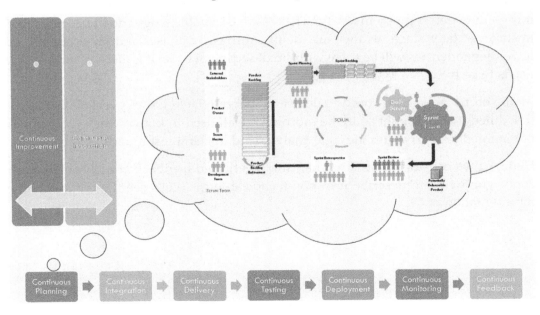

Figure 2.4: Continuous planning

- Backlog Grooming or Product Backlog refinement is one of the most important activities in a Scrum framework, as it improves estimation based on past learning. Hence, based on the understanding of the Scrum Team as well as stakeholders, Product Backlog items evolve.

Continuous integration

Continuous integration (CI) is a continuous DevOps practice in which Development Team commits bug fixes or feature implementation frequently, integrate them in shared repository such as GitLab or GitHub; every check in can be verified using an automated build that is scheduled or configured with hooks to trigger a build, execute unit tests, verify code quality, and create a package.

Recently, I came across a situation where the project team complained to us that after CICD configuration there were more failures in the build and it is a serious issue. All of us who were dealing with DevOps practices implementation were really surprised by this claim. We always came across a situation where CICD or automation or DevOps practices implementation helps to minimize issues. We discussed all the issues and finally came to the conclusion that the problem was not because of a CI configuration. The problem was different, and CI only highlighted the issues more than ever.

Hence, it helps to detect a problem early on so that it doesn't create issues later. Why it is good to detect problems early? The reason is, small changes don't become huge mistakes at later stages as they are identified in early phases and fixed quickly, as fewer dependencies will be there with small section of code. It is just the *mindset* that needs to be fixed.

In one of my projects, CI used to detect all merge-related issues every day, if any. I scheduled it at midnight so in the morning we all used to know which change was not merged properly with the code analysis and the Unit test reports.

Hence, if we consider CI as a mechanism to get rapid feedback at early stages then it is a good way to describe it in non-technical terms. Let's see the diagrammatic representation of CI:

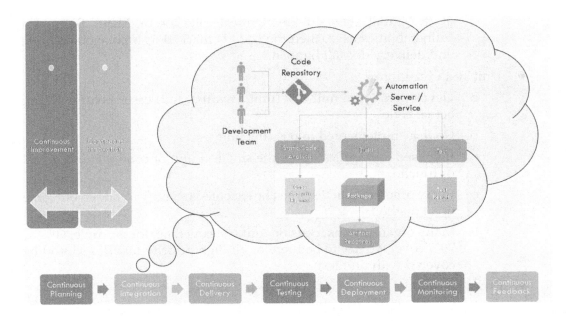

Figure 2.5: *Continuous integration*

Let's understand the flow – what happens in Continuous Integration.

- Developers commit code to central repositories such as GitLab, GitHub, Subversion, and Bitbucket in the following scenarios:
    - o Feature/user story is completed
    - o Bug is fixed
- CI build execution begins based on Push or Pull mechanism:
    - o Schedule based build trigger – inefficient, as CI server continuously Poll repository for changes
    - o Build trigger when developer commits code into repository – hook configured for repository triggers build in automation server or CI server – efficient, and works without delay
- Continuous code inspection: Static code analysis is configured with quality gates,
    - o SonarQube, Android Lint, ESLint, JSLint, FindBug, PMD, SwiftLint, OCLint, and other tools can be utilized for static code analysis
    - o Configure quality gate considering that the feature is available in the tool, so based on categories of issues, code analysis will fail and further processing won't happen
    - o Yes, most customers ask for maintaining code quality; I have seen many projects where SonarQube reports are used as benchmarks

at the initial stage. If any Critical, Blocker or Major Bugs and Vulnerabilities exist, then the code is marked as a poor quality one and delivery doesn't happen.

- Unit Test execution
  - o Developers write unit test (unit tests that fail) cases before writing actual code
  - o Code is implemented to pass the unit test
  - o It is used for verification of the smallest unit of code that is method or function
  - o Every time the Unit test must be executed to verify intended outcome of all methods
  - o Many organizations focus on unit test coverage, for example, 60% or 70% coverage has to be there or all high priority features should be covered with unit tests
- Package creation
  - o WAR / APK/ IPA files or packages or Artifacts are generated using Build tools, such as Apache Maven, Apache Ant, Make, Gradle, Nant, and MSBuild
- Artifact management
  - o Artifacts generated by build tools are stored in repositories, such as JFrog Artifactory or Nexus
  - o It is easy to manage binaries in such repositories
  - o Artifact repositories play a crucial role in Roll back process, considering the fact that they manage multiple versions
- What if the build breaks?
  - o Mail or slack notification can be configured
  - o Identify root cause or dependencies that triggered the failure
  - o Action must be taken to fix the build issues
  - o Identifying issues will be easier because of small changes and hence, the code that is responsible to break things needs to be attended to and fixed
- Continuous delivery tools: Azure DevOps, Travis CI, Jenkins, Bamboo, TeamCity, TFS.

Continuous delivery

Continuous delivery (CD) is an extension or continuation of CI. Sounds complex? Let take a look at the diagrammatic representation of CD:

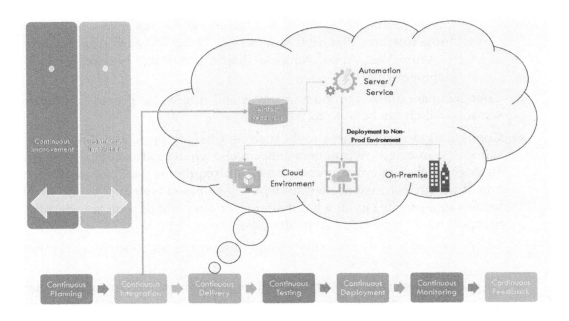

Figure 2.6: Continuous delivery

Let me rephrase it. Once CI is successful, it has a package as an outcome of this phase. Now, the important part is to deploy that package for further processing. CD deals with deploying the package into different environments. With the invention of cloud computing, multiple environments can be created for different types of testing. All the environments can be the same and created and destroyed within few minutes. Hence, the problem of huge cost is dealt with, through the use of cloud resources. Now, even containers can be used. Let's understand important aspects involved in the process of Continuous Delivery:

- Artifact repositories: Nexus or JFrog Artifactory can be utilized to retrieve the version of a package that needs to be deployed in a specific environment
- Environment can be Dev, QA, pre-prod, or any other non-prod; deployment environment can be cloud or non-cloud
  - o Cloud platforms such as AWS and Azure are utilized for deployment now a days
  - o Different cloud deployment models are popular, based on the criticality of the project; banking industry might not use public cloud, they prefer private clouds considering the security aspect; similarly, non-critical applications can use a public cloud
  - o Different cloud service models can be utilized for application deployment based on the requirements, for example, for more control and access, Infrastructure as a Service (IaaS - AWS EC2 instances,

Azure Virtual Machines) is utilized, while no responsibility of Infrastructure, Platform as a Service (PaaS - Azure App Services / Azure Web Apps, Amazon Elastic Beanstalk) is used for easy deployment

- Containers are utilized on premise; AWS and Azure also provide container services, which can be utilized

- Configuration management tools such as Chef, Puppet, and Ansible are utilized to manage environments effectively, while easily keeping efficient strategy to change environments based on requirements. For example, in one of the projects, we needed to deploy Java-based web application in 50 servers in a private cloud; what if after a certain point of time, it is decided that port needs to be changed in all of the 50 servers?

  o One way is to manually change the port in all 50 servers and that does sound good

  o Another way is to utilize configuration management tools so that such changes and many more things can be automated using this tool to swiftly make the changes

- Sprint-wise releases are not huge, and hence it is easy to detect issues and fix them before it goes to production (If you don't know about Scrum then go to *Chapter 1: Overview of Agile and Scrum Framework.*)

- Manual deployment to any environment can be a tremendous pain, considering the small size of the Sprints as multiple time deployment takes place all the time in all the environments; hence, automated deployment can be the best approach

- Automated deployment to any non-prod environment can be implemented using batch scripts, shell scripts, plugins, utilities, and tools

- What to use for deployment is very much decided on the basis of the culture of an organization

- Most of the automation tools provide facilities to deploy application packages in the form of plugins or integrating script

  o Azure DevOps, Jenkins, TeamCity, CircleCI, Atlassian Bamboo, IBM UrbanCode Deploy, Octopus Deploy, and other tools can be utilized to achieve automated deployment. Specific deployment tools are also supported by automation tools using plugins.

The objective of CD is to make product Increment ready to deploy with a faster time to market and with high quality. In addition, it brings a culture of discipline and standardizes deployment process. Faster time to market and high quality are the two major benefits that CD helps us in achieving.

Continuous Testing

Let's understand testing, automated testing, and continuous testing:

- **Testing:** Product Increment (Scrum terminology) is validated and verified against defined functional and non-functional requirements by the Product Owner. Outcome of the testing is the assurance of the level of quality the package satisfies. Effective and faster testing helps to improve the quality of a product Increment. Hence, manual testing creates a bottleneck when it comes to repeated testing in short Sprints. What if your application lifecycle phases are automated using CICD, where testing takes 2-5 days for verification and validation?

- **Automated testing:** In automated testing, testing teams write scripts using specific tools, considering the application type, such as web applications or mobile applications. It is useful to write automated test scripts for all high priority features to increase the coverage over time. Let us see the diagrammatic representation of automated and continuous testing:

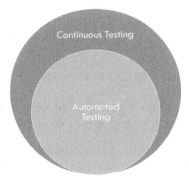

Figure 2.7: Continuous testing vs automated testing

- **Continuous testing:** Continuous testing is the accelerator in DevOps pipeline as it plays an important role of maintaining quality. It includes automated function, load/performance, security, and other tests. It plays an important role in the era of Agile, where development cycles are shorter and hence, multiple deployments take place every 3-4 weeks.

Continuous testing is a natural extension of CD. Once a package or application is deployed into non-prod environment and features are implemented, then it is ready for quality verification. It is best to decide the strategy of testing at the time of project initiation, so that planning and skills can be managed once the Sprint starts. Continuous testing is possible only with automated testing within short span of Sprints in Scrum. It is important to have the skill set with open source and commercial tools according to the culture of an organization. Additionally, processes need to be set for continuous testing. Essentially, it makes feedback continuous and quick, and hence, if actions are taken on time, quality of the product or an application is going to be better than before. Let us see the diagrammatic representation of continuous testing:

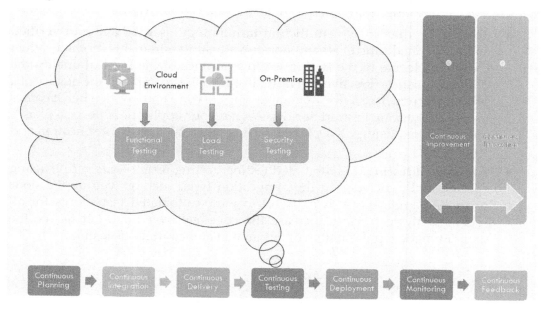

Figure 2.8: Continuous testing

Development methodologies, such as **test-driven development (TDD)** and **behavior-driven development (BDD)**, are very popular in DevOps practices implementation.

Test environment plays an important part in accelerating continuous testing. With cloud platforms and containers, it is easy to create Elastic environments for testing and getting away with it once the testing is done. Following are some important points related to testing in application lifecycle management:

- Unit test coverage is important to verify the smallest unit of the code that is a method or a function based on pre-defined input and output. As soon as the Development Team commits code into central/distributed repository, CI server / automation server compiles the code and execute Unit tests, and publishes reports in different forms based on the automation server. Unit testing comes with some challenges though:
  - o Culture of not writing unit tests
    - DevOps is all about changing the culture isn't it?
  - o Efforts are not estimated while negotiating with customers, and hence the Development Team feels Unit Tests are a burden
    - Convince the customer; convince the Development Teams and explain how it helps to identify defects early on, which results into faster time to market

- o Development team does not know the tools to write Unit test cases

    - ■ Arrange trainings; use video tutorials that are available online or use YouTube

- o Deadline to deliver the main product is an excuse for not writing unit test cases

    - ■ In my experience, a Java developer in my Scrum team developed 100s of unit tests within two days and he started enjoying writing it so much that it became a habit for him

- Create Test environments in cloud platforms, such as Microsoft Azure or AWS. Containers can be utilized for creating test environment. For example, Selenium Hub can be created using containers and functional test execution can start once the package is created using CI and deployed in QA environment using CD; For mobile applications, Appium can be used to perform automated functional testing.

    - o Once functional testing is completed, the Selenium Hub created using containers can be done away with.

- Cucumber is one of the popular tools for BDD.
- Pipeline can include configuration of load testing, using Apache JMeter or any other tool. The entire configuration can be configured in script and configured with automation server.

    - o Publish reports related to load testing, and based on the outcome, it can be decided whether further steps can be taken or not.

- Web application and mobile security testing tools can be utilized for integration of security testing in the DevOps pipeline.
- One of the important things for the testing team is to get the package on time for testing purpose. Using Artifact repository or automation server, artifact sharing becomes easier and multiple versions can also be managed

    - o Email and slack notifications can be highly effective for getting continuous updates of test failures, so that action against it can be performed.

In my discussions for automated testing, I have often found the following challenges:

- The Development Team is not writing codes in a way that we can automate it.

    - o There are problems in the existing development practices where developers don't care about standardization or coding standards and quality

    - o For example, ID or name attribute for HTML component is missing and that creates a problem for automation as it is difficult to identify the component using script. Many components are given the same name and hence it is literally impossible to find the component easily in a test automation script

o   Development teams complain about time issues because of deadlines. My answer to them is simple: Why do you follow all the standards when it comes from the customer? Writing good code is a habit and only you, yes your programmer is going to be benefitted by it in the long run.

● Testing team does not understand the features correctly and raises wrong defects

o   Involve testing team in all Product Backlog discussions, Sprint Planning, Sprint Review, Sprint Retrospective, and Product Backlog Grooming events so they are aware of all the things related to the project.

● Development and testing team don't see eye to eye because of the nature of their work

o   Culture shift is extremely important here.

o   All members of the Scrum Team have to understand that this is a team effort, and the goal of the entire activity is to create a better product, and hence collaboration and communication is vital.

Let's see the components of continuous testing:

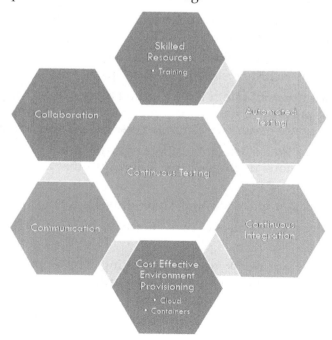

Figure 2.9: *Components of continuous testing*

Automated testing, CI, cost effective environment provisioning using cloud or containers, communication (Scrum events are helpful to achieve this), and collaboration (Scrum Framework incorporates this aspect) using tools such as slack or email notification, can be useful to accelerate time to market for a product Increment.

Continuous deployment

We have seen that objective of any organization is to deploy packages effectively and in a timely manner. CD achieves that in non-production environments such as Dev, QA, and stage. Let's see the diagrammatic representation of continuous deployment:

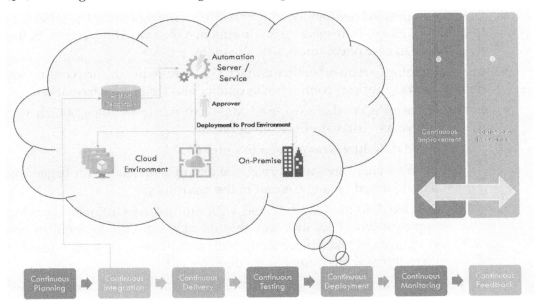

Figure 2.10: *Continuous deployment*

Continuous deployment is continuation of CD. In CD, a package is deployed in the production environment. Deployment may be based on approval workflow for better governance and verification from required stakeholder(s) that the package is good to go to the end users.

CD is a high-risk release, and hence governance needs to be setup for approval workflow. Approvals can be configured for one or multiple approvers based on the features available in the release automation team. There are cases where logical and/or conditions are configured in approval workflow.

Following are some important points for automated deployment in various environments:

- Automated deployment to prod environment can be implemented using batch scripts, shell scripts, plugins, utilities, and tools.

- What to use for deployment is very much decided by the culture of an organization.

- Most of the automation tools provide facilities to deploy application packages in the form of plugins or integrating script
  - o Azure DevOps, Jenkins, TeamCity, CircleCI, Atlassian Bamboo, IBM UrbanCode Deploy, Octopus Deploy, and other tools can be utilized to achieve automated deployment. Specific deployment tools are also supported by automation tools using plugins.

- CD and continuous deployment might use the same tool set or the same way to deploy package in respective environments; the only difference is better governance in case of continuous deployment.

- Important thing to remember here is that CD is a pre-requisite for a continuous deployment as it brings confidence of quality and faster time to market.

- In one of the project where we used Microsoft Azure DevOps, which was earlier known as Visual Studio Team Services
  - o Build definition was created to setup CI.
  - o Push mechanism was setup as the feature is available for triggering a build based on any commit in the repository.
  - o Release definition was created with multiple environments having approval workflow in a way that its successful deployment in one environment takes place along with approvals, only then it used to go to the next environment for deployment.
  - o Approval rights were given to the Product Owner, the Scrum Master and the Development Team based on the environments.
  - o Roll backs were managed in Microsoft Azure App Services using slots feature; slots in Azure App Services or Azure Web Apps take hardly few seconds to change the pointers to different slots and hence we can change environments in no time.

- In another project, we had configured roll back by using IBM Urbancode Deploy
  - o Two different implementations were successfully developed using Jenkins and Atlassion Bamboo.
  - o Jenkins had an IBM UrbanCode Deploy plugin so it was easier to integrate Jenkins and IBM UrbanCode Deploy.
  - o Artifact was retrieved from JFrogArtifactory in case of Atlassion Bamboo.

o Deployment workflows were created for deploying a web application in Tomcat Web Server.

o Approval workflow was set.

o In case of deployment failure, another workflow is used to trigger it, and it was a roll back workflow where the last successful deployment was done again to keep the application alive.

It is important to setup deployment environments quickly, and it can be achieved using cloud environments (IaaS or PaaS), configuration management tools, and containers. There are many ways to use infrastructure as a code that helps to create an entire environment in one go.

Approval workflows for deployment, monitoring of resources (infrastructure and application), and notification based on the status of success or failure of any phase in application lifecycle is critical to fix issues quickly.

Continuous monitoring and continuous notifications

Short Sprints, automated approach in managing application life cycle phases, and cloud environments bring speed and increased frequency to deployment activities. It is important to monitor all the activities related to application and environments to detect issues early and fix them before they affect the application to no point of return. Manual activities are no longer sufficient in a highly competitive and a fast world. Let's see the diagrammatic representation of continuous monitoring:

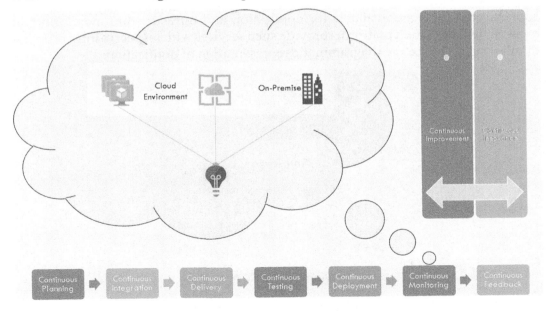

Figure 2.11: Continuous monitoring

It is important to monitor applications as well as Infrastructure, irrespective of production or non-production environments, as we move towards shift left movement in all activities. It is better to fail early when effect is not having high impact. Shift left approach is feasible now because of cost effectiveness and production like non-production environments provided by cloud platforms such as Microsoft Azure and AWS.

Now, the question is what are the examples of application and infrastructure monitoring?

In one of my projects, production and non-production environments were built using PaaS in Microsoft Azure Cloud. We configured the following:

- Scale in and scale out configuration based on CPU and memory utilization to deal with high-peak scenarios.
- Email notifications to respective stakeholders in scale in and scale out execution.
- Email notifications when errors occur while accessing web application.
- Any deployment failure would trigger email notification so release team can take actions quickly.

In one of the proof of concept, we integrated rollback scenario in case of deployment failure.

In another project, application monitoring tool was configured to keep track of all issues related to web servers and performance of database operations. Many sophisticated tools are available for application and infrastructure monitoring; in most of the cases, cloud platforms provide such services with respect to infrastructure monitoring. Let's see the diagrammatic representation of notification:

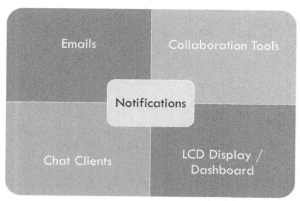

Figure 2.12: Notifications

Continuous monitoring should be part of DevOps pipeline and not an afterthought or a scheduled event once in a while. It is important to configure notifications based on emails or slack notification, considering the culture of an organization, to find out failures quickly so that they can be acted upon, and rectified quickly.

Continuous feedback

"We all need people who will give us feedback. That's how we improve."

- Bill Gates

Continuous feedback is one of the important phases in Agile development approach, where learning based on experience, feedback based on current market, or feedback based on expectations are integrated into the next Sprint to improve existing practices.

Remember Sprint Retrospective?

Sprint Retrospective marks an end of the Sprint, when constructive feedback is sought. Sprint retrospective often becomes a battle ground initially. Blame game starts and that is where Scrum Master comes into the picture to explain the real meaning and the purpose of a Sprint Retrospective meeting. Criticism, like rain, should be gentle enough to nourish the Development Team's growth without destroying their confidence.

Scrum Team decides, takes actions, affects the existing processes, receives feedback from stakeholders, incorporates it into the next Sprint, then the wise 'Scrum team makes more decisions, and so forth the circle of feedback and improvements go on and on.

Following are some important aspects of continuous feedback:

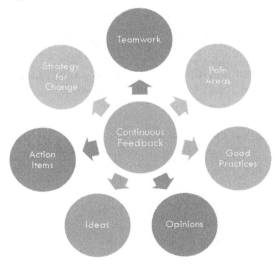

Figure 2.13: Continuous feedback

Make feedback a normal practice or a routine, rather than a once-in-a-while activity for performance review. It is important for a Scrum Team to identify the pain areas and the good practices, discuss them in openly, exchange ideas, prepare action items, and formulate a strategy to change the existing practices for improvement and innovations.

All the above continuous practices, along with automation, save time for the Development Team and increase their productivity. This can be utilized for continuous improvements and innovations to further enhance the time to market and the quality of the product or an application.

Continuous improvements

We cannot hope to build a better organization culture without improving the mindsets and the existing practices. To that end, each of us must work for our own improvement and, at the same time, share a general responsibility for the entire organization; our particular duty being to support, train, and share knowledge with those whom we think can be most useful in the business unit. DevOps practices implementation is a never-ending journey. There's always going to be growth, improvement, challenges, lessons; we need to take them all in and do what's right, continue to grow, live, market, and compete. *William Pollard* has correctly said that without change, there is no innovation, creativity, or incentive for improvement. Those who initiate change will have a better opportunity to manage the change that is inevitable. He also believed, *Learning and innovation go hand in hand. The arrogance of success is to think that what you did yesterday will be sufficient for tomorrow.* This is so apt for continuous improvement in DevOps culture.

For changing the organization culture towards continuous improvement, equal responsibility lies with the leadership as well as with other individuals. It is the responsibility of the leadership to provide opportunity to teams to improve by empowering them, and the responsibility of team is to contribute and improve with all available resources.

Continuous improvement requires attention to many details and Scrum events provide all the details and an opportunity to improve continuously, based on the combined learning of the Scrum Team.

The following diagram shows blocks of PDCA:

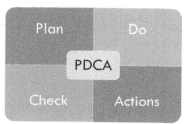

Figure 2.14: PDCA

Many organizations follow the PDCA technique for continuous improvements. This approach or technique is one of the most popular one in the Kaizen approach, where a specific issue is identified and improved upon, making continuous improvement an ongoing process, a part of the organization culture.

Continuous innovations

"Without change there is no innovation, creativity, or incentive for improvement. Those who initiate change will have a better opportunity to manage the change that is inevitable."

- William Pollard

Agile and DevOps practices are like winds of change. When the winds of change blow, some people/organizations build walls and others build windmills. It is all about being relevant in the market and business. Changes require innovation, and innovation leads to progress.

Innovation doesn't mean that you create something new; it can also mean to improve what exists. Remember, we discussed about the Waterfall and the Agile approach for software development? It is all about improving the existing practices by changing the culture of an organization.

Tom Freston rightly said, *Innovation is taking two things that already exist and putting them together in a new way.* Continuous practice, along with a desire to improve continuously, provides a way for continuous innovation.

Following are some of the phases for continuous innovation:

Figure 2.15: Continuous innovation

Agile development approach and DevOps practices implementation are something new, as well as re-arranging the old in a new way to improve existing practices. In my experience, Agile, Scrum Framework, and DevOps practices implementation are not a blanket implementation of what is available. It may differ in terms of certain small things, which are different which need to be identified. For example, automated deployment using deployment tools may not be a culture in a specific organization. That has to be brought in with conviction to convince stakeholders about its benefits and address their concerns to re-arrange existing practices for betterment. As *Socrates said, The secret of change is to focus all of your energy, not on fighting the old, but on building the new.*

How and why to innovate continuously? It is simple. You can't use up innovation. The more you innovate, the more ways you find to innovate. There's a way to do it better—find it, *Thomas Edison* said.

Benefits of DevOps culture and strategy

DevOps culture brings many benefits to an organization with respect to business and technical aspects. Let's understand the benefits of the same, and how to create a strategy to implement DevOps practices.

Benefits of DevOps

There are many benefits of the Agile approach and DevOps practices implementation. Refer to the following figure which includes the benefits of DevOps:

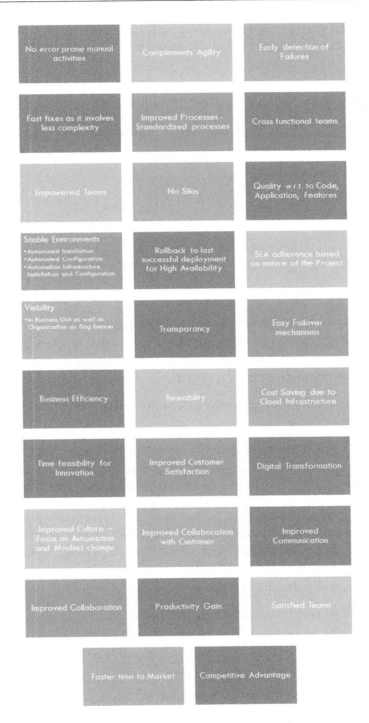

Figure 2.16: *Benefits of DevOps*

In the next section we will understand how to form a strategy and realize the benefits of DevOps practices implementation by adopting them in phases, considering the maturity model.

Strategy

A holistic DevOps practices implementation strategy should cover the following:

- Objective
- Maturity model
- Assessment framework
- Roadmap
- Plan
- Benefits measurement

Maturity model

DevOps practices implementation is better executed in a phased manner. It should be like plug and play in the DevOps pipeline, and hence it is important to work on all the practices in terms of planning and as and when an organization or a unit is ready, plug the new practice into the pipeline or orchestration.

DevOps maturity model indicates where are you in terms of defined maturity model at the start of the journey?

As DevOps and Agile both are journeys and not destinations, static maturity model doesn't work. You define your maturity model at the start and stick to it for the rest of the journey, is a scenario where you don't consider evolution of technology, knowledge, or best practices, and hence the culture.

As per my experience, the maturity model has to be defined as an **AS_IS** situation, and considering that, a **TO BE** scenario should be considered. However, over time, based on the technology and skill evolution, changes have to be considered and hence, maturity model should be dynamic.

This situation is similar to stretching your ability to lift eight when you reach a specific point of enhancing capability. However, care should be taken not to overstep in redefining it over and over again without any logical context to step up.

Another thing while considering the maturity model is to be flexible with respect to DevOps. It is a culture to improve speed and quality and not a technology hence, flexibility is needed. No single model or architecture or framework will fit all projects or application in the same projects or all business units.

Strange? Consider an application that requires mobile as well as web component. Your CI strategy, CD strategy, artifact repository-related decision will vary along with automated testing tools; it doesn't end there. You can't force customers to use specific tools if they have already established a culture of automation. You, as a service provider, need to work with the existing tools provided by customers. Not only that, scenarios can be different here as well. For example, implementation in customer environment with tools and resources provided by the customers; implementation in your environment and deployment in customer environment; implementation in your environment and deployment in cloud environment; implementation in customer environment while deployment in cloud environment. Additionally, different tools are used for different practices. For example, some organizations rely on open source tools while some have a Microsoft stack. In the same category, multiple tools are available. Hence, to go with a specific set of tools is not a good strategy to have at the outset. Rather, train your teams to work with multiple tools as practices are not going to change drastically. CI will be CI and CD will be CD, irrespective of the tools and the environment.

Usually, I follow a simple principle: work with the tool available and just try to find out manual activities in application life cycle phases and automate using best set of tools if they are available or suggest your tools. I prefer open source tools and it mostly works.

The following diagram represents sample maturity model:

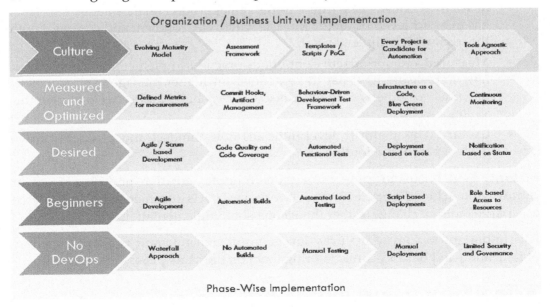

Figure 2.17: DevOps maturity model

The preceding diagram represents an indicative model and as I mentioned earlier, it should evolve continuously.

The model defines five maturity levels -- no DevOps, beginners, desired, measured and optimized, and culture. It is important to understand that at the beginning, organizations might be at different maturity levels in different categories.

For example, it is easier to configure static code analysis and CI, hence it might be the case where build automation, SCA, and CI might be higher in case of maturity levels than automated deployment. It is desired to bring all the projects at one standardized level, and then go upwards in maturity level. Once the base automation is achieved, then it is easier to scale up as resistance and other behavioral issues might not come as roadblock.

Following is the explanation of different maturity levels:

- **No DevOps:** AS IS situation with respect to automation; no defined practices or processes, and automation is driven by individuals rather than as a part of strategy.

- **Beginners:** Vision is defined and this maturity level covers minimal set of automation that needs to be achieved in each and every project irrespective of environments, and irrespective of who is controlling that environment to initiate a culture change.

- **Desired:** This is the level which we should keep as a base line from where to scale up, considering future improvements and enhancements. This level has to be achieved by all the projects where environment and control is with the team which implements it.

- **Measured and optimized:** Continuous practices implementation is good but how to measure it? It has to be defined for higher management as well as potential customers, with regards to clear visibility and gains to market this strategy well..

- **Culture:** This maturity level indicates how mindset and practices can be made a part of the routine.

Maturity model helps to gauge the success in implementation, and plan better for future work. Achieving maturity model works best if it is incremental and considered as a part of culture change, rather than a one-shot implementation.

It is important to convey maturity levels, improvements, and goals to the entire organization and business units to bring them on the same page.

Assessment framework

Many DevOps teams, tool vendors, and service providers create DevOps Assessment Framework. The following image depicts the results of sample assessment:

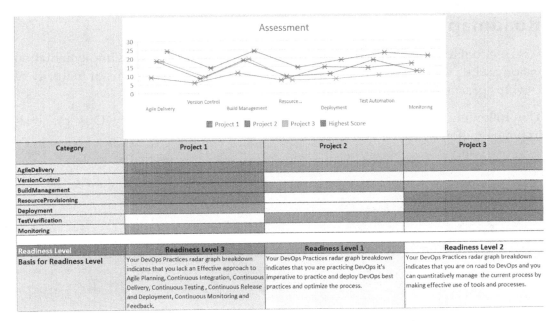

Figure 2.18: *DevOps Readiness Assessment Framework*

The previous image is just a sample for visualizing the assessment report. The assessment might include questions that are related to several topics, phases, or best practices:

- Process
- Culture
- Agile
- Version control
- Build management
- Resource provisioning
- Deployment
- Test automation
- Monitoring
- Measurement

Assessment framework helps to assess AS IS situation based on questionnaires, and decide the maturity of a project or business unit or organization. Based on it, further plan can be formed. This graph can be mapped with maturity levels as well.

Roadmap

It is essential to create definitive roadmap for the DevOps practices implementation vision and its success. Roadmap depends on where are you in terms of maturity of DevOps practices implementation.

The following figure depicts some phases of roadmap for DevOps practices implementation:

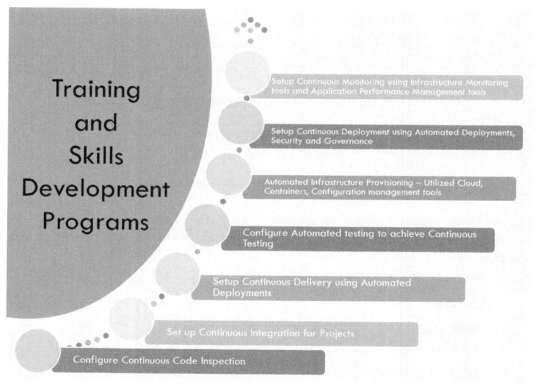

Figure 2.19: DevOps roadmap

Training and skill development across the DevOps journey help to accelerate progress towards the desired maturity levels in a speedy manner.

Plan

Create a plan based on the roadmap. Continuous practices implementation is always a phase-wise implementation.

Train people and spread awareness of DevOps practices. Define the goals and set a timeline to achieve it. Following are some of the DevOps phases:

Figure 2.20:DevOps phases

Once you achieve the goal, start implementing another phase and while doing it, plan to train resources for the requirements of the next phase or phases. It is important to identify, tools, trainings, project where we can implement DevOps practices.

Benefits measurement

Without measurements and visibility into benefits in numbers, it is difficult to convince management of an organization to not only continue its existing efforts but also to scale existing practices and future work.

Following are some measurement points in different phases:

- Continuous planning
  - o Sprint velocity
- CI
  - o Code quality in terms of bugs, vulnerabilities, and code smells
  - o Unit tests results
  - o Code coverage
- CD
  - o Deployment frequency
  - o Deployment time
  - o Deployment failures
  - o Roll back time in case of failed deployments
  - o Change in lead time
  - o Resource provisioning time

- Continuous testing
  - o Resource provisioning time
  - o Test execution time
  - o Frequency of test execution
  - o Automated functional tests (pass-fail ratio)
  - o Automated load/performance tests (pass-fail ratio)
  - o Automated security tests (pass-fail ratio)

In the case of continuous planning, velocity and continuous learning, to improve estimation of work for the next Sprint, help to measure the Development Team's capacity.

Over time, estimates become better, and the Development Teams knows their capabilities and plan implementation very well x. Velocity or speed of feature implementation becomes better with time, and it can be a useful metrics to measure the benefits of the Agile development approach.

In case of DevOps practices implementation, the easiest one to start measuring in terms of metrics is deployment time after and before DevOps practices are implemented.

In one of my projects, eight deployments were needed in the application servers hosted in Microsoft Azure Cloud. Before DevOps practices implementation, the Development Team used to deploy application in each environment manually.

Following were the hurdles in deployment:
- Size of the package
- Proxy/firewall
- Network speed
- Port opening in network to deploy a package from internal network to cloud

Due to the above constraints, the failure rate in deployment of an application was very high. It used to take a minimum of 15 minutes to deploy in one server and a maximum 30 minutes. Daily, 2-3 deployments were performed in all environments by two release engineers.

30 minutes * 2 deployments * 8 application servers of different environments

480 minutes a day

8 hours a day

4 hours a day in a deployment of application in different environments using release engineers.

Let's consider a scenario where deployment is done using Microsoft Azure DevOps. The moment code is checked in the Microsoft Azure DevOps repository, it will trigger build definition or CI process to be executed, Once it is successful, it will trigger deployments in multiple environments based on the extension/tasks configured in the release definition.

30 minutes was reduced to 5 minutes per deployment. All tasks were automated.

Release engineers took time initially to stable out the automation process but once it was stable, they hardly encountered failures. Notifications were configured for deployment failures so immediately they used to know about failures and they would act on it.

5 minutes * 2 deployments * 8 application servers of different environments

80 minutes is the total deployment time having no release engineer involved as it was an automated process.

40 minute a day, even if each release engineer wants to be present at the time of deployment activity.

1 hour and 20 minutes effectively in entire deployment. With parallel execution using multiple agents, time was further reduced based on the number of deployment agents.

This is just an indication of how measurements can be done in before and after scenarios to measure tangible benefits of DevOps practices implementation.

How to find DevOps skills

One of the major challenges is to get DevOps skilled resources. Often, it is not clear what kind of skills is required?

Personally, I look for good attitude in anyone who is going to be hired or is willing to work in my team. Next, it is important to have knowledge about continuous practices and how different tools can be utilized to implement automation pipeline for applying lifecycle management phases. Knowledge about cloud computing, cloud service models, cloud deployment models, containers, configuration management are a boon but can you expect all the things in one person?

Bit unrealistic, isn't it?

Hence, it is important to build a team and delegate work to resources who are expert in specific areas. For example, cloud engineers or security experts. Integrating cloud and security related things can be performed by DevOps engineer.

However, it is also important for DevOps engineer to know the basics of all the tools and technologies involved in automation of application lifecycle management phases.

One of the approaches which I don't endorse is hiring DevOps engineers to change culture. It is simply not possible as it is a team game, and collective effort is needed for the same. It is important to make people realize why DevOps is useful, train them and make them execute pilots, and make them realize how time is saved because of continuous practices implementation, and then your job is done.

I have a friend who was once involved in a project alongside me, and we implemented end-to-end automation for web application in Microsoft Azure. He realized the amount of time saved because of not doing manual deployment using FTP client. After that, he always looked to automate all the manual steps using Automation tools in the entire project on their own. That's how you build culture. By changing mindset of people who are working in the organization and not by hiring resources from outside organizations.

It is also important to spread awareness, irrespective of the roles and responsibility in the organization. Hence, introductory training is extremely important for spreading the word.

Effective way to influence the behavior and change mindset for DevOps adoption

There are many theories and concepts available that can be utilized for changing the mindset in the organization. Let us learn them.

Nudge theory

Richard Thaler was awarded the Nobel Prize in Economics 2017 for his contributions to behavioral economics. He is known as the Father of the nudge theory. In 2008, *Richard Thaler* and *Cass Sunstein* authored a book *Nudge: Improving Decisions About Health, Wealth, and Happiness*. It brought nudge theory to prominence.

Nudge theory is all about *nudging* people to make changes in policies and implementing things that are beneficial in the long term. Nudges are not about mandating something.

For example, putting apple at eye level counts as a nudge. Banning pizza doesn't count as a nudge.

DevOps team has to be a nudge unit to change the culture in an organization. That is how people's mindset and behavior are changed in a way without forcing them towards certain options or significantly changing their economic incentives.

Nudges are small changes in the overall culture that are easy and inexpensive to implement. There are many types of nudges that can help in cultivating DevOps culture in an organization.

Default Nudge

It is an effective way to influence behavior in the organization through DevOps practices implementation. Keep DevOps practices implementation as a default if it is not opted out with valid reasons. Research and experimental studies show that making an option a default increases the chance of it getting selected and performed; this is called the default effect.

Keeping DevOps practices implementation as a default is an important example of nudges or soft paternalist policy.

The social proof of Nudge

It is easy to convince customers and project teams by showcasing DevOps practices implementation by other teams and benefits they have achieved. Everyone wants to adopt new and efficient things and by providing proof of successful execution of DevOps practices implementation, it becomes easier to convince different stakeholders.

By demonstrating tools, processes, and frameworks, we can nudge others to change their mindset and go for tools as well as to implement DevOps practices.

Numerical anchors Nudge

Measurement Metrics with numbers can help nudge stakeholders or teams to change mindset. For example, before DevOps practices implementation, deployment used to take 30 minutes, while after its implementation it takes 5 minutes. Cumulative calculation becomes huge and teams understand gain in terms of time and productivity.

Option restriction Nudge

Keep specific options in terms of DevOps practices implementation, such as implement CI. Keep all critical and major bugs in solved state before deployment. Use open source tools for automation, use Jenkins or Azure DevOps for CICD automation. It works better than giving them option to use any tool they like and any DevOps practices which are feasible. It creates confusion and delays if multiple options are provided to the team.

Competition Nudge

One of the most important nudges in the business unit or an organization is competition nudge. Spread the word that a specific project or a unit is utilizing DevOps practices and managing productivity gains. It encourages other teams and units in the organization to compete and incorporate DevOps practices in their existing culture.

CAMS model

The CAMS model term was coined by *Damon Edwards* and *John Willis* after DevOps Days Mountain view 2010. Damon Edwards and John Willis are the authors of the famous Podcast *DevOps Cafe*. **CAMS** stand for **Culture, Automation, Measurement and Sharing**.

We have covered cultural aspect, automation using continuous practices, and measurement of metrics. Now refer the following image to understand the CAMS model:

Figure 2.21: CAMS model

Sharing is one of the important aspects to grow DevOps culture in an organization. Collaborative culture with communities to share technical knowledge and troubleshooting issues, breaking the walls of different projects or business units cultivate DevOps culture, which eventually benefits the organization.

> Read more DevOps Culture (Part 1) at **http://itrevolution.com/devops-culture-part-1/**. This article is written by *John Willis*.

Conclusion

DevOps culture can be affected by cognitive biases as it is all about changing culture and hence resistance is inevitable. Cognitive biases are patterns of deviation from the norm and are related to psychology and behavioral economics. Assessment framework, maturity model, frameworks, and processes help fix resistance due to culture change.

Ambiguity effect	The tendency to avoid options regarding automated approach and continuous practices implementation for which the probability of a favorable outcome is unknown. Phase wise implementation based on maturity model, realize the benefits and go for next phase.

Anchoring or vocalism	The tendency to rely too heavily on existing practices while making decisions, not to integrate feedback frequently and learn from lessons to improve practices to improve existing organization culture. Create a chart of things that went well and things which went wrong, introspect in Retrospective meeting and decide action items to improve on, create a plan to integrate action items in the coming sprints based on priorities.
Automation bias	The tendency to depend excessively on automated systems without verification and improvements based on learning, leading to erroneous automated information overriding correct decisions. **Try -> Analyze -> Revise -> Try Again** should be the cycle the Scrum team needs to focus on. Even with automation, it is important to analyses or monitor behavior of existing processes. Continuous monitoring, continuous improvements, and continuous innovations help to improve organization culture.
Availability cascade (Anti-Pattern)	Repeat something long enough and it will become true. In case of DevOps practices implementation, this is true in the context. The more you repeat the process of automation, the more you gain confidence and the more you realize its benefits.
Bandwagon effect	The tendency to do (or believe) things because many other people do (or believe) the same. Everyone is doing DevOps and that's why organizations want to do DevOps. It is better to have DevOps assessment framework and measurements in place to find out AS-IS scenario and benefits that can be achieved using DevOps practices.
Curse of knowledge	When better-informed DevOps evangelists find it extremely difficult to think about problems from the perspective of Project Teams or Development Teams.
Declinism	Often, the predisposition to view the past favorably and the future negatively is a common practice when any change in culture is going to take place. It is a game of patience.
Default effect	If DevOps practices implementation is considered as a choice between several options, the tendency to favor the default one helps in convincing the teams. It also applies to tools that are going to be utilized in automation.
Empathy gap	In cultivating DevOps culture, the tendency to underestimate the influence or strength of feelings, in either oneself or others, is a road block. Even if it is a resistance in practice implementation, that has to be taken seriously and addressed.

Exaggerated expectation	The tendency to expect or predict more extreme outcomes from automation or DevOps practices implementation than those outcomes that actually happen. It disappoints people and the growth stops. It is better to keep realistic expectations; learn from failures and improve.
Functional fixedness	Existing culture in terms of processes and technology limits a person to using an object only in the way it is traditionally used. It is important to find bottlenecks and improve existing practices in application lifecycle management.
Law of the instrument	An over-reliance on a familiar tool or methods of existing practices, ignoring or under-valuing alternative DevOps practices, which are more useful in terms of faster time to market and getting quality. It is important to have a vision for a cultural change and go ahead with it by using assessment framework or maturity models.
Mere exposure effect	The tendency to express undue liking for traditional practices, merely because of familiarity, and ignoring continuous practices of DevOps culture.
Neglect of probability	The tendency to completely disregard probability of failures of DevOps practices implementation due to cultural difference when making a decision under uncertainty.
Optimism bias	The tendency to be over-optimistic, overestimating favorable and pleasing outcomes.
Ostrich effect	Ignoring an obvious not so-effective traditional approach and ignoring better approaches.
Outcome bias	The tendency to judge a decision by its eventual outcome instead of based on the quality of the decision at the time it was made. Hence it is important to implement continuous practices phase wise; realize the benefits and then implement another practice.
Status quo bias	The tendency to like things to stay relatively the same and not to adopt new practices even though they are useful and in trend.

In the next chapter, we will cover how cloud computing plays a crucial role in changing existing organization culture.

## CHAPTER 3

Overview of Cloud Computing and Containers

Cloud computing is a disruptive innovation in recent times. This chapter will cover the definition of cloud computing and containers. We will discuss the benefits of cloud and containers. We will discuss cloud service models and deployment models along with their use. We will also cover the difference between virtual machine and containers. This chapter will cover how Agile, DevOps practices implementation, and cloud computing combination can be utilized effectively to transform the culture of an organization effectively.

Structure

In this chapter, we will discuss following:

- Cloud computing
- Cloud deploymentmodels
- Cloud service models
- Benefits of cloud computing
- Containers
- How Agile, DevOps, and cloud are effective together

Objective

The main objective of this chapter is to get familiar with cloud computing, its different models, and their benefits. It is important to understand how cloud can play a game changer in DevOps adoption.

Cloud computing

Let's understand some of the challenges in traditional environment and how cloud computing provides an answer to those challenges. Refer to the following diagram:

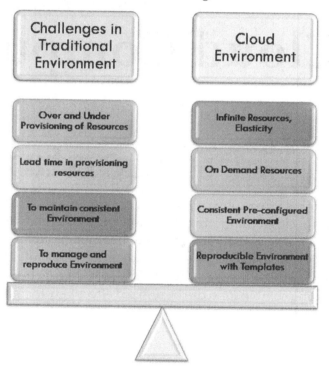

Figure 3.1: Traditional and cloud environment

Before discussing in details, let's understandwhat is cloud computing?

As per **National Institute of Standards and Technology (NIST)** definition, there are following aspects of cloud computing:

- Cloud deployment models
- Cloud service models
- Essential characteristics

The following figure refers to the NIST cloud computing:

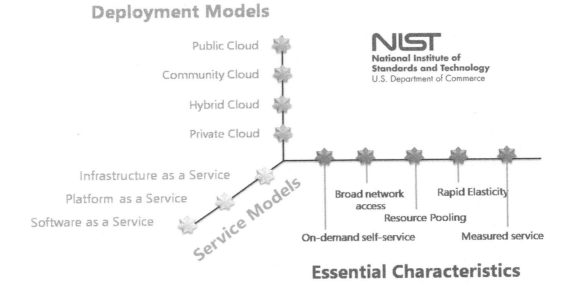

Figure 3.2: *NIST-cloud computing*

Let's discuss cloud deployment models and cloud service models in details.

Cloud deployment models

There are four cloud deployment models as per NIST definition:

- Public cloud
- Private cloud
- Hybrid cloud
- Community cloud

Let's understand each cloud deployment model in detail.

Public cloud

Public cloud is one of the most popular cloud deployment models. We can access public cloud services over internet. Anyone who has a credit card or enterprise account or free tier can access public cloud services.

Following are some important benefits of public cloud:

- Compute, storage, and network resources are available as service.

- Self-service model.
- Resources such as VM, storage, network, security,among others, are provided over the internet.
- Resources are shared (multi-tenant) and dedicated, based on the services made available by the cloud service providers.
- Privacy is considered using multi-tenant architecture.
- Free tier for 1 year or free usage using credit amount of month is available for trial purpose.
- Pay as you use, just like utility services - electricity - pay as per usage.
- Third-party is responsible for purchasing infrastructure, managing and maintaining infrastructure effectively.
- Quick provisioning of resources.
- Infinite scalable resources - sometime limited as per account or based on cloud services providers' rules.
- Management, monitoring, and security are the responsibilities of cloud service providers based on the cloud service models used by the user.
- No heavy capital expenditure is required to manage and maintain on-premises IT resources.
- Public cloud provides infinite scalable resources with multiple regions and data centers to design application architecture that supports high availability and fault tolerance.
- Less waste of resources due to agility.
- Complete control over resources and hence any customization related to installations and security can be performed.

Let's see the use cases of them. Following are some important use cases of public cloud:

- Most popular for test environments
- Non-critical applications to start with
- Good candidate for applications that has unusual flow of traffic
- Storage backup and archive
- Big Data processing applications

Following are some examples of public cloud provider:

- Microsoft Azure Cloud
- Amazon Web Services (AWS)
- Google Compute Engine (GCE)
- Digital Ocean
- Rackspace

My Experiences

It all started in 2010, when I changed my job,I first encountered cloudcomputing with respect to actual hands-on. In 2009, I worked on a Java-based application that used to store compressed and encrypted database backup in cloud.

Initially, public cloud was just used for experiments and non-critical applications. However, over time things have changed based on the experiences and confidence in cloud services in different organizations.

Nowadays, security is one of the important things in application lifecycle management activities, and it is one of the focal points irrespective of where application is hosted and hence, public cloud has become more acceptable, considering improved security practices and increased capabilities of different organizations as well.

I have used both Microsoft Azure and AWS in some projects, and most of the time environments were provided by customers themselves and hence we could understand the increased level of maturity in market as well.

Scalability and load balancer are eye catching and widely-used features in public cloud adoption for maintaining high availability and fault tolerance.

While security is still a debatable point, public cloud is gaining momentum for wider adoption based on increased confidence and maturity.

Let's compare services provided by Microsoft Azure and AWS:

Category	Microsoft Azure	Amazon Web Services (AWS)
VMs	Azure Virtual Machines	Elastic Compute Cloud (EC2) Instances
Containers	Azure Container Service	EC2 Container Service
Kubernetes	Azure Kubernetes Service	Elastic Container Service for Kubernetes
Function as a Service or Serverless Computing	Azure Functions	AWS Lambda
Object storage	Azure Storage	Simple Storage Services
Disk storage	Azure Storage Disk	Elastic Block Store
Hybrid storage	StorSimple	Storage Gateway
Data transfer	Import/Export	AWS Import/Export Disk
Virtual Network	Virtual Network	Virtual Private Cloud
Cross connectivity	Azure VPN Gateway	AWS VPN Gateway
Domain name system service	Azure DNS	Route 53

CDN	Azure Content Delivery Network	CloudFront
Dedicated network	ExpressRoute	Direct Connect
Relational database	SQL database	RDS
Authentication and authorization	Azure Active Directory Azure Active Directory Premium	Identity and Access Management
DevOps	Azure DevOps	AWS CodeBuild AWS CodePipeline

Table 3.1: Microsoft Azure and AWS Services

This is only a limited list of services provided by AWS and Microsoft Azure. In the next section, we will discuss private cloud.

Private cloud

Private cloud is a cloud deployment model that serves the need of a single organization that builds it and owns it. Private cloud is built behind the organization firewall and the whole infrastructure is under the control of an organization; hence, the organization can design and implement all the practices and experience over the years. It is easy to convince internal business unit for cloud usage as it is secure, and is only utilized by the organization. Private cloud provides the same kind of features that public cloud provides. Major difference can be the cost and control. The following explains the private cloud reference architecture:

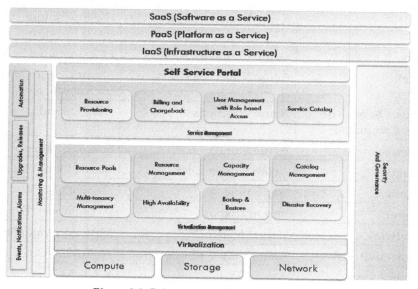

Figure 3.3: Private cloud reference architecture

Private cloud vendors provide product(s) which can be utilized to build enterprise level private cloud with all the features similar to public cloud services. Virtualization and virtualization management products are used to manage resource pools while multiple services are available, such as the following:

- High availability
- Fault tolerance
- Resource management
- Backup and restore
- Resource provisioning
- Billing and chargeback
- Role-based access
- Service catalogue

Once all the layers are installed and configured properly, the self-service portal can be utilized for using all computing, storage, and network resources effectively using resource pools.

Let's understand the different challenges an organization faces, and how private cloud can address all those challenges:

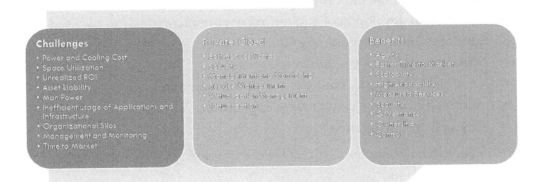

Figure 3.4: Private cloud benefits

Following are the challenges faced by organizations:

- Dynamic market scenario requires agility and rapid provisioning of IT resources to deploy product increment faster.
- End users need better quality of product/software/application.
- Silos with underutilized capacity leads to inefficient utilization.
- High security and industry compliance requirements make large organizations vary of using public cloud.
- Monitoring, measurement, and chargeback for consumption of resources per business unit.

Following are the benefits of using a private cloud:

- Private cloud provides agility through on-demand, pay as you go, scalable, and rapidly-deployable resource pools.
- Private cloud provides architecture that provides agility, performance, scalability, availability, security, and manageability.
- Virtualized resources, resource pools, and self-service portal help to reduce complexities and increase efficient utilization of resources.
- On-premise design and control, along with ownership of all resources, help organizations with compliances and business requirements.
- Private cloud platforms provide sophisticated offerings or features for management, monitoring, measurement, high availability, and chargeback related features or solutions.

Following are some of the important use cases of Private cloud:

- Application development and testing environment
- Special compliance requirements
- Special configuration requirements
- Centralized resources with security and governance
- Adoption of cloud – cloud native applications
- Research and innovation

Following are some examples of private cloud provider:

- VMware vCloud
- OpenStack
- CloudStack

My Experience

Private cloud was more popular and is still more popular because of the security-related aspects, considering the deployment location of private cloud behind the firewall of an organization. However, purchasing sufficient physical resources such as compute, storage, and network components is a task that takes a lot of time.

In most organizations, there is a process that is followed for acquiring new resources and there are budget-related constraints too. It took more than 3-4 months for the acquisition, and even 100 GB RAM and two blade servers were found to be limited for advanced level of proof of concepts.

We majorly used VMware and OpenStack for building private cloud. We worked more on VMware-based cloud. We utilized products such as VMware ESX, VMware ESXi, VMware vCenter, and VMware vCloud Director.

A team that starts with building a private cloud gains more insights into work with cloud computing as they build the entire cloud with sophisticated products provided by cloud vendors.

OpenStack was gaining popularity at that time and we started working on PoC for OpenStack as well.

Our main objective was to build a private cloud initially and then try to automate this entire process. Yes, building a private cloud in an automated manner. We utilized different CLIs and APIs available for VMware and created scripts to build private cloud in minimum time.

Multiple scripts, open source tools and CLIs or APIs are available to install virtualization software on bare metal resources. It can be used to discover physical hosts and install necessary software on it to make it virtualization enabled.

Once the virtualization layer is successfully installed and configured, the next step is to install management layer over virtualization layer to manage it more effectively. Virtualization management layer provides more features in terms of high availability, fault tolerance, and resource pools compared to only virtualization layer.

Once virtualization management layer is installed and configured using CLI or API that is made available by the private cloud vendor; the next step is to install the security layer, create service catalogues and policies. It is an essential part of service providers to provide ease of use on self-service portal.

It is advisable to use CLIs or APIs provided by private cloud vendor rather than using third-party tools to manage automation scripts.

Flow can create phase-wise implementation of private cloud that can be easily replicated, which is also represented in a diagrammatic manner below:

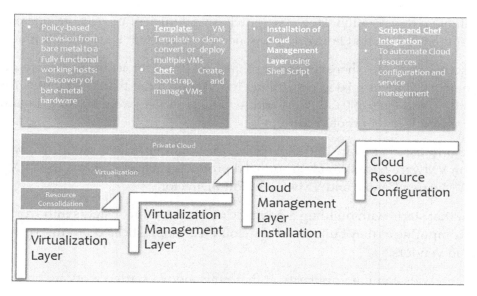

Figure 3.5: Phase-wise implementation of private cloud

In the next section, we will discusshybrid cloud.

Hybrid cloud

Hybrid cloud is a cloud deployment model that has a mixture of other cloud deployment models such as public cloud and private cloud. The main objective of this design is to keep business-critical applications and data on-premises (behind firewall) in a more secure environment or perceived to be more secure environment such as on a private cloud, while keeping the rest of the components on a public cloud. Hence, it addresses concerns of organizations and also brings cloud benefits into picture. At times, it is a combination of on-premise resources or virtualized resources or private cloud resources and public cloud resources.

Following are some of the benefits of hybrid cloud:
- Best of both worlds
    - **Public cloud:** agility, scalability, and economy of scale
    - **On-premise resources or virtualized resources or private cloud:** ownership, security, and governance
- Deploy critical application on premise or keep sensitive data on premise to maintain security

Following are some of the popular use cases of hybrid cloud:
- Dynamic or highly changeable or spike usage applications
- Big Data processing
- Backup

Following are some of the providers that give facility to manage multiple clouds (tools for hybrid cloud management):

- Scalr
- RightScale Cloud Management
- VMware Suite

My Experiences

In my experience, I have worked on two projects and many more RFPs where the customer was willing to use public cloud only for non-critical components of the entire architecture. In one of the RFP, database was available on premise and application was required to be hosted on AWS. AWS provides services with which we can connect to on-premise resources and utilize effectively.

Network connectivity can be established between the Amazon VPC and the on-premises network using a **virtual private network (VPN)** or AWS Direct Connect services. The database available on premise can be accessed from public cloud resources.

The following diagram explains hybrid cloud scenario:

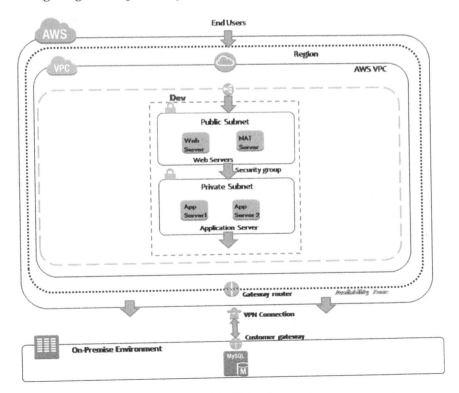

Figure 3.6: Hybrid cloud scenario

In another project, we used to have a third-party service hosted on the vendor's resources. Our Java-based middleware was hosted on Microsoft Azure Web Apps or Azure App services. All the data to the front end was made available using Java middleware but data was supplied from third-party vendor.

It was a tricky situation where we had to whitelist IP addresses of Azure App Services at the third-party vendor's firewall so our middleware could access API service hosted on the vendor's infrastructure.

Azure App Service is a PaaS, so as an end user we don't have any control but they provide the list of IP addresses in the Microsoft Azure portal that can be utilized for such integration.

Community cloud

Community cloud is a deployment model where resources are shared among the organizations who share common interests or security requirements or compliance requirements or performance requirements.

Following are some of the benefits of community cloud:
- Available to a set of organizations or users.
- Cloud features with specific security and compliance requirements considering users or organizations.

Following are some of the popular use cases of community cloud:
- Banking, government or utilities
- Life Science industry

After the overview of all the cloud deployment models, let's try to understand the difference between public cloud and private cloud:

Features	Public cloud	Private cloud
Scalability	• High • On demand provisioning to unlimited expansion • Economy of scale is applicable	• Low to Medium • Scalability to a limited extend based on resources available in the organization • Economy of scale is not applicable or limited
Reliability	• Medium to high, based on cloud service provider • SLAs are mapped with each service • Dedicated hardware offerings are available	• High, as resources are on-premise behind organization firewall

Security	• Good, but depends on security measures of service provider • Special security services are provided by cloud service providers yet configuration depends on cloud service model, that is,PaaS or IaaS	• Highly secure, all resources are on-premise • Traditional control can be established based on experience of specific organization • Resources are not shared with any other organizations
Performance	• Uses shared resources performance is based on the selection of resources in configuration considering the cost- low to medium	• Dedicated resource pool provides very good performance
Cost	• Low to Medium • No upfront cost • No need to procure hardware or software • Pay-as-you-go model • Cloud service providers provides services accessed by internet	• High • High upfront cost, requires on premise resources such as data center space, security, electricity, cooling, management, and monitoring related expenses • Open source and commercial products are available for private cloud setup
Control (hardware resource)	• Minimal control as per service provider rules and regulation • Dedicated hardware offerings are available	• Greater control, as they are self-owned and available on premise
Time to market	• Quick availability of resources or runtime environments	• More time is required to procure resources • Expertise is needed for installation and configuration of private cloud
Maintenance	• Cloud service provider is responsible for maintenance	• Organization or business unit is responsible for maintenance
Examples	• Amazon Web Services • Microsoft Azure • Google Cloud Platform	• VMware • OpenStack • Cloudstack

Table 3.2: Public cloud vsprivate cloud

Cloud service models

There are three cloud service models as per NIST definition, which are as follows:

- **Infrastructure as a Service (IaaS)**
- **Platform as a Service (PaaS)**
- **Software as a Service (SaaS)**

Infrastructure as a Service (IaaS)

Infrastructure as a Service (IaaS) provides resources such as compute, storage, network and others, where end users have more control and responsibility. End users don't have any control over cloud infrastructure as it is multi-tenant. However, end user has control over configurations such as OS and security.

In other words, it is similar to plain burger. If you buy it from the market, filling up with eatables and making it tasty is your responsibility. Similarly, in IaaS, all configurations and customizations should be done by the end user, and in case of failure to do so; the cloud service provider is not responsible.

The following diagram shows the example of IaaS:

Figure 3.7: Base Burger - IaaS

Let's see VMs available in Microsoft Azure:

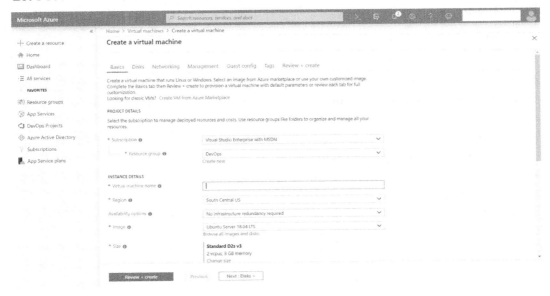

Figure 3.8 *Microsoft Azure IaaS*

The following screenshot provides details of image section, which has all the available images to create a VM:

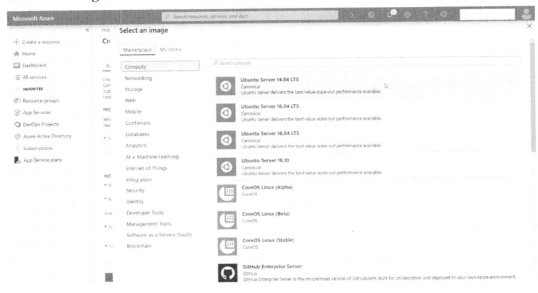

Figure 3.9: *Microsoft Azure VM images*

Hence, after VM is ready, all runtime environment installation and configuration is the end user's responsibility.

Following are some of the benefits of IaaS:

- No upfront investment/capital expenditure.
- Pay as you go pricing model.
- Scalability, high availability, fault tolerance can be configured with extra cost.
- More control over resources, virtual machines are available for security configuration and other hardening.
- User is responsible for all installation and configuration of runtime environment.
- Many services are made available by cloud service providers to easily administer or clone all resources.
- Expert knowledge is required to setup environments.

Following are some of the use cases of IaaS:

- Customization in runtime environment or specific versions of web server or application server is needed.
- Need complete control over runtime environment.
- Cost-effective option.
- Dynamic needs of resources.

Following are some of the examples of IaaS provider:

- Microsoft Azure Virtual Machines
- Amazon Elastic Compute Cloud (EC2)
- Simple Storage Services (S3)
- Azure Storage—Block Blob
- Elastic Block Store (EBS)
- Azure Storage Disk—Page Blobs
- Elastic File System
- Azure Files
- Virtual Private Cloud (VPC)
- Azure Virtual Network

My Experiences

Let's see an example of IaaS in AWS:

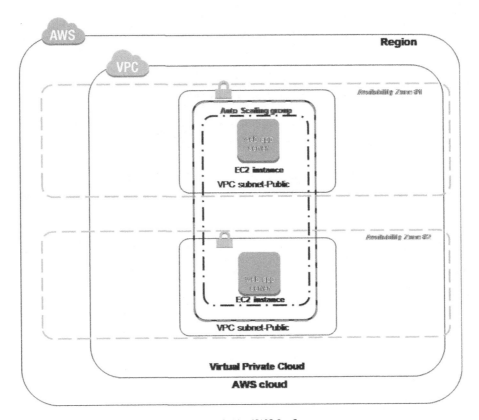

Figure 3.10: AWS IaaS

In most of the projects initially, AWS was used by the customer and IaaS was the service model that was very close to an on-premise environment, so customers were more comfortable in using IaaS. Initially it was all about VMs and no other service.

We used to configure virtual private cloud, subnets, security groups, auto scaling groups, load balancer, and all for high availability. Availability zones and regions were utilized to make application fault tolerant. Obviously, cost is a factor while configuring any application across regions but customer priority is more important, and according to need such configurations are useful.

Platform as a Service (PaaS)

Platform as a service (PaaS) is a cloud service model that provides different runtime environments in which a user can directly deploy application.

The following diagram shows the example of PaaS:

Figure 3.11: Burger - PaaS

In other words, it is similar to a burger with some pre-decided or pre-defined filling. Pre-configured platforms are available. Cloud service provider is responsible for managing the underlying infrastructure and the runtime environment.

For example, in Azure App Services, the following configuration is available, as shown in the following screenshot:

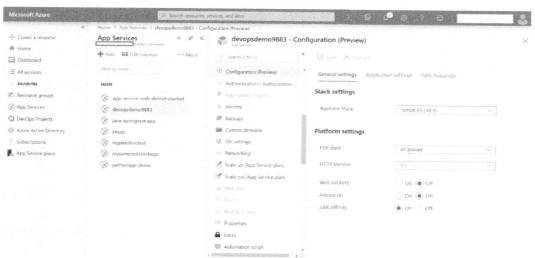

Figure 3.12: Azure App Services - PaaS

The following screenshot shows that the run-time stack gives details on available platforms:

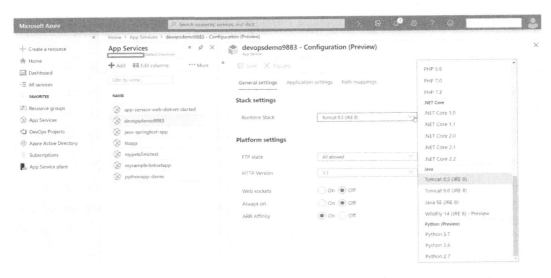

Figure 3.13: *Azure App Services - PaaS - runtime*

Following are some of the benefits of PaaS:
- No upfront investment/capital expenditure.
- Pay as you go pricing model.
- Usually no extra cost for available runtime environments; user only pays for underlying resources, however, it differs from one service provider to another.
- Easy configuration of scalability, and high availability.
- Most of the administrative tasks are configured from the cloud portal itself.
- Expert knowledge is useful, but all underlying resources and runtime management is done by the cloud service provider.
- Faster time to market,
  - o Resources are available for deployment much faster than IaaS as everything is available.
- Deployment requires drag and drop or package selection box in cloud portal.
- Users or organization can focus on core tasks, while the rest of the activities, such as environment provisioning, installation and configuration of runtime environment, and security configuration of the environment,are managed by experts from the cloud service providers.
- Backup and upgradation is the responsibility of the cloud service providers.

Following are some of the use cases of PaaS:
- Need speed and flexibility.
- No specific requirements in terms of runtime environment and all the components are provided by PaaS offerings.

Following are some of the examples of PaaS provider:

- Microsoft Azure App Services
- Amazon Elastic Beanstalk

My Experiences

For most of my projects, I have worked on the PaaS model only in the latter part of my work. Azure App Services was the main service in one of my last two projects. I have realized that Europe-based project is using Microsoft Azure more.

Azure App Services are easy to configure, and all the configurations are available in the portal. Portal settings and UI have been changed multiple times in the last couple of years but as per my understanding, it has become better with time. For both the projects, we used to host Java-based middleware in Azure App Services in Tomcat web server.

Runtime stack is available with specific versions for Java. If those versions are not feasible for a project then Azure App Services is of no use. Better to go for IaaS in such scenarios.

Azure App services can be easily configured with Azure Active Directory. Multiple pricing models are available and some of the best features are available in Azure App Services, such as deployment slots or troubleshooting, notifications, scaling configuration, and so on. Deployment slot is an amazing feature of Azure App Service that can be utilized for rollback. It requires only few seconds to change versions across slots or environments.

Azure App Service Environment is a premium service that allows you to get Azure App Services in a virtual network, and hence you can configure firewall rules and make it more secure. Essentially, you get more control with the flexibility of PaaS.

Software as a Service

Software as a service (SaaS) is a cloud service model that provides direct access to a hosted application. No need to install infrastructure or deploy packages. Application can be accessed on internet from anywhere. All data resides with the service provider and so does all the responsibilities.

Following are some of the benefits of SaaS:

- No upfront investment/capital expenditure.
- Subscription model.
- Scalability and high availability are the responsibility of the cloud service providers.
- Faster time to market.

- Backup and upgradation are the responsibility of the cloud service providers.
- All responsibilities lie with the cloud service providers.

Following are some of the use cases of SaaS:
- Short-terms requirements.
- To use already-established applications and to avoid installing and configuring them for quick usage.

Following are some of the examples of SaaS provider:
- Microsoft Office 365
- Salesforce.com
- Google Apps
- Dropbox
- Slack

My Experiences

In most of the organizations, we utilized Microsoft Office 365 or Microsoft SharePoint using SaaS. In daily usage, we use many SaaS based applications.

Just think about the applications that are not installed or configured and directly used using the internet in a browser!

Containers

Containers can package application code, libraries, and configurations. Container engine is installed on host OS. Hence, all containers share a single host and that can be a security threat. However, all containers are run as isolated process and managed by container engine. Many containers can run on a single Host operating system.

Let's understand how containers are different from VMs. Each VM requires own guest OS. Type 1 virtualization needs host OS while Type 2 virtualization product can be directly installed on the hardware:

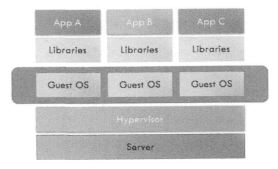

Figure 3.14: Virtual machine

One hosted OS can be used to run multiple isolated containers, as shown in the following diagram:

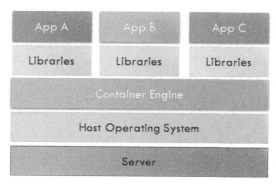

Figure 3.15: Containers

Docker is an open source tool that is used to create, deploy and manage containers on different host operating systems, using resource isolation features, such as cgroups and Linux kernels. Docker comes in two flavors:

- Docker Community Edition
- Docker Enterprise Edition

Docker Hub is a SaaS that provides the facility of publishing and sharingDocker images through a common library. Docker swarm supports cluster load balancing, where multiple Docker resource pools act as one and that results into scalability and high availability.

An organization utilizes orchestration to manage containers in an effective manner.

Following are some of the benefits of containers:

- Less complexities in management
- Portability
- Minimum size as no guest OS is involved
- Faster to spin up/deployment

Following are some of the use cases of containers:

- PaaS
- Testing infrastructure
- Application migration
- Microservices – each service that can be considered as application can be packaged in container; scalability and high availability of the application or service can be managed independently based on the usage of the microservice

Following are some of the examples of containers providers:

- Docker
- Kubernetes
- EC2 Container Service (ECS)
- Azure Container Service
- EC2 Container Registry
- Azure Container Registry
- Elastic Container Service for Kubernetes (EKS)
- Azure Kubernetes Service (AKS)

My Experiences

In one of the proof of concepts, we implemented DevOps pipeline using containers. Code inspection, build, deployment, and functional testing are executed on Docker containers. All the containers were created using customized images. The moment a specific container completes its job, it is destroyed. In this way resources are managed effectively and the outcome of a specific stage is saved.

All containers used to take a maximum of 5 GB of space, while same could have demanded 50 GB or more space if VMs or physical machines would have been used.

How Agile, DevOps, and Cloud are effective together

An important question when we discuss the improvement in organization is: How can we get better? Let's ask ourselves, what we need to stop? What can we do differently? How can we?

According to *Ryan Lilly, we are not creators; only combiners of the created.* Invention isn't about new ingredients, but new recipes. And innovations taste the best. There is never just one thing that leads to success. Alone, Agile, DevOps, or Cloud is still not the best. It is always their combination and utilizing them in the right place at the right time which makes a difference. Let's see the diagrammatic representation of the same:

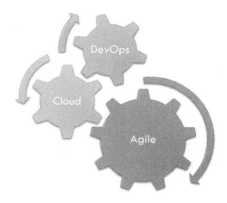

Figure 3.16: Agile, Cloud and DevOps

Digital transformation is a pre-requisite. Combination of Agile development model, DevOps, and cloud computing is the recipe to increase competitiveness in today's dynamic world!

Let me make it very clear at the beginning, Agile needs DevOps to be more effective and to get results which are envisioned. Similarly, DevOps practices implementation needs cloud computing and containers to get the envisioned results. DevOps is more about culture and mindset with automation, while cloud and containers are more about technology and service with automation. Agile methodology needs DevOps and cloud to get effective results. None is mutually exclusive. Each one complements the other.

The following diagram explains the relevance of Agile, DevOps, and cloud:

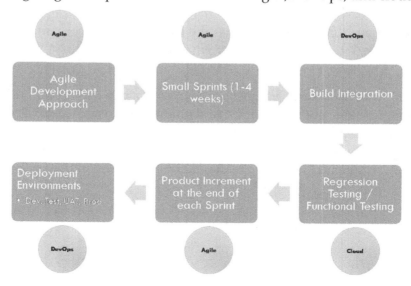

Figure 3.17: Relevance of Agile, DevOps and Cloud

Even with automation in application lifecycle management activities, infrastructure provisioning can be a hurdle. There is a big lead time for resource provisioning and many departments are involved in it. Cloud computing eliminates all such issues with self-service portal, pay as you go billing model, and scalable resources. Multiple environments can be provisioned and de-provisioned quickly. Hence, it not only brings agility but also cost benefits.

Whenever a cloud environment is available in any project, we can easily create resources; the development team can try new things, some things may fail or the environment may need some change or they may not be usable, and in that condition a new environment with new capabilities can be created easily so that experiments can be undertaken. Due to economy of scale, all environments can have consistent configuration and hence all the issues occurring from different kinds of environments can be eliminated in the beginning itself. Fail fast,recover fast!

Cloud not only brings agility to IT infrastructure but also brings automation into picture. Infrastructure as a code is a new norm and will be used in the future for all requirements. Multiple cloud service vendors provide ways to create environment using templates or some kind of script. It is reusable and programmable. Hence, it brings IT transformation.

DevOps practices implementation gives pace to product Increment, and cloud computing complements it by provisioning the environment faster. IaaS can be integrated in DevOps orchestration or pipeline easily, and hence the entire application lifecycle management can be automated. Continuous operations can be automated using continuous practices. It is repeatable and hence takes little time to mature. Once the orchestration piece is mature, most of the things are executed with a few mouse clicks.

With DevOps and cloud, scalability, high availability, fault tolerance, quick and easy deployment, and rollback can be configured seamlessly.

This combination brings stability with speed and quality, and that is rare.

To summarize, Agile development approach, DevOpspractices (continuous code inspection, CI, CD, continuous testing, continuous deployment, continuous feedback, continuous improvements, continuous innovation), and cloud computing bring speed and quality in application lifecycle management, hence it change the existing culture.

Conclusion

There is competitiveness in the market. Organizations want faster time to market. It essentially means that you can't do application development in a traditional way. Application needs to be available in the market quickly; with limited set of features and then product increments with new features can be released.

This is a huge culture change. Short development cycles result into issues and delays because of manual activities in environment provisioning or deployment. It is a hurdle. That is where DevOps practices implementation helps in bringing pace for the application lifecycle management activities. However, security is a major obstacle in cloud adoption. Based on the criticality of applications, different cloud deployment models can be utilized.

Hence, Agile, DevOps, and cloud make digital transformation effective and worth it.

In the next chapter, we will cover Azure DevOps Boards for planning.

CHAPTER 4
Azure Boards

Azure DevOps Boards helps to manage backlogs, built-in scrum boards, reporting, Kanban boards, sprint planning features, traceability, tracking of different ideas, dashboards, health, and status of your project, and so on.

Structure

We will cover the following topics in this chapter:

- Azure DevOps organizations
- New project in Azure DevOps
- Work item processes
- Work items
- Boards
- Backlogs
- Sprints
- Queries
- Retrospectives
- Product vision
- Dashboard

Objective

The main objective of this chapter is to gain understanding of Azure DevOps Boards service to manage multiple processes such as basic, CMMI, Agile, and Scrum.

Azure DevOps organizations

Organization in Azure DevOps provides you access to a portal where you can create projects with multiple processes, such as basic, CMMI, Agile, and Scrum; you can create a repository and manage source code, either in Git or in **Team Foundation Version Control (TFVC);** you can setup CICD using build and release definitions; you can set up multiple environments, and configure approval process before deployment for a specific environment; you can use hook mechanism to integrate with other services; use existing and multiple other extensions to integrate with other services.

Create a new organization in Azure DevOps portal

How to organize, and manage multiple related projects? There are different horizontals or verticals or business units or individual projects or customer specific projects. In Azure DevOps, you can manage such sections using organization.

Each organization has free tier. Limits are as given in the following table:

Service	Description
Azure Boards	Work item tracking and Kanban boards
Azure Repos	Unlimited private Git repositories
Load testing	20,000 VUMs per month (Note: cloud-based load testing service is deprecated)
Azure Pipelines	One hosted job with 1,800 minutes per month for CI/CD and one self-hosted job
Azure Artifacts	Package management
Users	Up to five users for each service type

Table 4.1: Azure DevOps Services

Let's see the structure in Azure DevOps:

```
|___

    Organization (s)

        |____ Project (s)
```

|____ Dashboards (Summary)

|____ Wiki

|____Boards (Agile, Scrum, CMMI, other Process management)

    |____ Work Items

    |____ Boards

    |____ Backlogs

    |____ Sprints

    |____ Queries

    |____ Retrospectives

    |____ Product Vision

|____Repos (Source Code Management: Git and TFVC)

    |____ Files

    |____ Commits

    |____ Pushes

    |____ Branches

    |____ Tags

    |____ Pull Requests

|____ Pipelines (DevOps Practices such as Continuous Integration and Delivery)

    |____ Builds

    |____ Releases

    |____ Library

    |____ Task Groups

    |____ Deployment Groups

|____ Test Plans (Continuous Test integration)

    |____ Test Plans

    |____ Parameters

    |____ Configurations

    |____ Runs

    |____ Load Test

|____ Artifacts (Artifact Repository)

Creating a new organization

Follow the following steps to create a new organization:

1. Go to **https://dev.azure.com**
2. Click on **New organization.**
3. Click on **Continue** as shown in the following screenshot:

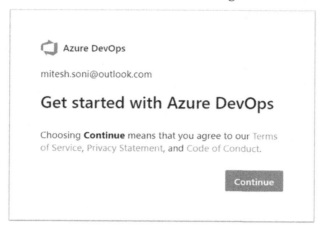

Figure 4.1: Create new organization

4. Provide name of an organization.
5. Select where you want to host project.
6. Name your project, and click on **Continue** as shown in the following screenshot:

Figure 4.2: Organization in Azure DevOps

7. Verify the newly created project in Azure DevOps Summary:

Figure 4.3: Organization Summary

Before working on different aspects of Azure DevOps, let's see a template project using Azure DevOps Demo Generator, and then individually work on creating similar kind of structure, or work on action items.

Azure DevOps Demo Generator

Azure DevOps Demo Generator provides you a portal where you can create projects from available templates that have different configurations. Templates have available sample data.

Before using Azure Boards, let's see the entire picture using Azure DevOps Demo Generator. Go to **https://azuredevopsdemogenerator.azurewebsites.net/**

You will get the following screen displayed:

Figure 4.4: Azure DevOps Demo Generator Portal

Sign in with valid credentials for Azure DevOps. Go through different permissions, as shown in the following screenshot:

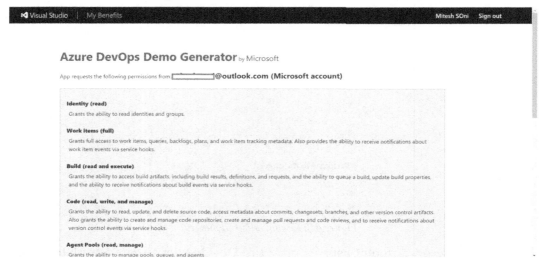

Figure 4.5: Permissions

Read them carefully and accept the permissions, as shown in the following screenshot:

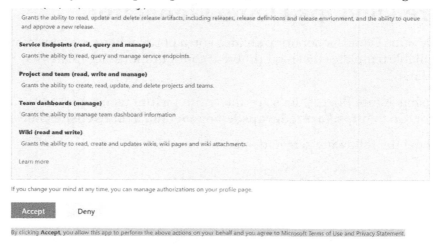

Figure 4.6: Accept permissions

By clicking **Accept,** you allow this app to perform the above actions on your behalf, and you agree to **Microsoft Terms of Use and Privacy Statement.** In our case, we have selected **MyShuttle** template as we are also going to work on Java-based projects using Scrum processes. Refer to the following screenshot to select a specific template according to your need:

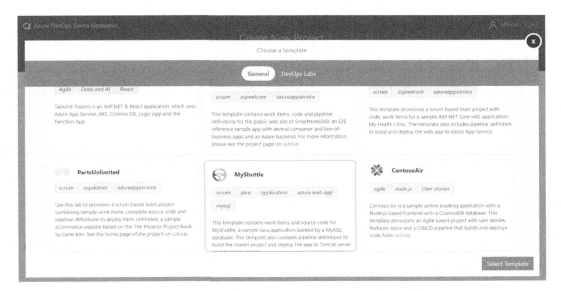

Figure 4.7: DevOps demo template in Azure DevOps

After selecting a template, you can select an organization. Give the project name, select a template, and then click on **Create Project**, as shown in the following screenshot:

Figure 4.8: New project in Azure DevOps Demo Generator

The process of creating the project based on the output is shown once you click on **Create Project**. It will be similar to the following screenshot:

Figure 4.9: *New project in Azure DevOps Demo Generator - Progress*

Once your project is created, click on **Navigate to project**, as shown in the following screenshot:

Figure 4.10: *New project in Azure DevOps Demo Generator - Navigate to project*

Here, you are on a newly created project with selected template, as shown in the following screenshot:

Figure 4.11: *Template project in Azure DevOps Summary*

Click on **Dashboards** and verify the following widgets:

- **All Work Items**
- **Bugs**
- **Team**
- **Different tiles**
- **Pie Chart**
- **Sprint related details**

We should create similar, if not the same kind of dashboard, for visibility when we work on Scrum process:

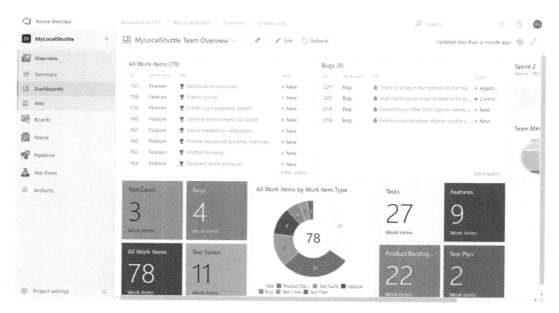

Figure 4.12: *Template project dashboard in Azure DevOps*

Let's create a new project in the next section.

New project in Azure DevOps

Let's create a project in Azure DevOps portal which will have different services, such as **Azure Boards, Repos, Pipelines, Test Plans,** and **Artifacts**, related to a specific project. Each project may have multiple teams, and they can have multiple builds and release definitions for DevOps practices implementation.

Each project can have multiple agents or agent pools available on cloud or on premise. Following are the sections or features available in Azure DevOps for each project.

```
|____ Project (s)

    |____ Dashboards (Summary)

    |____ Wiki

    |____Boards (Agile, Scrum, CMMI, other Process management)

    |____Repos (Source Code Management: Git and Team Foundation Version
    Control (TFVC))

    |____ Pipelines (DevOps Practices such as Continuous Integration
    and Delivery)
```

```
|____  Test Plans (Continuous Test integration)

|____  Artifacts (Artifact Repository)
```

Click on **Create Project** in organization in Azure DevOps Dashboard. Provide project name and select visibility of project. The following table shows the visibility of the options present in the project:

Visibility	Description
Private	Need to sign in to gain read only access to most of the services available in Azure DevOps; need to add and manage user access explicitly
Public	No need to sign in to gain read only access to most of the services available in Azure DevOps

Table 4.2: Project Visibility

Click on **Create** button as shown in the following screenshot:

Figure 4.13: New project in Azure DevOps

In the next section, you will know about different processes.

Work item processes

Click on the **Advanced** button to get more options to select **Version control** and **Work item process** as shown in the following screenshot:

Figure 4.14: Project Visibility in Azure DevOps

And, we have our first project ready. It will be similar to the following screenshot:

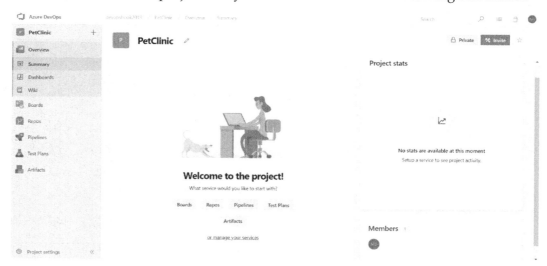

Figure 4.15: PetClinic project summary

Click on **Dashboards**, which is empty as no widget has been added, as you can see in the following screenshot:

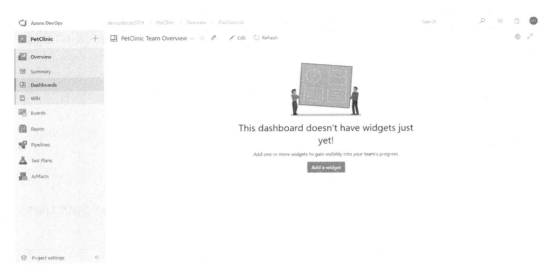

Figure 4.16: *PetClinic project dashboard*

Click on **Project settings** and verify the different options available for the **PetClinic** project in Azure DevOps. The screen will be similar to the following screenshot:

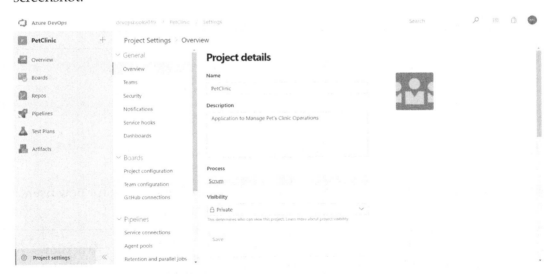

Figure 4.17: *PetClinic project details*

Go to **Organization Settings** and verify the available projects under the organization created in Azure DevOps portal, as shown in the following screenshot:

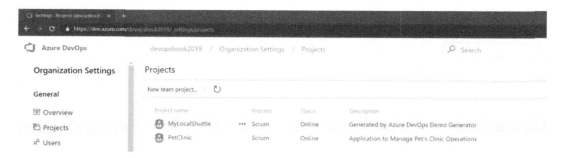

Figure 4.18: Projects in organization

Let's understand the different work item processes. Go to **Organization Settings|** **Process,** as shown in the following screenshot:

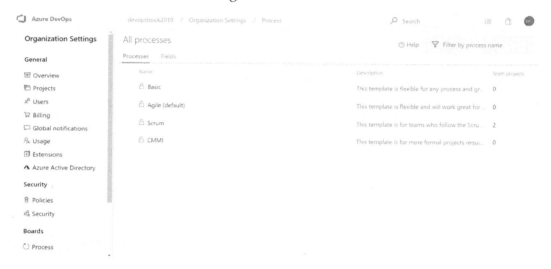

Figure 4.19: Processes in organization

Basic process is a simple module which is in selective preview mode for new users. The following table lists the work item types used in **Basic** process:

Portfolio backlogs	Product planning	Task and sprint planning	Bugs, issues, risk management	Workflow states
Epic	Issue	Task	Issue	• To Do • Doing • Done

Table 4.3: Basic process

The **Basic** process screen will be similar to the following screenshot:

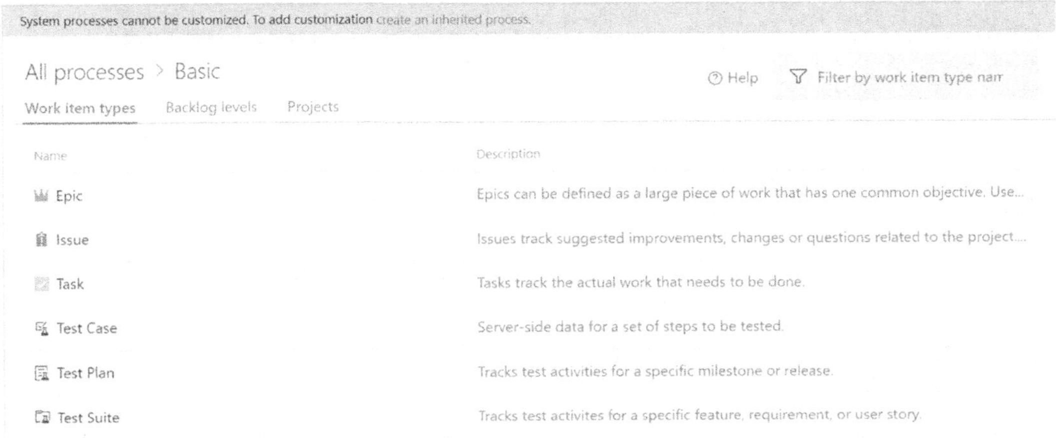

System processes cannot be customized. To add customization create an inherited process.

All processes > Basic   ⓘ Help   ▽ Filter by work item type nam

Work item types   Backlog levels   Projects

Name	Description
ᴟ Epic	Epics can be defined as a large piece of work that has one common objective. Use...
🔖 Issue	Issues track suggested improvements, changes or questions related to the project...
☑ Task	Tasks track the actual work that needs to be done.
▦ Test Case	Server-side data for a set of steps to be tested.
▤ Test Plan	Tracks test activities for a specific milestone or release.
▤ Test Suite	Tracks test activites for a specific feature, requirement, or user story.

Figure 4.20: Basic process

Agile process helps you to use Agile planning methods, where you can use stories on Kanban Board. Tasks can have original estimate, remaining work, and completed work. The following table describes the work item types used in Agile process:

Portfolio backlogs	Product planning	Task and sprint planning	Bugs, issues, risk management	Workflow states
Epic Feature	User story Bug	Task Bug	Bug Issue	New Active Resolved Removed

Table 4.4: Basic process

The **Agile** process screen will be similar to the following screenshot:

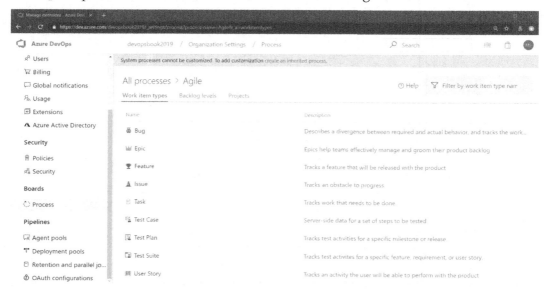

Figure 4.21: Agile process

Scrum process helps to use Scrum framework, where you can use PBIs on Kanban Board. Tasks can have only remaining work. The following table describes the work item types used in Scrum process:

Portfolio backlogs	Product planning	Task and sprint planning	Bugs, issues, risk management	Workflow states
Epic Feature	Product backlog item Bug	Bug Task	Bug Impediment	New Approved Committed Done Removed

Table 4.5: Agile process

The **Scrum** process screen will be similar to the following screenshot:

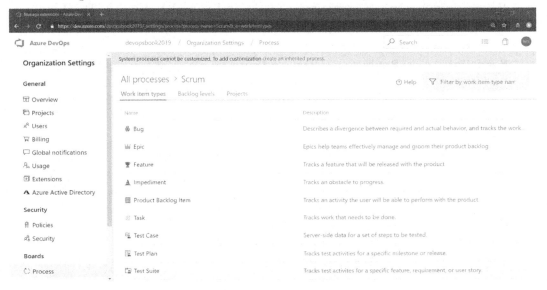

Figure 4.22: *Scrum process*

Go to **Backlog levels** to understand different levels and their importance. Refer to the following screenshot:

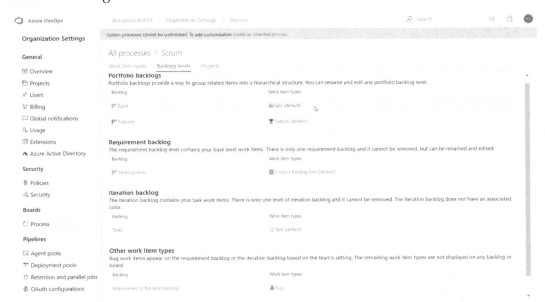

Figure 4.23: *Scrum process Backlog levels*

CMMI process helps to track requirements, change requests, risks, and others. Tasks can have original estimate, remaining work, and completed work. The following table describes the work item types used in CMMI process:

Portfolio backlogs	Product planning	Task and sprint planning	Bugs, issues, risk management	Workflow states
Epic	Requirement	Task	Bug	Proposed
Feature	Bug	Bug	Issue	Active
			Risk	Resolved
			Review	Closed

Table 4.6: CMMI Process

The **CMMI** process screen will be similar to the following screenshot:

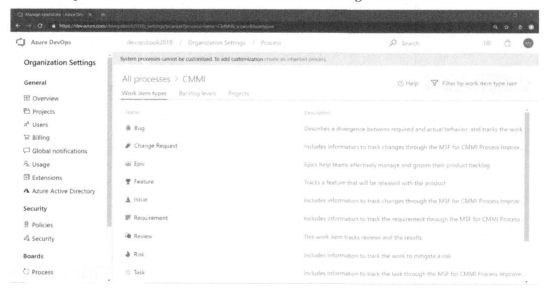

Figure 4.24: CMMI process

To get more details on workflow states, transitions, and reasons, visit: **https://docs. microsoft.com/en-us/azure/devops/boards/work-items/guidance/choose-process**

There are different agent pools that are used to build definition execution for continuous integration pipelines. Windows, Ubuntu, and macOS are available for execution, with different software packages pre-installed. You can create on premise agent pool, if required.

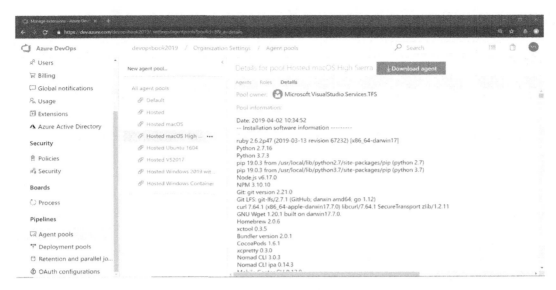

Figure 4.25: Agent Pools

In the next section, we will understand some project settings and Azure Boards for Scrum process.

Work Items

The Scrum process supports **Portfolio Backlog (Epic, Feature, Product Backlog Item, Task; Bug, Task), Test (Test Plan, Test Suite, Test Case), Feedback (Feedback Request, Feedback Response),** and **Code Review (Code Review Request, Code Review Response)** to plan and manage implementation of application-related work.

Go to Azure DevOps Portal, click on **PetClinic** project, and then navigate to **Boards | Work Items | New Work Item** to verify available options for Scrum process (as discussed earlier). The following screenshot shows the available list for the **Work Item:**

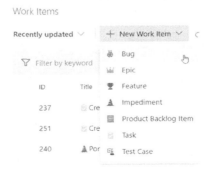

Figure 4.26: Work Items

Let's create a **Bug**.

Bug

Click on **Boards | Work Items | New Work Item | Bug.** Assign the **Bug** to an existing user in the team.

Select **Area/Team.** Select **Iteration** or **Sprint**/existing Sprint, which is going to start. The following screenshot shows the same:

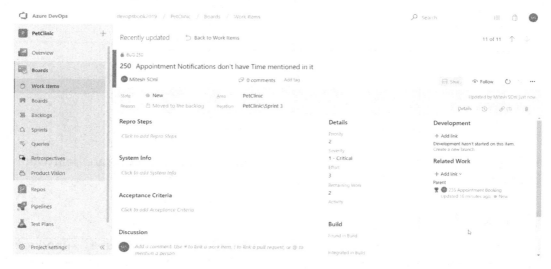

Figure 4.27: Bug

Let see the details of area and iteration paths:

- **Area paths:** Work Items grouped by team, product, or feature.
- **Iteration paths:** Work Items grouped by sprints most of the times.

If the state is approved, it means the Product Owner has approved the bug and that it should go for a fix. We can select the reason and save the Bug as shown in below screenshot.

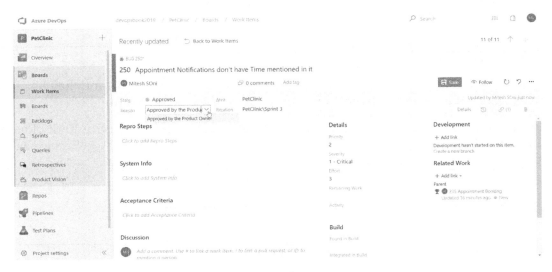

Figure 4.28: *Bug state*

Epic

Epic represents the business aspect of an application. Epics define the vision broadly. Unlike user stories, epics can span across different Sprints.

Feature

Feature represents the technical aspects of an application. Click on **Boards | Work Items | New Work Item | Feature.** Give **Title**, assign it to an existing user from the team. Refer to the following screenshot:

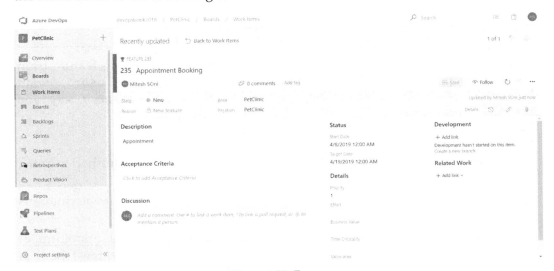

Figure 4.29: *Feature*

Assign **Area** and **Iteration** path too.

Impediment

Impediments are known issues that are reasons for pending activities and they have to be resolved as soon as possible by active efforts of the Scrum team.

In this case, it is important to open a port to access Azure App Service to deploy an application package. Link **Impediment** to task of creation Azure App Service as shown in the following screenshot:

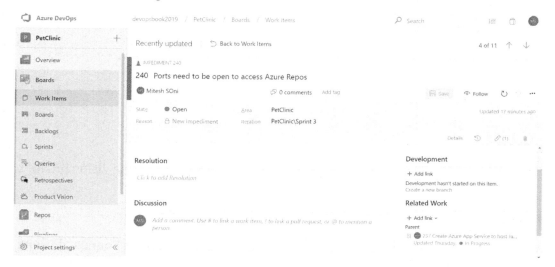

Figure 4.30: Impediment

Product Backlog Items (PBIs)

A **Product Backlog Item** provides simplified description of any feature from the end user's perspective. The PBI Format: As a **<role / type of user>**, I want **<feature / what you want to be implemented>** so that **<reason / why you want this feature>**.

Example of a PBI is as follows:

- **Title:** As a Pet Owner, I want to know the availability of veterinarians on a specific date
- **Description:** As a Pet Owner, I want to know the availability of veterinarians on a specific date
- **Acceptance Criteria:** Pet Owner should be able to know the appointment time on a given date, and if the time slot is unavailable then suggest the next 5 available slots.

Refer to the following screenshot:

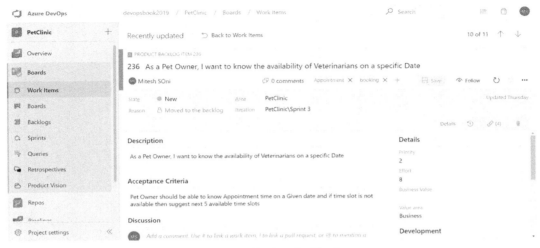

Figure 4.31: *Product Backlog Item*

Let's see a task in the next section and how to link tasks with PBI.

Task

Product Backlog Item can be broken into a number of tasks that will achieve implementation of the Backlog Item. It is the fastest way to implement and deliver. Click on **Boards | Work Items | New Work Item | Task.**

Create a task with a tile: **Create Azure App Service to host Java based Web Application** as shown in the following screenshot:

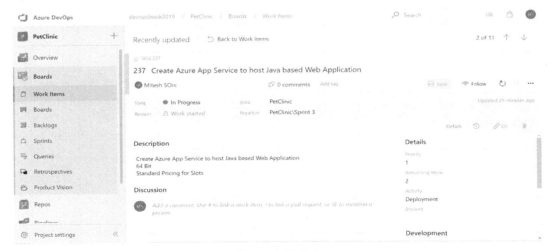

Figure 4.32: *Task*

To assign this task to an existing PBI, click on **Add link | Existing item** as shown in the following screenshot:

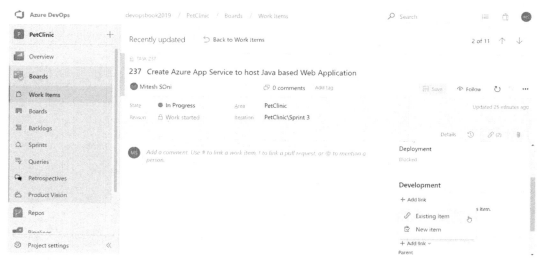

Figure 4.33: Task - Add link

Select **Parent** as a **Lint type**, and also as a related **Parent Backlog Item**. Click on **OK** as shown in the following screenshot:

Figure 4.34: Task - Add link - Parent

Look at the **Related Work** section and verify child and parent links as you can see in the following screenshot:

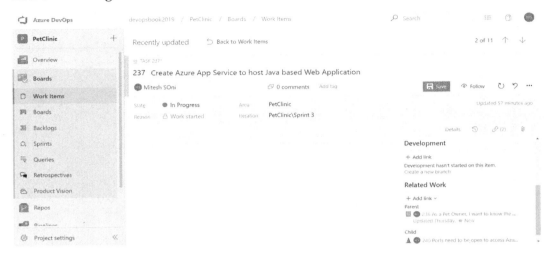

Figure 4.35: Task - Parent and Child relations

In the next section, we will discuss Boards.

Boards

Navigate to Boards in Azure DevOps Portal. Select a specific **Team Backlog** according to your suitability. You can switch over from one team to another for different PBIs. Select a team and features. Refer to the following screenshot:

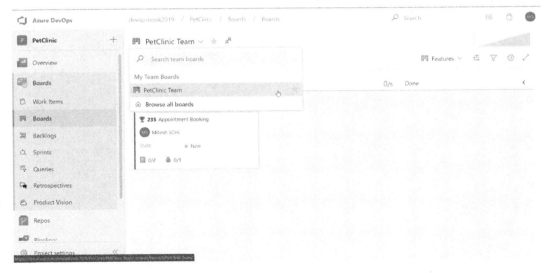

Figure 4.36: Azure Boards - Team Selection

Select Backlog items in the Boards and verify the portal as shown in the following screenshot:

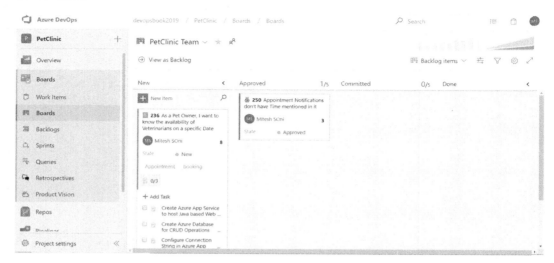

Figure 4.37: *Azure Boards - Product Backlog Items*

In the next section, we will discuss about Backlogs.

Backlogs

Backlog is a collection/a set of desired and prioritized features that a customer wants to see as a final outcome. The sample screen of Backlog is shown in the following screenshot:

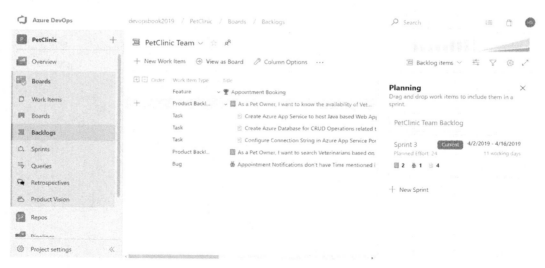

Figure 4.38: *Backlogs*

You can select **Features** or **Product Backlog** specific to Team Backlog as shown in the following screenshot. Make the **Parents** toggle to see the relationships between different **Work Items:**

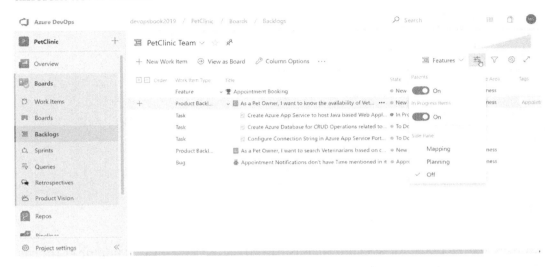

Figure 4.39: *Backlog - Parents*

In the next section, we will discuss Sprints.

Sprints

Sprint is a Scrum event that ends with potentially releasable product Increment. Prioritized Product Backlog contains n number of features or PBIs that may not be completed in one sprint. In simple words, Sprint Backlog is a subset of Product Backlog, which contains PBIs selected to be developed in the coming Sprint.

Go to **Project settings**. Click on **Project configuration | New child**. Create multiple Sprints based on your requirements, as shown in the following screenshot:

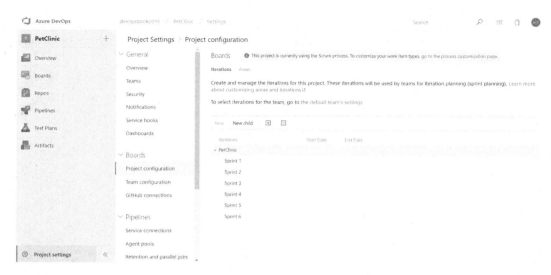

Figure 4.40: *Sprint - Project configuration*

You can set the dates for specific Sprints directly from **Project configuration**, as shown in the following screenshot:

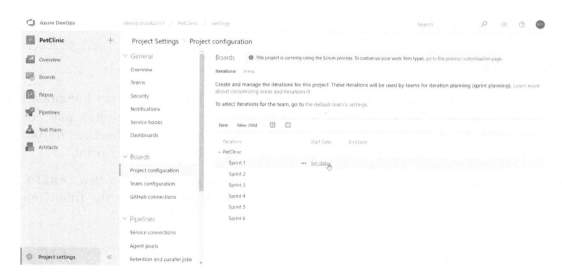

Figure 4.41: *Sprint - dates*

Provide a name of the Sprint. Select **Start date** and **End date**, along with the **Location**, as shown in the following screenshot. Click on **Save and close** button:

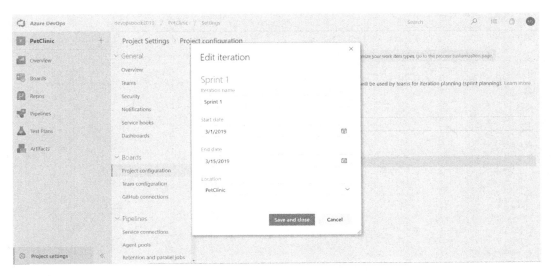

Figure 4.42: Sprint - Edit iteration

If you want to delete a Sprint, then click on three dots **(...)** and select **Delete** button, as shown in the following screenshot.

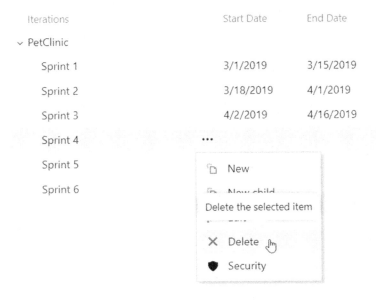

Figure 4.43: Delete Sprint

Delete multiple sprints available in Azure DevOps if no more than 3 Sprints are required, and verify the project configuration dashboard, as shown in the following screenshot:

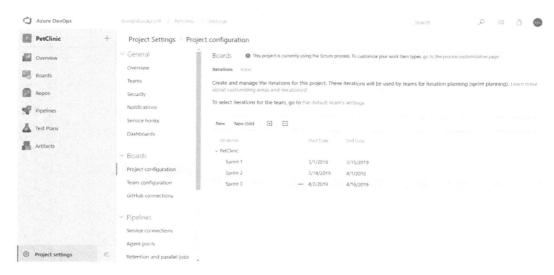

Figure 4.44: *Project configuration - Sprint*

Configure **Backlog navigation levels, Working days** for the team under **Team configuration**, as shown in the following screenshot:

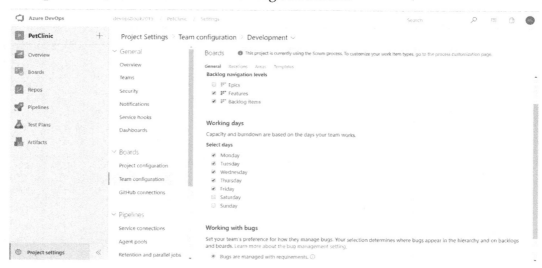

Figure 4.45: *Team configuration*

Verify available **Agent pools**. We have Java-based application, so in case of Build and Release **definitions**, we will use related **Agent pools**, as shown in the following screenshot:

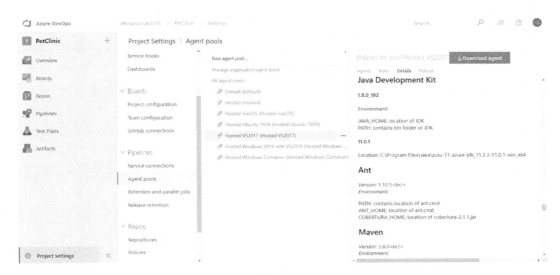

Figure 4.46: Hosted Agent pool - Java

For a specific Sprint, we can set days off, in cases of planned leave of an employee. Click on Sprints, select a specific Sprint from the dropdown, and then click on **Capacity| Days off.** Select **Start** and **End** date, and then click on **OK**, as shown in the following screenshot:

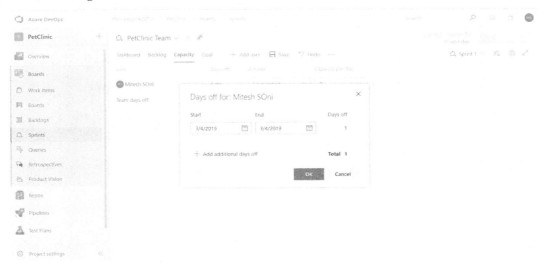

Figure 4.47: Days off for team members in Sprint

Hours will be calculated based on the overall capacity minus the hours of days off. Assign the activity and the number of hours for daily work at the same location for a specific user or for all the team members individually.

It might be possible that different team members have different working hours based on availability and requirement. Refer to the following screenshot:

Figure 4.48: Capacity of team members in Sprint

In the next section, we will discuss about shared queries and how useful they are for other activities.

Queries

Queries help us to list bugs, PBIs, features, or other work items based on field criteria.

Click on **Queries | New query,** as shown in the following screenshot:

Figure 4.49: New queries

In **Editor**, provide the values to filter results, as shown in the following screenshot:

Figure 4.50: Query Editor

Click on **Run query**, and verify results in the bottom section of the Azure DevOps Dashboard, as shown in the following screenshot:

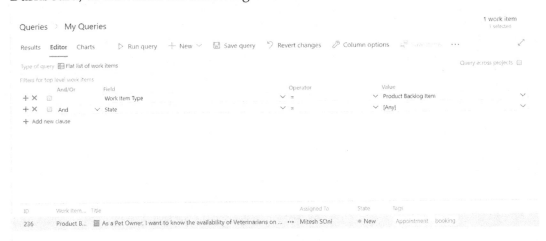

Figure 4.51: Query results

To save a query, click on **Save query** and provide a name. Select **Shared Queries** in **Folder**. We will discuss why is it necessary to save a query in this folder. Click **OK**, as shown in the following screenshot:

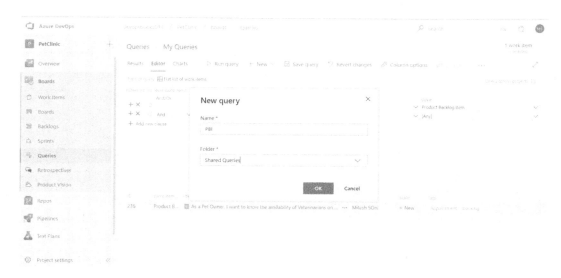

Figure 4.52: Save query

In the next section, we will discuss Retrospective section.

Retrospectives

Sprint Retrospective marks an end of the Sprint. It is a time of constructive feedback and improvements, rather than being a blame game. Navigate to the **Retrospective** in Azure Dashboard.

To create a board, click on **Create Board**, as shown in the following screenshot:

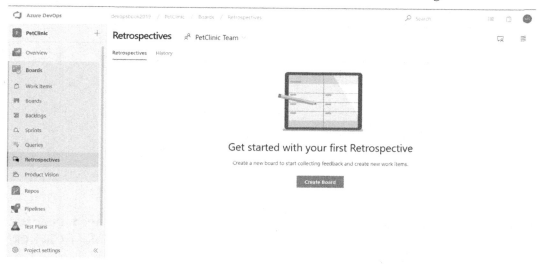

Figure 4.53: Azure DevOps - Retrospective

The Scrum team collaborates and introspects on what went well and what didn't in the Sprint; what kind of actions can be taken to improve the things that went wrong to avoid them in future Sprints.

Add new columns, if required, in addition to the existing ones, such as **what went well and what didn't,** as shown in the following screenshot:

Figure 4.54: *New Retrospective*

Add new feedback in a specific column based on experience of the sprint. All team members can give their feedback as, as shown in the following screenshot:

Figure 4.55: *Retrospective dashboard*

Click on **Vote**, and allow team members to decide if they agree with specific feedbacks within specific sections. Refer to the following screenshot:

Figure 4.56: Retrospective dashboard - Act

Click on **Act** tab, which has a facility to add a feature to act upon **Action Items,** so that it can be tracked. We can add different **Work Items** as **Action Items** based on the discussions, as shown in the following screenshot:

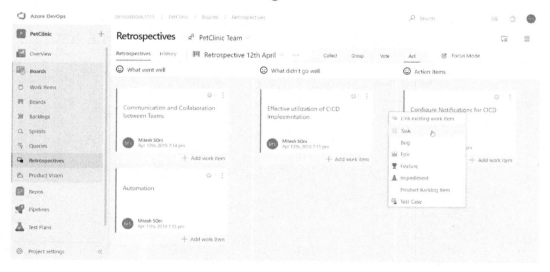

Figure 4.57: Task related to Retrospective Action

Verify that the task has been created. Click on the **History** tab to verify the existing status of the Retrospective, as shown in the following screenshot:

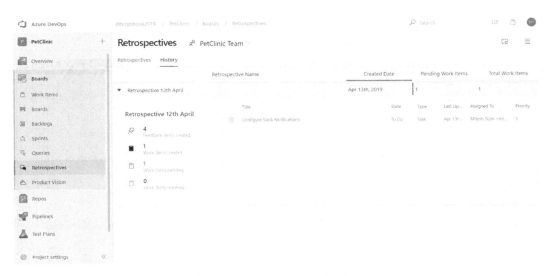

Figure 4.58: *Retrospective History*

In the next section, we will discuss Product Vision.

Extensions

The Microsoft Azure Extensions provide a way to integrate other applications, so that multiple tools can be used in **Build** or **Release** definitions in a **Pipeline**.

Go to **https://marketplace.visualstudio.com/azuredevops** to get details of Extensions for Azure DevOps, as shown in the following screenshot:

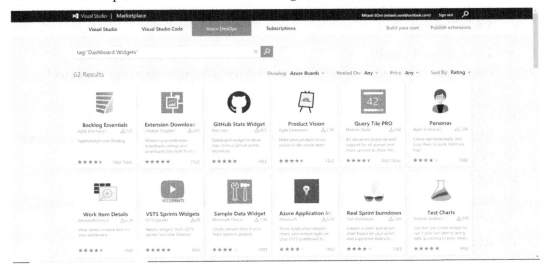

Figure 4.59: *Azure DevOps Extensions*

Select a specific Extension and install it using the wizard. Select an organization and download and install it, as shown in the following screenshot:

Figure 4.60: Azure DevOps Extensions - organization

Some of the popular Extensions are as follows:

- Project Teams
  https://marketplace.visualstudio.com/items?itemName=davesmits. VSTSTeams

- Team Project Health
  https://marketplace.visualstudio.com/items?itemName=ms-devlabs. TeamProjectHealth

- Product Vision
  https://marketplace.visualstudio.com/items?itemName=agile-extensions. product-vision

- Sprint Goal
  https://marketplace.visualstudio.com/items?itemName=keesschollaart. sprint-goal

- Work Item Visualization
  https://marketplace.visualstudio.com/items?itemName=ms-devlabs. WorkItemVisualization

- SonarQube
  **https://marketplace.visualstudio.com/
  acquisition?itemName=SonarSource.sonarqube**

- Code Coverage Protector
  **https://marketplace.visualstudio.com/items?itemName=davesmits.
  codecoverageprotector**

- Quality Gate Widget
  **https://marketplace.visualstudio.com/items?itemName=yuriburgernet.
  qualitygatewidget**

- Test Charts
  **https://marketplace.visualstudio.com/
  items?itemName=NebbiaTechnology.nebbia-test-charts**

- Release Stats
  **https://marketplace.visualstudio.com/items?itemName=WandrilleHubert.
  ReleaseStats**

- Release Approvals
  **https://marketplace.visualstudio.com/items?itemName=YodLabs.
  RMApprovals**

- HockeyApp
  https://marketplace.visualstudio.com/items?itemName=ms.hockeyapp

- Azure Artifacts
  https://marketplace.visualstudio.com/items?itemName=ms.feed

- Generate Release Notes Build Task
  **https://marketplace.visualstudio.com/
  items?itemName=richardfennellBM.BM-VSTS-GenerateReleaseNotes-
  Task**

- Zip and unzip directory build task
  **https://marketplace.visualstudio.com/
  items?itemName=petergroenewegen.PeterGroenewegen-Xpirit-Vsts-
  Build-Zip**

- New Relic Dashboard Widgets
  **https://marketplace.visualstudio.com/items?itemName=jonathan-
  mezach.new-relic-dashboard-widgets**

- Slack Integration
  https://marketplace.visualstudio.com/items?itemName=ms-vsts.vss-services-slack

- Azure DevOps CLI
  https://marketplace.visualstudio.com/items?itemName=ms-vsts.cli

- Jenkins Integration
  https://marketplace.visualstudio.com/items?itemName=ms-vsts.services-jenkins

- Cordova Build
  https://marketplace.visualstudio.com/items?itemName=ms-vsclient.cordova-extension

- Export As PDF
  https://marketplace.visualstudio.com/items?itemName=onlyutkarsh.ExportAsPDF

Product Vision

Product vision is at the root of the roadmap for successful product creation. Following is one of the templates that can be utilized to create a vision:

For (Target user / customer base)
Who (Need)
The (application / product name) is a (application / product category)
That (Main benefit or feature that addresses the need)
Unlike (Existing solutions)
Our application / product (What differentiates your application / product from others)

Let's try to create a vision for our organization:

For (Pet Lovers)
Who (wants a quick way to access Clinics)
The (The Pet Clinic) is a (Web based application)
That (allows Pet Lovers to access contacts of Clinics from the Web)
Unlike (existing solutions that require Pet lovers to access information from General dictionaries)
Our application / product (will provide a total web-based Pet Care experience)

Install Product Vision extension from

https://marketplace.visualstudio.com/items?itemName=agile-extensions. product-vision

Figure 4.61: Product Vision

Let's try to put all sentences together, as shown in the following screenshot:

For **Pet Lovers** who want a quick way to access clinics, The PetClinic is a web-based application that allows Pet Lovers to access contacts of Clinics from the Web unlike existing solutions that require Pet lovers to access information from General dictionaries; **PetClinic** application will provide a total web-based Pet Care experience.

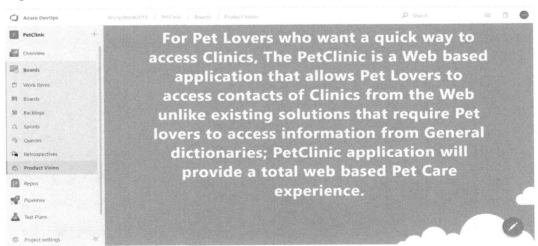

Figure 4.62: Final Product Vision

In the next section, we will discuss Dashboard.

Dashboard

Let's customize the Dashboard areas by selecting different widgets.

In our case, let's select **Query Tile** widget. Click on **Add**, as shown in the following screenshot:

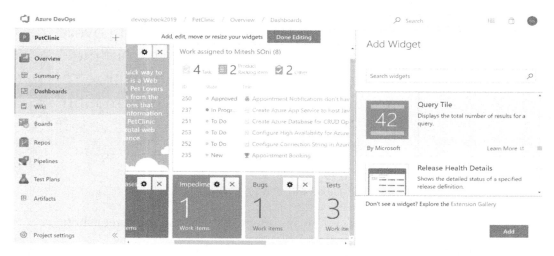

Figure 4.63: Project dashboard - Query Tile

Provide **Title** and in the **Query** list box, click on **Shared Queries** to find all the queries created in the shared folder in the earlier section. Select a specific query and click on **Save** button, as shown in the following screenshot:

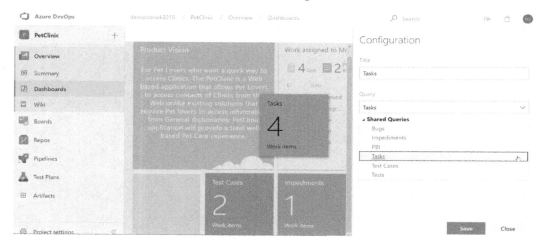

Figure 4.64: Project dashboard - Shared Query

Add widgets, such as **Product Vision, Work Assigned to Me,** and other **Query Tiles**.

Click on the **Done Editing** button and verify the dashboard, as shown in the following screenshot:

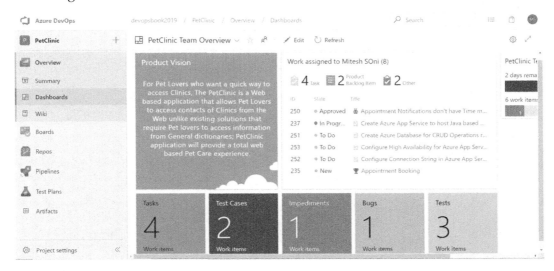

Figure 4.65: Project dashboard - Widgets

Conclusion

We have covered all the important topics available in Azure Boards section. In the next chapter, we will have hands-on activities for Azure Repos.

Azure Repos

Azure Repos consists of two version control tools that help you to manage source code for your projects. Azure Repos enable you to edit the code, create branches, fork repositories, tracks the code, snapshots, and so on. Version control plays an important role in managing code.

As of now, Azure Repos provides two version control tools. One is Git and the other is **Team Foundation Version Control (TFVC).** Git is a distributed version control system, while TFVC is a centralized version control one.

Structure

We will cover the following topics in this chapter:

- Hosted Git Azure Repo
- Clone Repository in Azure DevOps
- Fork Repository in Azure DevOps
- Branches
- Tags
- Code management in Azure DevOps dashboard

Objective

The main objective of this chapter is to gain understanding of Azure Repos, and the best practices for branch management.

Hosted Git Azure Repo

Git is one of the most popular distributed version control system in the recent times. It has almost become a synonym for version control. Discussion on Git in detail is out of this chapter's scope. To access Git in Azure Repos, use tools such as Git for Windows and others.

To get more details on Git, visit **https://git-scm.com/doc** and **https://git-scm.com/docs/gittutorial**.

We have already created a project named **PetClinic**. Click on **Repos**, as shown in the following screenshot:

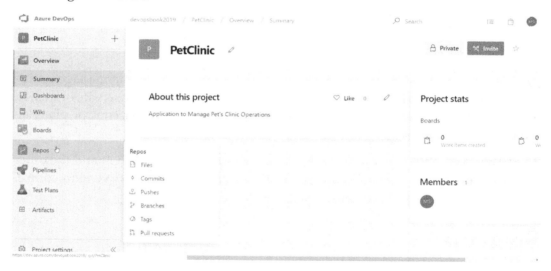

Figure 5.1: Repos

Click on Files and verify the URLs:

https://devopsbook2019@dev.azure.com/devopsbook2019/PetClinic/_git/ PetClinic

git@ssh.dev.azure.com:v3/devopsbook2019/PetClinic/PetClinic

Refer to the following screenshot:

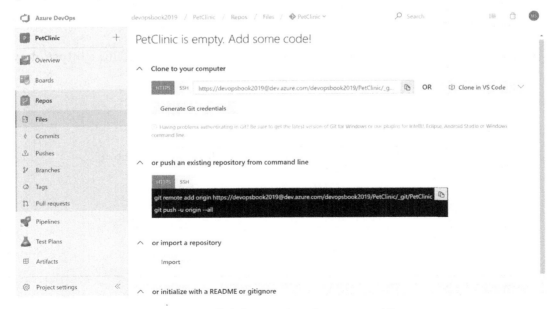

Figure 5.2: Clone URLs

Click on **HTTPS** and verify the commands, as shown in the following screenshot:

git remote add origin https://devopsbook2019@dev.azure.com/devopsbook2019/
PetClinic/_git/PetClinic

git push -u origin —all

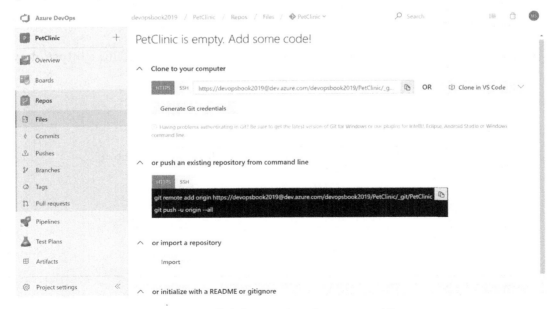

Figure 5.3: Existing repository from command line

Click on **SSH** and verify the commands. It will be similar to the following:

```
git remote add origin git@ssh.dev.azure.com:v3/devopsbook2019/PetClinic/
PetClinic

git push -u origin -all
```

You can create Git credentials to access Azure Repos using Git clients. Provide name, password, confirm password, and then click on **Save Git Credentials**, as shown in the following screenshot:

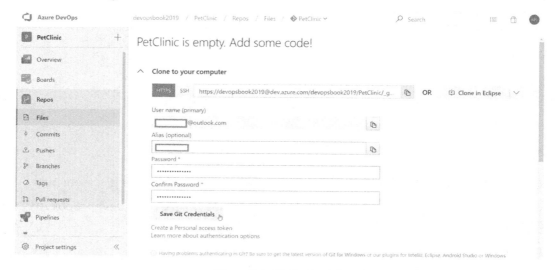

Figure 5.4: Git Credentials

Go to source code directory in local system. Use the following URL: **https://dev. azure.com/devopsbook2019/PetClinic/_git/PetClinic**

Execute Git push command, which is as follows:

```
$git push -u origin -all
```

Dialogue box appears to sign in, as shown in the following screenshot:

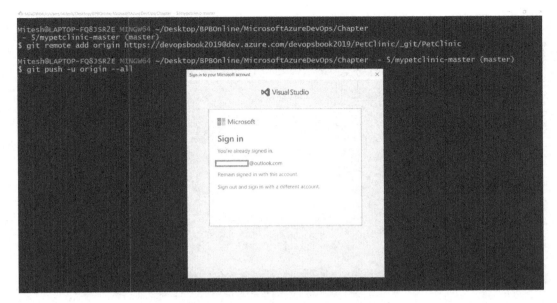

Figure 5.5: Sign in to Microsoft Account

Provide email address, as shown in the following screenshot:

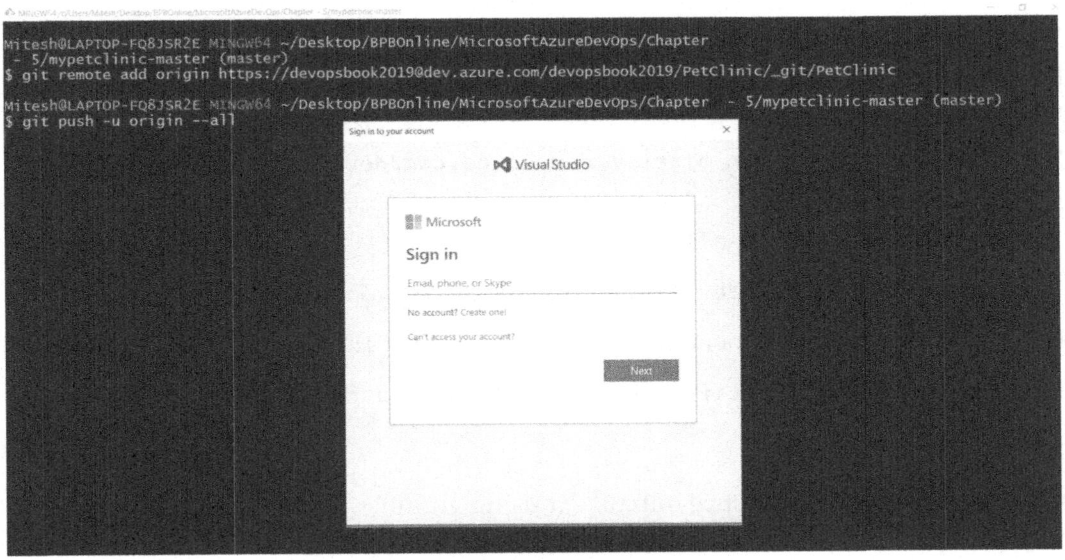

Figure 5.6: Sign in to your Account

Provide password and click on **OK**, as shown in the following screenshot:

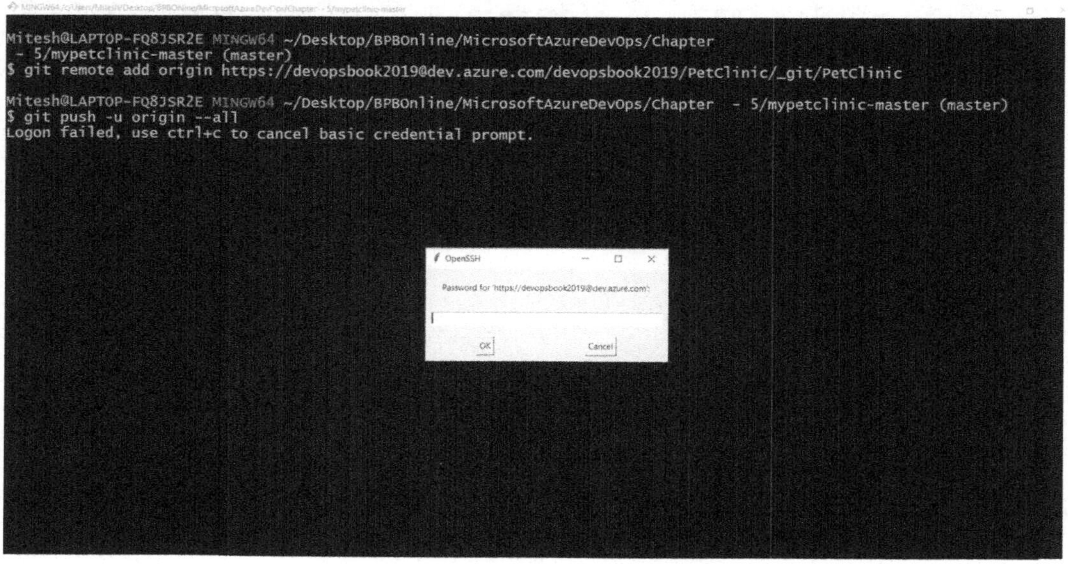

Figure 5.7: *Password for Git*

Let's push the existing repository to Azure Repo for the project we have already created. Refer to the following:

```
Mitesh@LAPTOP-FQ8JSR2E MINGW64 ~/Desktop/BPBOnline/MicrosoftAzureDevOps/
Chapter   - 5/mypetclinic-master (master)
```

```
$ git remote add origin https://dev.azure.com/devopsbook2019/PetClinic/_
git/PetClinic
```

```
$ git push -u origin --all
```

Username for 'https://dev.azure.com': xxxxxxxxx@outlook.com

No refs in common and none specified; doing nothing.

Perhaps you should specify a branch such as 'master'.

Everything up-to-date.

Git was not initialized. Hence initialize it using git init:

```
$ gitinit .
```

Initialized empty Git repository in

```
C:/Users/Mitesh/Desktop/BPBOnline/MicrosoftAzureDevOps/Chapter      -   5/
mypetclinic-master/.git/
```

Execute Git add command:

```
$ git add .
warning: LF will be replaced by CRLF in .bowerrc.
The file will have its original line endings in your working directory
warning: LF will be replaced by CRLF in .editorconfig.
The file will have its original line endings in your working directory
warning: LF will be replaced by CRLF in .gitignore.
The file will have its original line endings in your working directory
warning: LF will be replaced by CRLF in .mvn/wrapper/maven-wrapper.
properties.
The file will have its original line endings in your working directory
```

Execute commit command to save changes to local repository:

```
$ git commit -m "My first commit"
[master (root-commit) a08d5b9] My first commit
 496 files changed, 89072 insertions(+)
 create mode 100644 .bowerrc
 create mode 100644 .editorconfig
 create mode 100644 .gitignore
 create mode 100644 .mvn/wrapper/maven-wrapper.jar
 create mode 100644 .mvn/wrapper/maven-wrapper.properties
 create mode 100644 .springBeans
 create mode 100644 .travis.yml
 create mode 100644 Jenkinsfile
 create mode 100644 Readme.txt
```

Push all changes to remote repository using git push command:

```
$ git push -u origin --all
Username for 'https://dev.azure.com': xxxxxxxxxxxxxxx@outlook.com
Enumerating objects: 550, done.
Counting objects: 100% (550/550), done.
```

```
Delta compression using up to 4 threads
Compressing objects: 100% (533/533), done.
Writing objects: 100% (550/550), 1.37 MiB | 44.00 KiB/s, done.
Total 550 (delta 87), reused 0 (delta 0)
remote: Analyzing objects... (550/550) (41110 ms)
remote: Storing packfile... done (103 ms)
remote: Storing index... done (36 ms)
To https://dev.azure.com/devopsbook2019/PetClinic/_git/PetClinic
 * [new branch]      master -> master
Branch 'master' set up to track remote branch 'master' from 'origin'.
```

Let's visit the Azure DevOps portal to see the effect of push operation from command line.

Go to Azure DevOps Portal. Click on the **Pushes** section and verify the latest commit, as shown in the following screenshot:

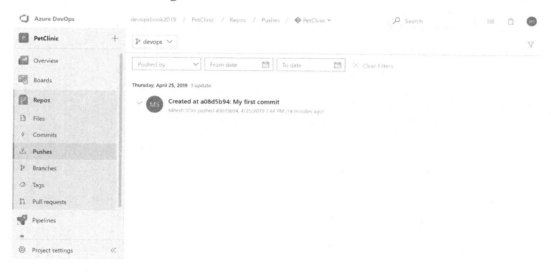

Figure 5.8: Pushes in Azure Repos

Click on **Commits** to verify the recent one and verify the description, as shown in the following screenshot:

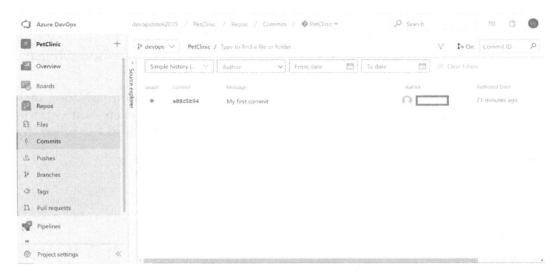

Figure 5.9: Commits in Azure Repos

In the next section, we will cover how to clone repository.

Clone repository in Azure DevOps

To clone a repository, go to **Files | Clone.** You can use HTTPS and SSH URLs or **Generate Git credentials**, as shown in the following screenshot:

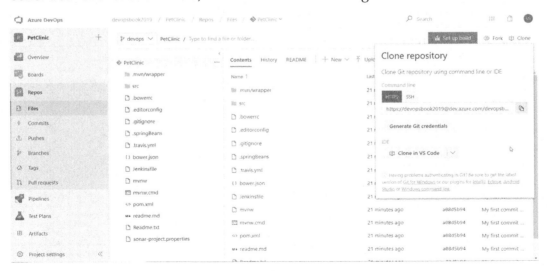

Figure 5.10: Clone repository

In the next section, we will cover how to fork repository.

Fork repository in Azure DevOps

Forking a repository helps you to create a copy of the existing one. You can make changes to the repository, which won't affect the existing one.

To fork an existing repository, click on **Fork**. A window pops-up to ask for a new **Repository name** or keep default one. Select the **Project** where you want to fork the existing repository. Click on the Fork button, as shown in the following screenshot:

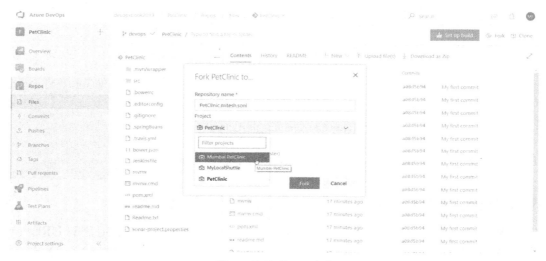

Figure 5.11: Create fork

Verify the forked repository. Refer to the following screenshot:

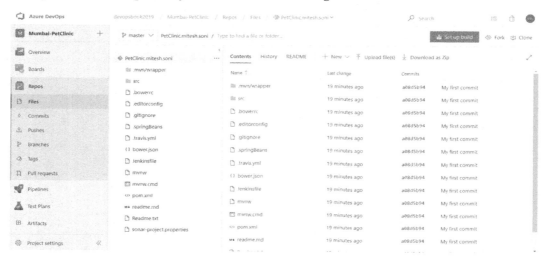

Figure 5.12: Forked repository

In the next section, we will discuss branches.

Branches

Branches help teams to collaborate in a better way by sharing and reviewing codes. It is important to understand the branching strategies, using pull requests for reviewing code, managing releases, and using tagging.

The following diagram will give an end-to-end scenario in short:

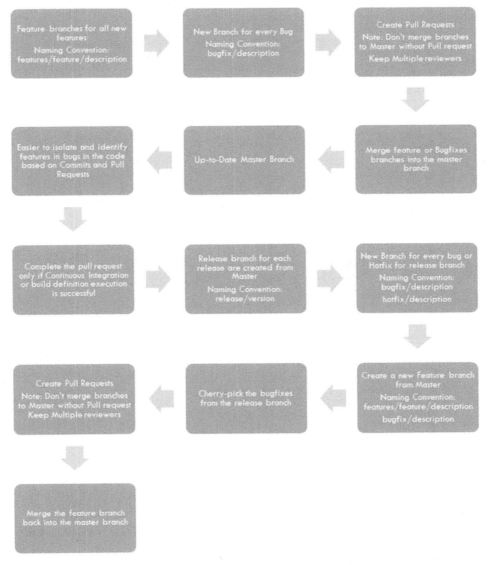

Figure 5.13: *Branching strategy*

Let's see how to create a Branch in Azure DevOps portal.

To verify the available branches, go to Azure Repos and click on the drop-down, as shown in the following screenshot:

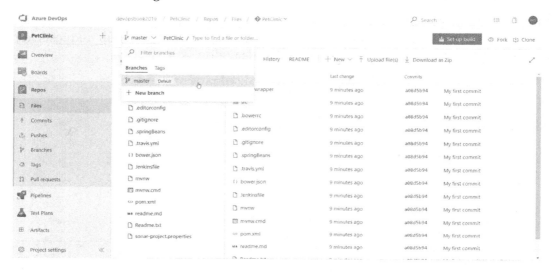

Figure 5.14: Existing branches

To create a new branch, select **New branch**. Refer to the following screenshot:

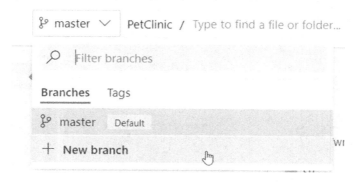

Figure 5.15: New branch

Provide a name for the new branch and select a branch on which the new branch should be based upon.

If you want to link this new branch with any work item that has been created in Azure Repos, then link it by clicking on **Create branch**, as shown in the following screenshot:

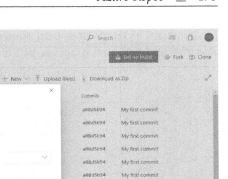

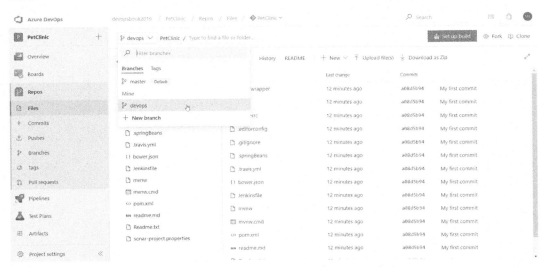

Figure 5.16: Create branch

Click on the drop-down to verify the newly created branch. Refer to the following screenshot:

Figure 5.17: Newly created branch

Let's verify if there any pull request is available. No pull requests are available in Azure DevOps portal according to the following screenshot:

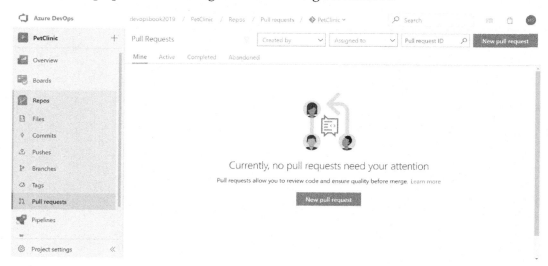

Figure 5.18: Pull Request

To create a feature specific branch or work item-specific branch, open the **Work Items** in Azure Boards. Click on **Create new branch**, as shown in the following screenshot:

Figure 5.19: Branch related to Work Item

Give a name to the branch and select a repository and the main branch. The reason to select a **master** branch is based on the earlier discussion, where we would like to keep the **master** branch up-to-date.

Work items that are to be linked are already selected. Click on **Create branch** as shown in the following screenshot:

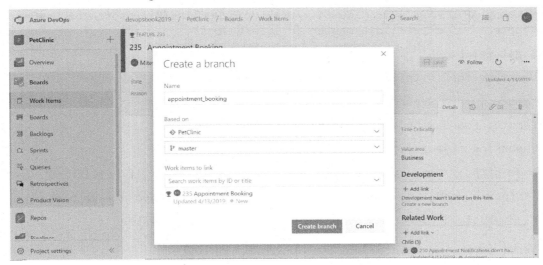

Figure 5.20: *Create branch related to Work Item*

Verify the drop-down for the newly created branch that is linked to **Work Items/ Feature**. Refer to the following screenshot:

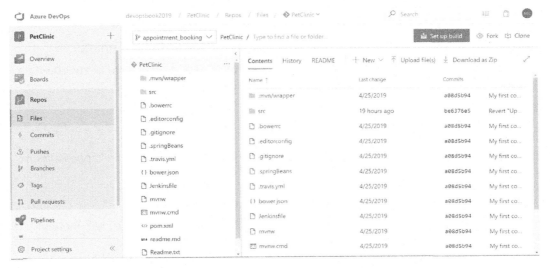

Figure 5.21: *Newly created branch for Work Item*

Let's try to get details in the command window. Fetch the details from Azure Repos. Find the details related to the newly created branch, which is as follows:

```
Mitesh@LAPTOP-FQ8JSR2E MINGW64 ~/Desktop/BPBOnline/MicrosoftAzureDevOps/
Chapter  - 5/mypetclinic-master (origin/devops)
```

$ git fetch

```
Username for 'https://dev.azure.com': xxxxxxxxxxx@outlook.com

remote: Azure Repos

remote: Found 2 objects to send. (7 ms)

Unpacking objects: 100% (2/2), done.

From https://dev.azure.com/devopsbook2019/PetClinic/_git/PetClinic
 * [new branch]       appointment_booking -> origin/appointment_booking
   75b5da1..3c25804  master                 -> origin/master
```

Verify the existing branch using the following command:

```
Mitesh@LAPTOP-FQ8JSR2E MINGW64 ~/Desktop/BPBOnline/MicrosoftAzureDevOps/
Chapter  - 5/mypetclinic-master (origin/devops)

$ git branch

master

* origin/devops
```

Let's move to the newly created branch. Refer to the following command:

```
Mitesh@LAPTOP-FQ8JSR2E MINGW64 ~/Desktop/BPBOnline/MicrosoftAzureDevOps/
Chapter  - 5/mypetclinic-master (origin/devops)
```

$ git checkout appointment_booking

```
Switched to a new branch 'appointment_booking'

Branch 'appointment_booking' set up to track remote branch 'appointment_
booking' from 'origin'.
```

Verify the existing branch again using the following command:

```
Mitesh@LAPTOP-FQ8JSR2E MINGW64 ~/Desktop/BPBOnline/MicrosoftAzureDevOps/
Chapter  - 5/mypetclinic-master (appointment_booking)
```

$ git branch

```
* appointment_booking

master

origin/devops
```

Let's try to change some files and create a pull request. We will perform this operation on another branch. Refer to the following command:

```
$ git commit -m "bgcolor changed of Homepage"

On branch origin/devops

Changes not staged for commit:

modified:   src/main/webapp/WEB-INF/jsp/welcome.jsp

no changes added to commit
```

Why did we receive this message? We need to add files for commit. Let's use git add command, which is as follows:

```
Mitesh@LAPTOP-FQ8JSR2E MINGW64 ~/Desktop/BPBOnline/MicrosoftAzureDevOps/
Chapter  - 5/mypetclinic-master (origin/devops)

$ git add .

warning: LF will be replaced by CRLF in src/main/webapp/WEB-INF/jsp/
welcome.jsp.
```

The file will have its original line endings in your working directory.

Commit the changes to the local repository using the following command:

```
Mitesh@LAPTOP-FQ8JSR2E MINGW64 ~/Desktop/BPBOnline/MicrosoftAzureDevOps/
Chapter  - 5/mypetclinic-master (origin/devops)

$ git commit -m "bgcolor changed of Homepage"

[origin/devops 3f755c4] bgcolor changed of Homepage

 1 file changed, 1 insertion(+), 1 deletion(-)
```

Verify the status now. It says nothing to commit. The working tree is clean because we have committed the changes. Check the status using the following command:

```
$ git status .

On branch origin/devops

nothing to commit, working tree clean
```

Push changes to Azure Repos using the following command:

```
$ git push -u origin –all

Username for 'https://dev.azure.com':

Enumerating objects: 15, done.

Counting objects: 100% (15/15), done.
```

```
Delta compression using up to 4 threads
Compressing objects: 100% (8/8), done.
Writing objects: 100% (8/8), 677 bytes | 84.00 KiB/s, done.
Total 8 (delta 5), reused 0 (delta 0)
remote: Analyzing objects... (8/8) (5 ms)
remote: Storing packfile... done (66 ms)
remote: Storing index... done (34 ms)
To https://dev.azure.com/devopsbook2019/PetClinic/_git/PetClinic
 * [new branch]      origin/devops -> origin/devops
Branch 'master' set up to track remote branch 'master' from 'origin'.
Branch 'origin/devops' set up to track remote branch 'origin/devops' from
'origin'.
```

Verify the latest commit, as shown in the following screenshot:

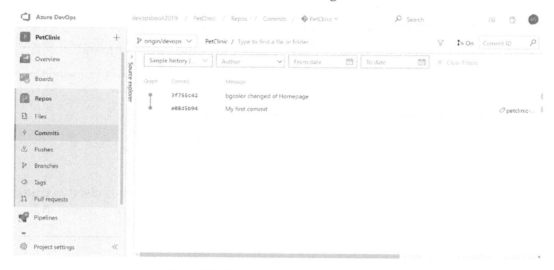

***Figure 5.22:** Existing commits in Azure Repos*

Click on the **Pull requests** section and click on **New Pull Request**. Keep the default values as we want to merge the change in the master branch. Refer to the following screenshot:

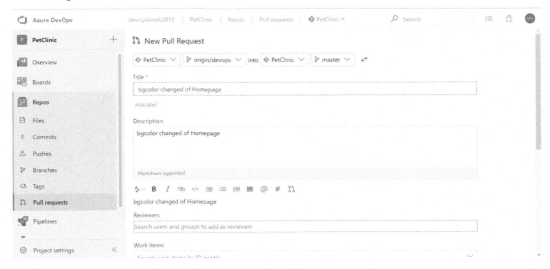

Figure 5.23: Pull request

Select the name of the reviewer. Verify the changes in the files and click on **Create** button, as shown in the following screenshot:

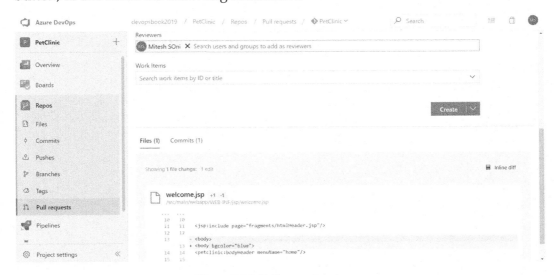

Figure 5.24: Pull request reviewers

In this case, I have assigned the pull request to myself. Go to **Pull requests** section and verify **Created by me** and **Assigned to me** headers, as shown in the following screenshot:

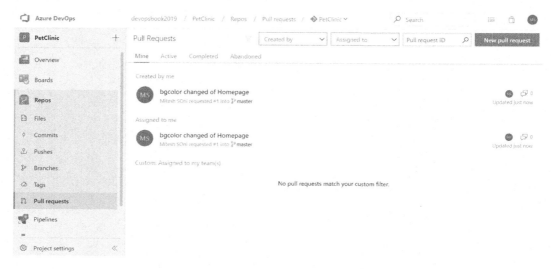

Figure 5.25: Pull request dashboard

Review the changes and if everything looks fine, then approve or approve with suggestions. Refer to the following screenshot:

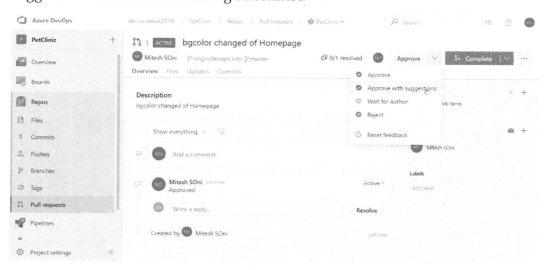

Figure 5.26: Pull request approval

Once the pull request is approved, as a best practice you should execute the build and make sure that the build is clean. If the build is clean then the pull request can be completed.

Go to **Pull requests** and click on **Complete**. Provide the description and the merge type. If you want to delete the branch after cleaning the build then select the option. Click on **Complete merge** button, as shown in the following screenshot:

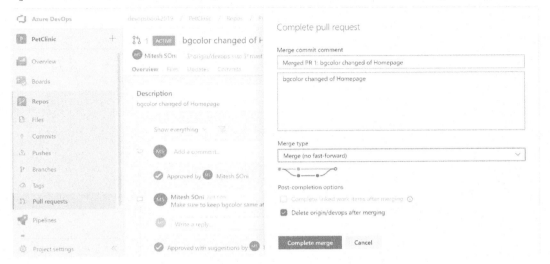

Figure 5.27: Complete Pull Request

Verify the completed status of the **pull request**. In the Pull requests section, go to the **Competed** section and verify the pull request we recently completed. Refer to the following screenshot:

Figure 5.28: Completed Pull Request

If we find any issue then we can revert as well. Click on **Revert**, as shown in the following screenshot:

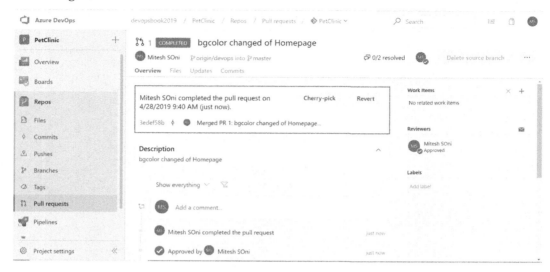

Figure 5.29: Pull Request - Revert

Another topic branch will be created with the reverted changes. Prompt will be available to create a pull request to the target branch. Refer to the following screenshot:

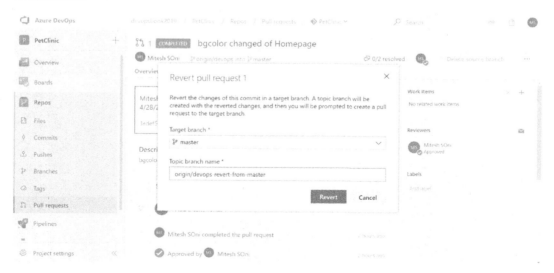

Figure 5.30: Revert the Pull Request

In the next section, we will discuss tags.

Tags

Azure DevOps Repos support annotated and lightweight tags. Let's understand the difference between the two in the following table:

	Annotated tags	**Lightweight tags**
Description	Provides additional details such as tag name, commit, message, tagger, and date	Pointer to specific commit and a tag name
How to create it	Can be created using web portal	Can be created using Visual Studio

Table 5.1: *Types of Tags*

To create a tag, go to **Commits**, click on … and click on **Create tag**…, as shown in the following screenshot:

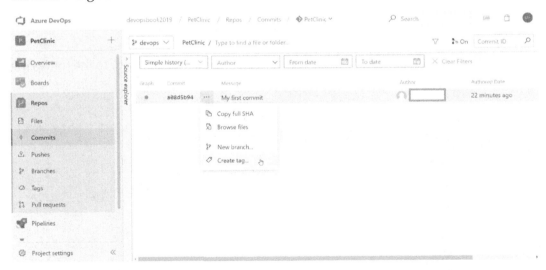

Figure 5.31: *Create Tag*

Provide a name for a tag. Select a commit to create the tag and provide the description. Click on the **Create** button, as shown in the following screenshot:

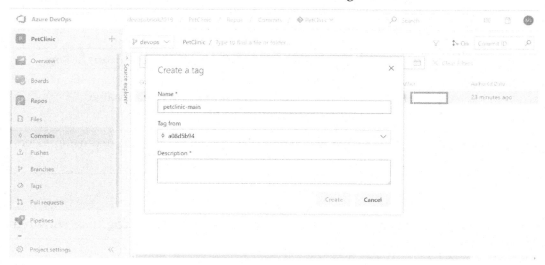

Figure 5.32: Tag description

Click on **Tags** and verify the newly-created tag in Azure Repos. Refer to the following screenshot:

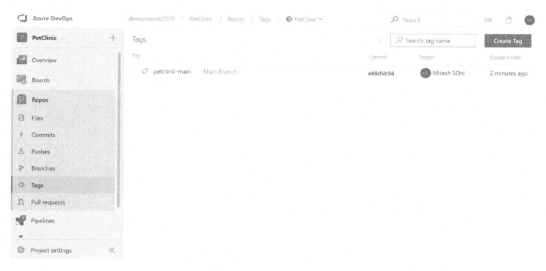

Figure 5.33: Tags in Azure Repos

Click on the **Tags** section to verify files, as shown in the following screenshot:

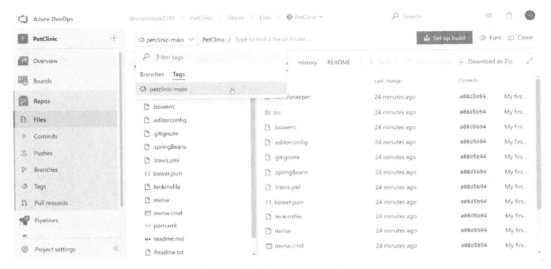

Figure 5.34: Files related to Tag

To get the details on the tag, move your mouse pointer to tag in the **Commits** section, as shown in the following screenshot:

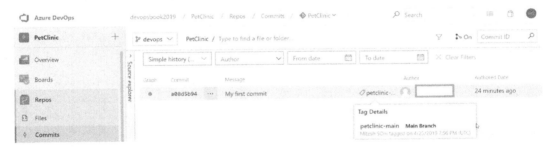

Figure 5.35: Tag Details

Let's go to the **Tags** section again. Click on the tag, as shown in the following screenshot:

Figure 5.36: Tag dashboard

Verify all commit numbers in the existing tag. Refer to the following screenshot:

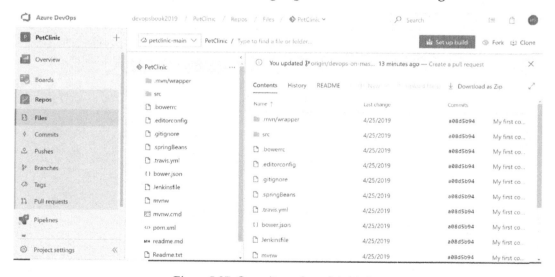

Figure 5.37: Commit number related to tag

Go to the current version of Azure Repos to verify the commit ID of src folder. Refer to the following screenshot:

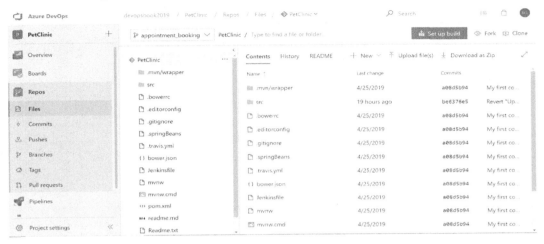

Figure 5.38: Existing Commit number in Azure Repo

For more details on tagging, visit: **https://git-scm.com/book/en/v2/Git-Basics-Tagging.**

Code management in Azure DevOps Dashboard

Source code can be easily managed in the Azure DevOps portal. Click on Azure Repos and then click on `Files | src` folder. Refer to the following screenshot:

Figure 5.39: Code in Azure Repos

You can compare the existing file with past versions by selecting a specific commit, as shown in the following screenshot:

Figure 5.40: Compare files in Azure Repos

To verify changes to a specific file over a period of time, click on the **History** section, as shown in the following screenshot:

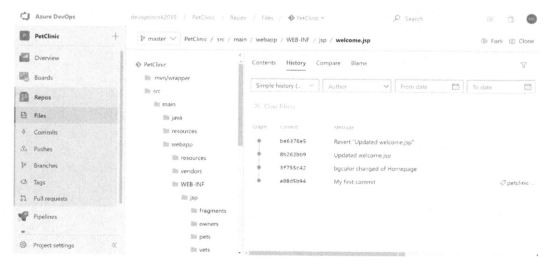

Figure 5.41: History of files in Azure Repos

Conclusion

We have covered all the important topics available in Azure Repos section, especially Git repository. In the next chapter, we will have hands-on activities for Microsoft Azure Cloud.

CHAPTER 6
Microsoft Azure Cloud

Microsoft Azure is one of the most popular cloud platforms available in the market, and it is a direct competitor to Amazon Web Services. Cloud computing plays a vital role in DevOps culture. The existing culture of resource management to deploy application for various environments is not effective, and it works as a bottleneck in the end-to-end automation pipeline. Cloud resources help in faster provisioning and de-provisioning of resources, scaling, high availability, and fault tolerance. The pricing model is also attractive compared to **CAPEX (Capital Expenditure).** We will discuss multiple services offered by Microsoft Azure that are useful for cloud deployments.

Structure

We will cover the following topics in this chapter:

- Azure regions, geographies, availability zones
- Microsoft Azure
- Resource groups
- Role-based access
- Microsoft Azure Services

Objective

This chapter will provide a brief description of Microsoft Azure Services and other important details about Microsoft Azure Cloud.

Azure regions, geographies, availability zones

Microsoft Azure has 54 regions worldwide, and is available across 140 countries/ regions. The number of regions helps to configure application runtime environment in a way that is closer to the end user. There are security, governance, and compliance requirements specific to the countries, making it necessary to configure infrastructure in a compliant way. The following image shows the regions that are available across 140 countries/regions:

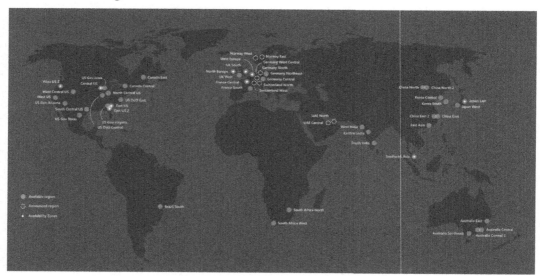

Figure 6.1: Azure Regions
(Reference: https://azure.microsoft.com/en-in/global-infrastructure/regions/)

Those geographies are fault-tolerant which contain two or more regions for compliance requirements and data storage. The following diagram states the same:

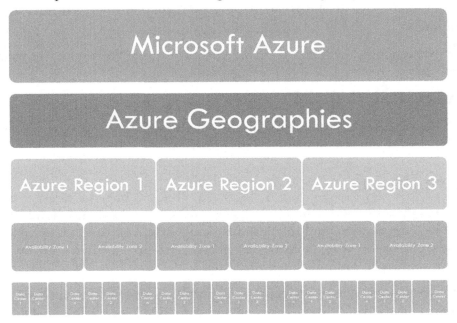

Figure 6.2: *Azure regions, geographies, availability zones*

Each region has availability zones, and each availability zone has one or more data centers. The following screenshot displays the services based on regions:

Figure 6.3: *Services or products are available based on regions*

Services or products are available based on regions, which can be verified via: **https:// azure.microsoft.com/en-in/global-infrastructure/services/**. To get more details on geographies, visit: **https://azure.microsoft.com/en-in/global-infrastructure/ geographies/**

In the next section, we will take a tour of Microsoft Azure Portal and its services.

Microsoft Azure

In the Microsoft Azure Portal, we will try to discuss those services which are more related to the implementation of DevOps practices.

Azure Portal

The Microsoft Azure portal allows end users to create and manage cloud resources using a web application, and the portal is being improved continuously since last few years. End users can manage the dashboard as per his/her own wish, by pinning specific resources according to their priorities.

As a Microsoft Azure user, we can access portal on all kinds of different devices available in the market, and browsers having different Color scheme customization.

1. When you visit **https://portal.azure.com**, the following screenshot shows the home page:

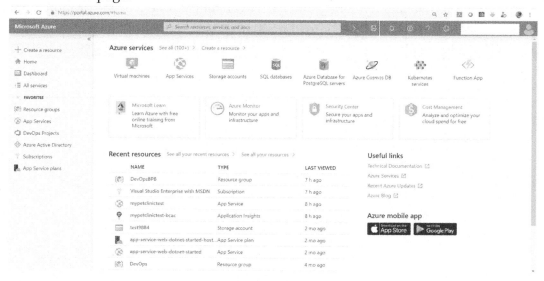

Figure 6.4: Microsoft Azure Portal

2. Click on the **Dashboard**.

3. You can create a new dashboard. Add tile from the **Tile Gallery**.

4. Resize the tile based on the need and availability of the size for the tile.

5. Click on **Done customizing** once you are done. Refer to the following screenshot:

Figure 6.5: *Microsoft Azure Dashboard*

6. After customization, the new dashboard looks like the following screenshot:

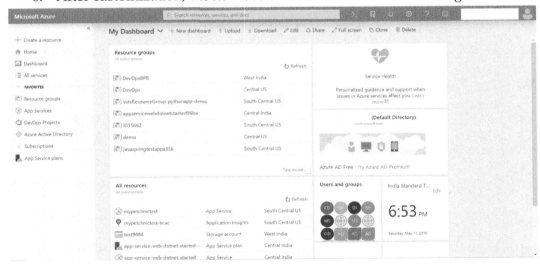

Figure 6.6: *Customized Microsoft Azure Dashboard*

7. You can download the dashboard as JSON file, and then upload it on Azure Portal. Refer to the following sample dashboard JSON file:

```json
"properties": {
  "lenses": {
    "0": {
      "order": 0,
      "parts": {
        "0": {
          "position": {
            "x": 0,
            "y": 0,
            "colSpan": 6,
            "rowSpan": 4
          },
          "metadata": {
            "inputs": [
              {
                "name": "resourceType",
                "value":"Microsoft.Resources/subscriptions/
                resourcegroups","isOptional": true
              },
              {
                "name": "filter",
                "isOptional": true
              },
              {
                "name": "scope",
                "isOptional": true
              },
              {
                "name": "kind",
```

```
                        "isOptional": true
                    }
                ],
        "type": "Extension/HubsExtension/PartType/BrowseResourceGroupPinnedPart"
                }
            },
            "1": {
                "position": {
                    "x": 6,
                    "y": 0,
                    "colSpan": 4,
                    "rowSpan": 2
                },
                "metadata": {
                    "inputs": [],
        "type": "Extension/HubsExtension/PartType/ServicesHealthPart"
                }
            }
        }
    },
    "metadata": {
        "model": {
            "timeRange": {
                "value": {
                    "relative": {
                        "duration": 24,
                "timeUnit": 1
                    }
```

```
                },
                    "type": "MsPortalFx.Composition.Configuration.ValueTypes.
        TimeRange"
                }
            }
        }
    },
    "name": "My Dashboard",
    "type": "Microsoft.Portal/dashboards",
    "location": "INSERT LOCATION",
    "tags": {
        "hidden-title": "My Dashboard"
    },
    "apiVersion": "2015-08-01-preview"
}
```

8. To change the color, just double click on the **Dashboard**. Following are the colours:

Figure 6.7: *Microsoft Azure Dashboard Colors*

9. In Azure Portal/Dashboard, you can add Azure Services in the favourites list.

10. There is a Cloud Shell that is available on the Azure Portal as well. We can use it for Azure CLI execution. It is similar to the following screenshot:

Figure 6.8: Microsoft Azure Cloud Shell

In the next section, we will discuss resource groups.

Resource groups

Resource groups are logical containers in Microsoft Azure Portal. You can create a resource group that contains all the resources for a web application or for a business unit or for a specific project that contains multiple modules. We can assign role-based access to the entire resource group. By deleting resource group, all the resources or Azure Services in the resource group will be deleted. Follow the steps given below to create a resource group:

1. Sign in to the Microsoft Azure portal.

2. Go to the left pane, select **App Services**, and search **Resource groups**. Refer to the following screenshot:

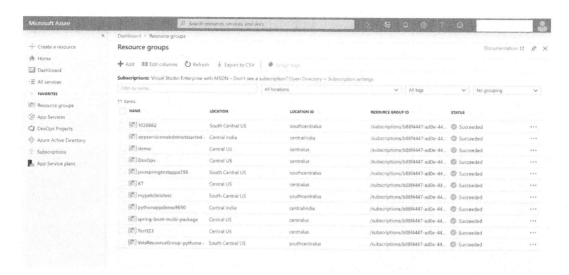

Figure 6.9: Microsoft Azure Resource Groups

1. Click on **Add**.

2. Select **Subscription** and provide **Resource group** name.

3. Select the **Region** and click on **Review + Create** button, as shown in the following screenshot:

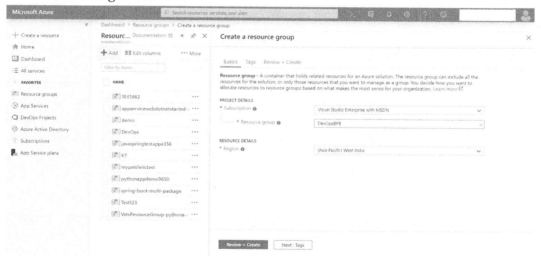

Figure 6.10: Creating a Resource group

4. Review the details and then click on the **Create** button, as shown in the following screenshot:

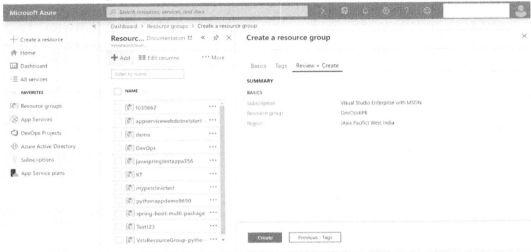

Figure 6.11: Resource group - Review

5. Click on the newly-created resource group in the resource group dashboard in Azure portal, as shown in the following screenshot:

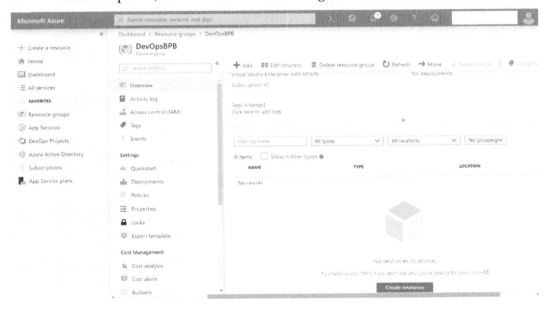

Figure 6.12: New Resource group

We will create all our resources in this particular resource group in the rest of the book. In the next section, we will discuss Azure mobile app.

Azure mobile app

Cloud resources make management and monitoring of resources easier as all resources can be accessed via the internet. It is easy to find issues and troubleshoot with handheld devices, such as mobiles and tablets. Azure mobile app helps to view metrics, check for alerts, start and stop Azure App services, browse App Services, and so on.

For Apple, follow the following steps:

First download it using this link: **https://itunes.apple.com/us/app/microsoft-azure/id1219013620?ls=1&mt=8**

1. Go to App Store in your iPhone.
2. Search for Microsoft Azure App.
3. Click on **GET**. Once it is installed, click on the app icon.
4. Sign in with your Microsoft Azure credentials.
5. On the mobile app dashboard, click on the resource group that we had created earlier.
6. Verify **Activity log, Properties, Access Controls (IAM),** and **Resources** of the resource group.
7. For Azure App Service, verify **Metrics, Resource health,** and **Properties.**
8. As an end user, you can **Start, Stop, Restart,** and **Browse** the application as shown in the following screenshot:

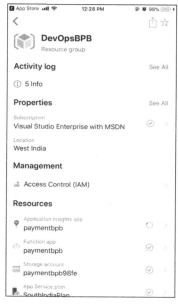

Figure 6.13: iOS App - Resource group   *Figure 6.14*: iOS App - App Services

For Android users, the app is available in the Google Play Store:

https://play.google.com/store/apps/details?id=com.microsoft.azure.

In the next section, we will discuss role-based access.

Role-based access control - RBAC

Role-based access control (RBAC) provides access management of Azure resources or resource groups. In a project or a business unit, if you want to provide access based on designation or a team's work profile then RBAC is very important. For example, you only want to provide access to development team for development and QnA environment only.

Let's understand role-based access with a diagram:

Figure 6.15: *Role-based access*

In role assignment, role definition is attached to a user or a group that has a defined scope to allow access to resources available in Microsoft Azure.

Let's make a co-administrator first, and then we will try to create role assignment using the following steps:

1. Go to the Microsoft azure Portal.

2. Click on **Subscriptions** in the left pane.

3. Select specific **subscription**.

4. Click on **Add | Add co-administrator**, as shown in the following screenshot:

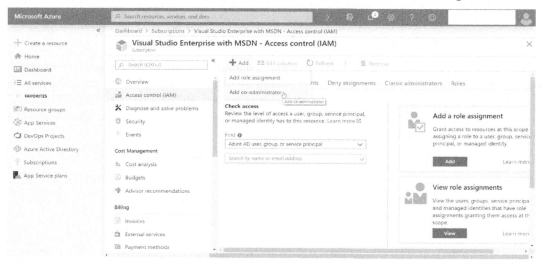

Figure 6.16: Co-administrator

5. Select a specific user to make him/her a co-admin, and then click on **Add** button, as shown in the following screenshot:

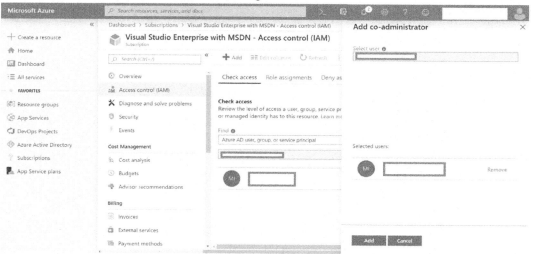

Figure 6.17: Microsoft Azure Subscription - Co admin

6. To verify an assignment, go to **Subscriptions**.

7. Select the specific subscription.

8. Click on **Classic administrators** section, and verify added co-administrator, as shown in the following screenshot:

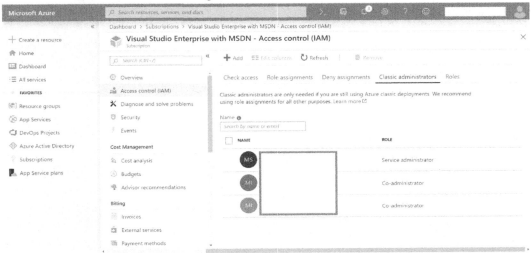

Figure 6.18: Microsoft Azure Classic administrators

9. Go to newly-created resource group and select **Access Control (IAM)**. Click on the user and find details about role assignments, as shown in the following screenshot:

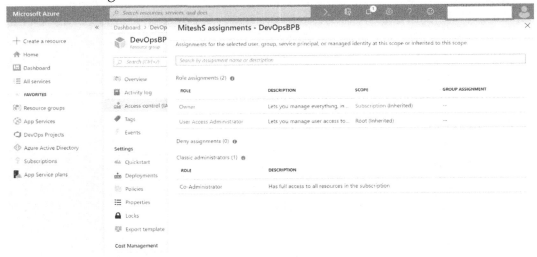

Figure 6.19: Microsoft Azure - Role assignments

10. Verify **Classic administrator** for the resource group as well. Refer to the following screenshot:

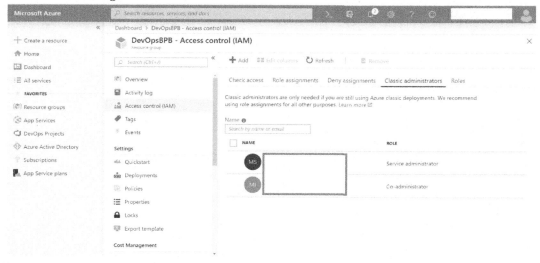

Figure 6.20: *Microsoft Azure Access Control*

11. We can check various roles by clicking on the **Roles** link available in **Access Control (IAM)** for the resource group, as shown in the following screenshot:

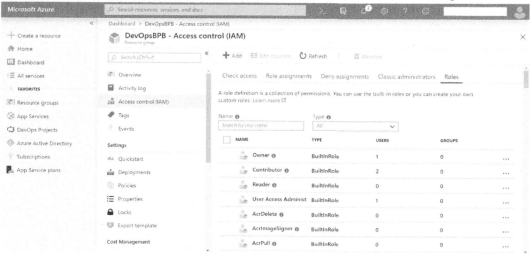

Figure 6.21: *Microsoft Azure roles*

12. Click on **Add | Add Role Assignment.**

13. Select **Role**, and select security principal and member.

14. Click on **Save** button, as shown in the following screenshot:

Figure 6.22: Microsoft Azure Role Assignment to User

15. Verify **Role assignments** in Azure Portal for resource group, as shown in the following screenshot:

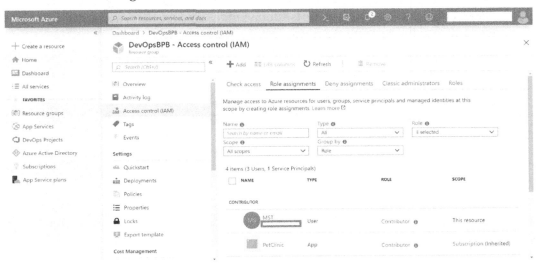

Figure 6.23: Microsoft Azure Role Assignment to resource group

In the next section, we will discuss the different Microsoft Azure Services.

Microsoft Azure Services

Let's get some overview of the services that we will try to use in the coming chapters for implementing DevOps practices.

Azure Cost Management

Azure Cost Management and billing is a cost management and billing solution that helps us monitor and manage cost. It helps us to utilize resources in a better way.

As a Microsoft Azure consumer, we can do the following things:

- Cost analysis (accumulated, daily, monthly)
- Cost analysis group by different parameters
- Pie charts (service name, location, resource group name by default)
- Manage budgets
- Advisor recommendations
- Cost alerts
- Exporting of billing data

Let us perform the following steps to understand the cost analysis:

1. Go to **Home** | **Cost Management + Billing**. Read access to one or more subscriptions, billing accounts, departments, enrolment accounts, resource groups, or management groups is required.
2. Click on **Budgets| Add.**
3. Select **Amount, Resets, Expiration date, Alerts,** and so on, as shown in the following screenshot:

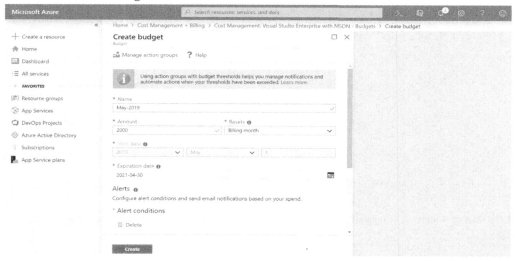

Figure 6.24: *Microsoft Azure Cost Management- Budget*

4. Budgets can be set for **Monthly, Quarterly,** or **Annually,** as shown in the following screenshot:

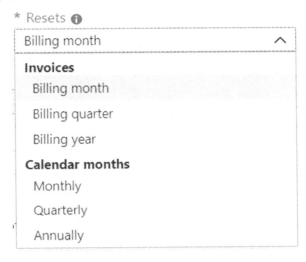

Figure 6.25: Microsoft Azure Cost Management Budget - Resets

5. Click on **Cost analysis** to know more details on what services are leading to cost, location-wise cost, and resource group-wise costs as well. Many other configurations are available for pie charts. Refer to the following screenshot:

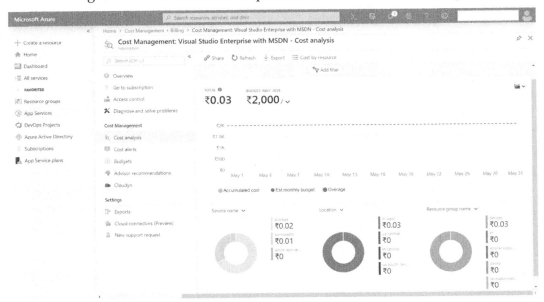

Figure 6.26: Microsoft Azure Cost Analysis

For more details visit: **https://docs.microsoft.com/en-us/azure/cost-management/**

Cloudyn is a Microsoft Azure service that will be eventually replaced by Azure Cost Management. Cloudyn helps to track cloud usage and cost for Azure, AWS, and Google resources.

In the next section, we will see Azure Policy.

Azure Monitor

Azure Monitor helps to monitor resources to find out the performance of an application and its issues. Azure Monitor includes Log Analytics and Application Insights. Hence, the availability of application increases.

1. Go to the Azure Portal, click on **All services | Monitor**, as shown in the following screenshot:

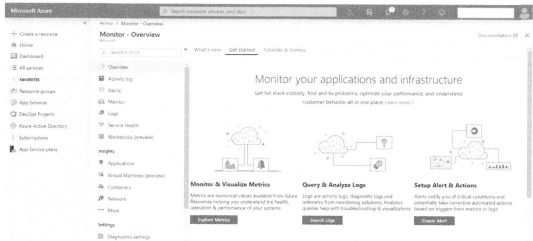

Figure 6.27: Microsoft Azure Monitor overview

2. In **Monitor**, click on **Metrics** and click on **New Chart**. Select Azure App Service for monitoring. Click on **Add metric** and add **Connections, CPU Time, Average Response Time, HTTP 2xx, Thread Count, Requests,** and observe the changes in the chart. We can change the types of chart,

as well as time duration, in the Azure Portal itself. Refer to the following screenshot:

Figure 6.28: Microsoft Azure Monitor Metrics

3. Click on **Alerts**. We need to **Create a rule** for setting up alerts and select **Resource – App Service** plans, as shown in the following screenshot:

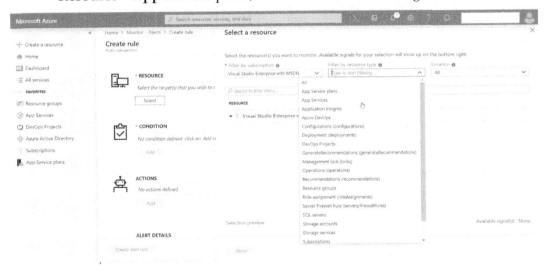

Figure 6.29: Microsoft Azure Monitor Alerts

4. Select **CONDITION** as suitable. Configure **ACTIONS** and click on **Create alert rule,** as shown in the following screenshot:

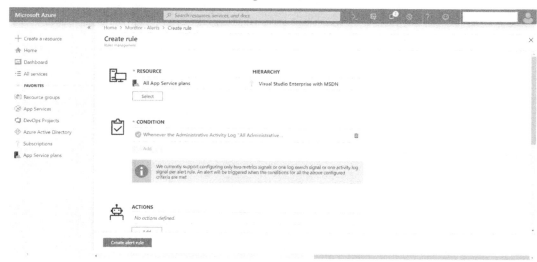

Figure 6.30: Microsoft Azure Alert Condition

Monitoring is an important part in DevOps. Azure Monitor collects data from application monitoring data, guest OS monitoring data, Azure resource/subscription /tenant monitoring data. Continuous monitoring of applications and infrastructure helps improve the DevOps culture. By setting up Azure Monitor in an appropriate way, performance and availability increases if proper action is taken in time.

App Services

Azure App Service is a **Platform as a Service (PaaS)**. It supports applications written in .NET, Node.js, PHP, Java, Python (on Linux), and HTML. It helps to host web applications, mobile middleware or Restful APIs. Infrastructure management is the responsibility of Microsoft. A cloud consumer only needs to worry about applications. Configuration of high availability is also the responsibility of the cloud consumer.

Following are some essential features of Azure App Services:

| Support for Java, ASP.NET, ASP.NET Core, Ruby, Node.js, PHP, or Python | Horizontal and vertical scaling – Auto and Manual | Deployment Slots – to manage different environments as well as Rollback |

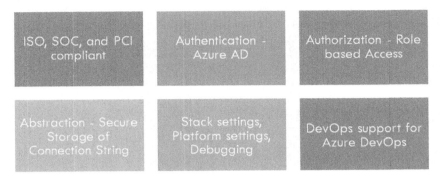

Figure 6.31: *Microsoft Azure App Service features*

App Services are available on the Azure portal, click on **All services | App Services**, as shown in the following screenshot:

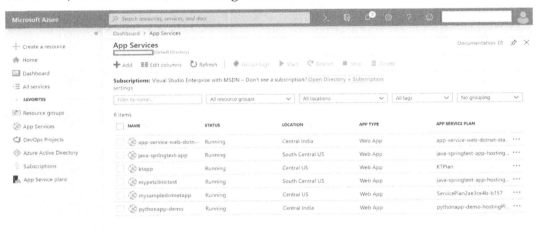

Figure 6.32: *Microsoft Azure App Service Portal*

App Service plan is a home where App Service is running. It contains a set of computable resources. One App Service plan can have more than one App Service but one App Service can't run on multiple App Service plans. It is created in a specific region, and hence an App Service is hosted in the region where the App Service plan is hosted.

Free, shared, basic, standard, premium, premiumV2, and isolated pricing plans are available for App Service plans. Refer to the following screenshot:

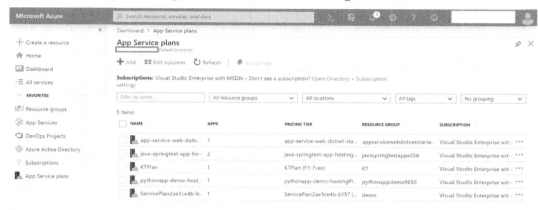

Figure 6.33: Microsoft Azure App Service Plans

App Service Environment (ASE) is a premium service provided by Microsoft Azure where we can host Azure App Services in isolated environment/virtual network where we can configure security on our own.

In the next section, we will discuss the Azure Functions in brief.

Azure Functions

Azure Functions is a serverless solution from Microsoft Azure. It allows us to execute function or method in the cloud. As a cloud consumer, we don't need to manage infrastructure, which is the responsibility of Microsoft Azure. In Azure Functions, we can write functions or methods in Java, PHP, C#, F#, or Node.js.

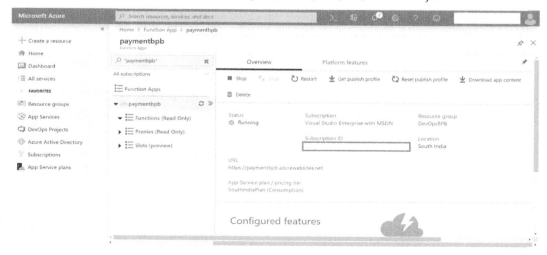

Figure 6.34: Microsoft Azure Functions

There are two types of pricing plans available with Azure Functions, which are as follows:

- Consumption plan - Pay as you use
- App Service plan.

Containers

Azure Kubernetes Service (AKS), Azure Container Instances, and Azure Container Registry are some of the container services provided by Microsoft Azure. The following diagram describes the same:

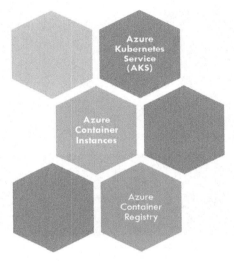

Figure 6.35: Microsoft Azure containers

Introduction of containers in the cloud and virtual world has helped in the evolution a lot. It is one of the popular ways to manage resources effectively by using it in build, package, and deployment. Azure Container Instances help us to create and run containers without managing underlying infrastructure.

Kubernetes allows us to work with declarative approach of deployments. It manages applications that are container-based. DevOps practices can be integrated easily to make the cultural shift easier. By using AKS, we can deploy Kubernetes cluster in Microsoft Azure. It is a hosted Kubernetes service. Microsoft Azure is responsible for the management and the maintenance of resources. Pricing is based on the usage of nodes or agents.

With the use of Azure Container Registry, we can create, manage, and maintain private Docker container images. It helps to store Docker images safely, which can be accessed without them being made publically available. We can utilize Azure Container Registry for deployment pipelines.

To get more details on containers, visit **https://docs.microsoft.com/en-in/azure/containers/**.

Azure Cloud Shell

How would you feel if Bash or Powershell are available in a browser without installing anything on your system? Azure Cloud Shell is a browser-based shell for managing Microsoft Azure Cloud resources.

We can utilize the shell from **https://shell.azure.com/** or from Microsoft Azure Portal itself. Refer to the following screenshot:

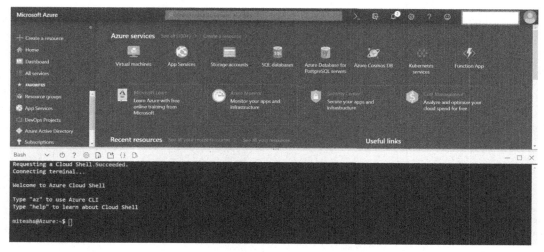

Figure 6.36: *Microsoft Azure Cloud Shell Bash*

For Linux users, use BASH, as shown in the following screenshot:

Figure 6.37: *Microsoft Azure Cloud Shell - BASH*

For Windows users, use PowerShell, as shown in the following screenshot:

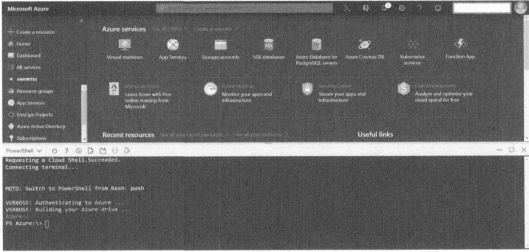

Figure 6.38: Microsoft Azure Cloud Shell - PowerShell

Let's try some commands. Execute `dir` command. It will provide Subscription Name, which is as follows:

PS Azure:\>dir

```
     Directory: Azure:

   Mode SubscriptionNameSubscriptionIdTenantId                State
   ----     ---------------         --------------    --------    -----
```

+   Visual Studio Enterprise with MSDN b88f4447-ad0e-44d4-a662-2eb5c950f091
b76e984d-14f8-48b9-940c-dceca5c43ad0 Enabled

Azure:/

PS Azure:\> cd './Visual Studio Enterprise with MSDN/'

Azure:/Visual Studio Enterprise with MSDN

Let's verify available resource groups using following command:

PS Azure:\> cd ./ResourceGroups/

Azure:/Visual Studio Enterprise with MSDN/ResourceGroups

PS Azure:\>dir

```
     Directory: Azure:/Visual Studio Enterprise with MSDN/ResourceGroups
```

```
Mode ResourceGroupName                     Location         ProvisioningState Tags
---- -----------------                     --------         ----------------- ----
+    1035662                               southcentralus Succeeded
+    appservicewebdotnetstarted96bacentralindia    Succeeded
+    cloud-shell-storage-centralindiacentralindia  Succeeded
+    democentralus        Succeeded
+    DevOpscentralus         Succeeded
+    DevOpsBPBwestindia         Succeeded
+    javaspringtestappa356southcentralus Succeeded
+    KT                                    centralus        Succeeded
+    mypetclinictestsouthcentralus Succeeded
+    petclinicbook-rgsouthcentralus Succeeded
+    pythonappdemo9650centralindia    Succeeded
+    spring-boot-multi-package             centralus        Succeeded
+    Test123                               centralus        Succeeded
+    VstsResourceGroup-pythonapp-demo southcentralus Succeeded
+    VstsRG-devopsbook2019-cc91            centralus        Succeeded
```

```
Azure:/Visual Studio Enterprise with MSDN/ResourceGroups
PS Azure:\>
```

Let's visit the web app we have created in a specific resource group using following commands:

```
PS Azure:\> cd ./mypetclinictest/
```

```
Azure:/Visual Studio Enterprise with MSDN/ResourceGroups/mypetclinictest
PS Azure:\>dir
```

```
   Directory: Azure:/Visual Studio Enterprise with MSDN/ResourceGroups/
   mypetclinictest
```

```
Mode ProviderName
---- ------------
+    microsoft.insights
```

```
+    Microsoft.Web
```

```
Azure:/Visual Studio Enterprise with MSDN/ResourceGroups/mypetclinictest
```

Hence, it is easier to view and manage resources from Cloud Shell in a browser. In the next section, we will discuss Azure DevOps in brief.

Azure DevOps projects

DevOps projects helps you to **Bring Your Code, Bring Your Repository (BYCBYR).**

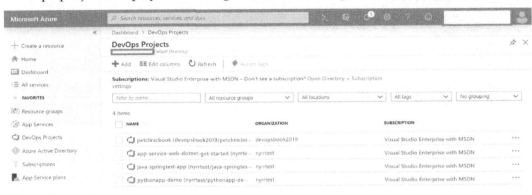

Figure 6.39: Microsoft Azure DevOps Projects Dashboard

DevOps projects performs the following activities:

- Setting up Git repository
- Setting up CICD pipeline
- Creating an Application Insights for monitoring

We can Monitor code repository status with commit details, build execution with status, and release execution with status on Azure DevOps projects dashboard.

Figure 6.40: *Microsoft Azure DevOps Project Overview*

Azure DevOps project flow is as follows:

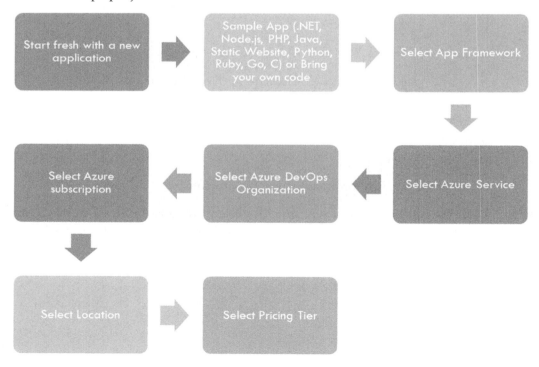

Figure 6.41: *Microsoft Azure DevOps project flow*

In the next section, we will discuss Azure Pipelines.

Azure Pipelines

Azure Pipelines is a feature available in the Azure DevOps that helps you to automate application life cycle management phases using build and release definition with Classic Pipelines or YAML file (Pipeline as a Code) based pipeline. **Continuous Integration and Continuous Delivery (CICD)** can be setup using Azure Pipelines.

Conclusion

We have covered all the important topics available in Microsoft Azure Cloud, which are more related to DevOps, such as Azure App Services, Monitoring, Cost Management, Azure DevOps Projects, and so on. In the next chapter, we will have hands-on activities for Microsoft Azure Services where we can deploy applications.

## CHAPTER 7

Microsoft Azure Cloud– Iaas and PaaS

Microsoft Azure is one of the most popular Cloud Services Providers in the market. Agile leads to DevOps and DevOps leads to Cloud Computing. All three can work in isolation but combination of them makes the entire scenario extremely effective in terms of quality and faster time to market. With Cloud computing, we can provide compute resources within very less time with proper governance and security. We will discuss multiple services offered by Microsoft Azure that are useful for cloud deployments.

Structure

We will cover following topics in this chapter:

- Infrastructure as a Service - Virtual Machines
- Platform as a Service - Azure App Services
- Monitoring of resources
- High availability and fault tolerance

Objective

In this chapter, we will provide a brief description about Microsoft Azure Services and other important details about Microsoft Azure Cloud.

Infrastructure as a Service - Virtual Machines

Azure **Virtual Machines (VMs)** is an **Infrastructure as a Service (IaaS)** offering from Microsoft where as a cloud consumer, it is your responsibility to manage all resources such as network, OS, hardening, installation, and configuration of runtime stack. Azure VM service supports the following:

- RedHat Linux
- Ubuntu
- Suse
- CentOS
- Debian
- Windows 10 Pro
- Windows Server
- SQL Server
- Oracle
- IBM
- SAP

Let us try to create a VM by performing the following steps. We have a Java-based application, so let us try to install the runtime environment and observe the efforts:

1. Login to the Microsoft Azure Portal, select **All services** | **Virtual machines**, as shown in the following screenshot:

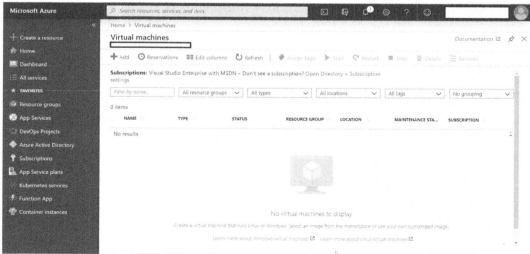

Figure 7.1: *VMs in Microsoft Azure*

2. Now, click on **Add** to open a side pane, which displaysthe `Create a virtual machine` window, as shown in the following screenshot:

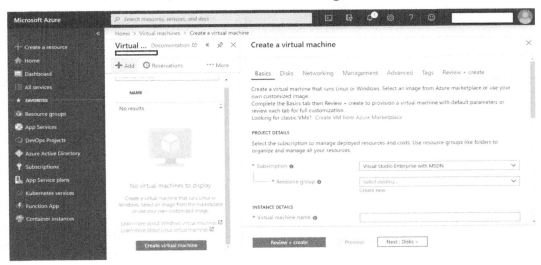

Figure 7.2: Create a new VM

3. Select a `Resource group` that we created earlier. Provide the unique name for a VM. Verify with the tooltip available for it and click on **Review + create**, as shown in the following screenshot:

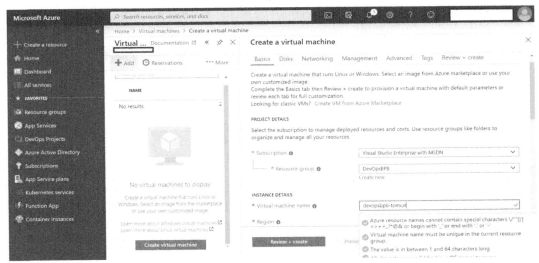

Figure 7.3: VM - Instance details

4. Select **Image** and **Authentication type**; provide **Username, Password,** and click on **Confirm password**. Now, click on **Next : Disks>,** as shown in the following screenshot:

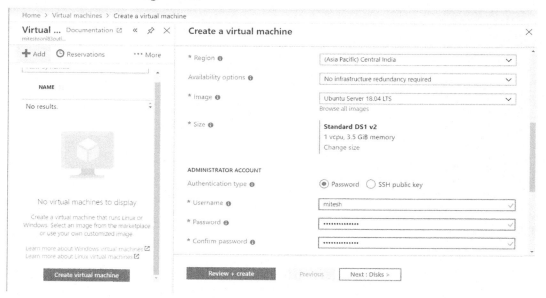

Figure 7.4: VMAdministrator account

5. Select **OS disk type** and click on **Next : Networking>,** as shown in the following screenshot:

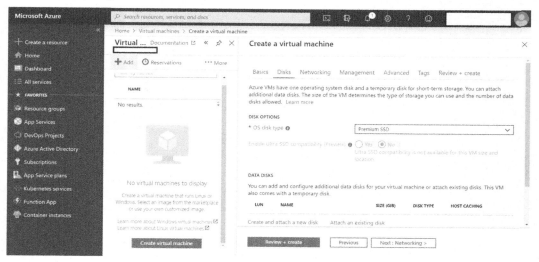

Figure 7.5: VMDisk

6. Select or keep the default settings for **Virtual network, Subnet, Public IP, NIC network security groups,** and so on. Click on **Next : Management>,** as shown in the following screenshot:

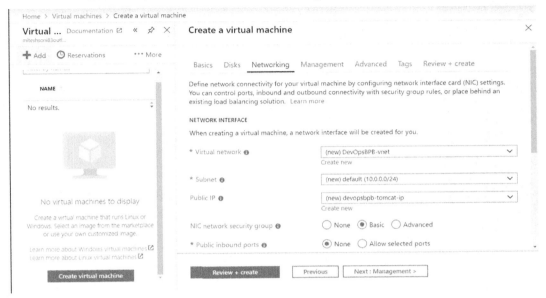

Figure 7.6: *VMnetworking*

7. Keep the default settings for **MONITORING** and click on **Next : Advanced>,** as shown in the following screenshot:

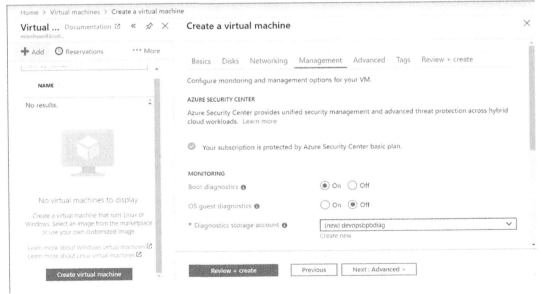

Figure 7.7: *VMmanagement*

8. Select **EXTENSIONS** if required and click on **Next : Tags >,** as shown in the following screenshot:

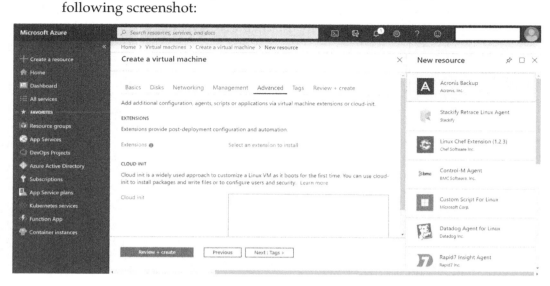

Figure 7.8: VMTags

9. Review all the details and click on **Create**, as shown in the following screenshot:

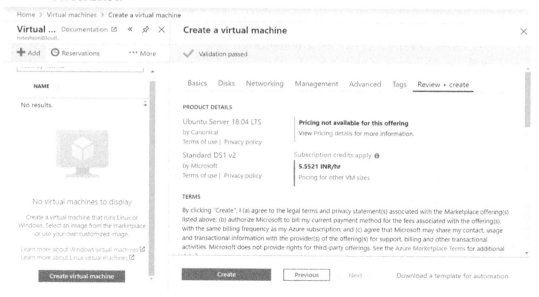

Figure 7.9: VMReview and Create

10. Observe the progress of the new deployment in form of the VM, as shown in the following screenshot:

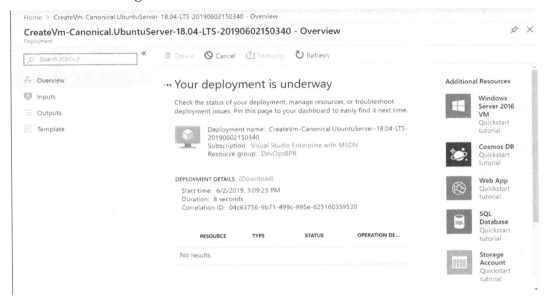

Figure 7.10: VMDeployment underway

11. Once the deployment is completed, you will be notified. It will look similar to the following screenshot:

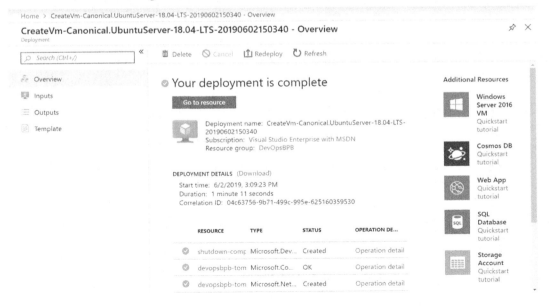

Figure 7.11: VMDeployment Completed

12. Click on **Virtual Machine** and select the name of the VM that is created recently. Click on the **Overview** link to verify more details, as shown in the following screenshot:

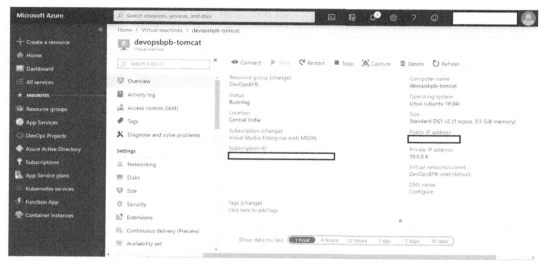

Figure 7.12: VMOverview

13. Verify the default inbound port rules, as shown in the following screenshot:

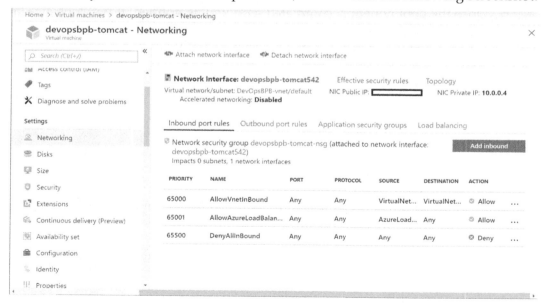

Figure 7.13: VMInbound Rules

14. Open PuTTY to access the Ubuntu-based VM. Use the hostname or IP address and give the port numberand click on **Open**, as shown in the following screenshot:

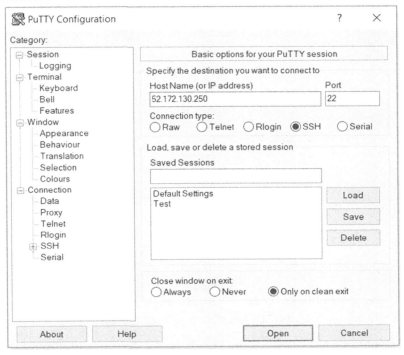

Figure 7.14: VMConnect using PuTTY

15. You will get a network error similar to the following screenshot:

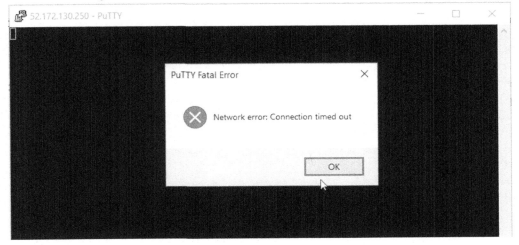

Figure 7.15: VMNetwork error

16. The reason for the error is that the SSH port is not open in inbound rules. For this, go to the Azure Portal, select **Networking | Add.** Enter 22 in **Destination port ranges** and then click on **Add**, as shown in the following screenshot:

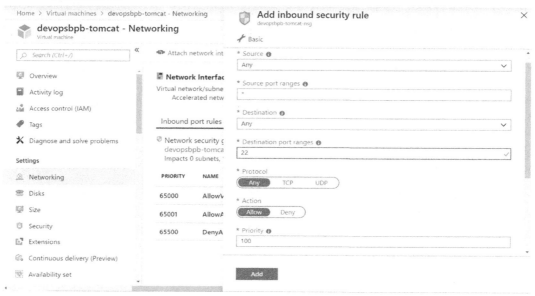

Figure 7.16: VMAdd inbound security rule

17. Verify the newly added inbound rule in the Azure portalby referring to the following screenshot:

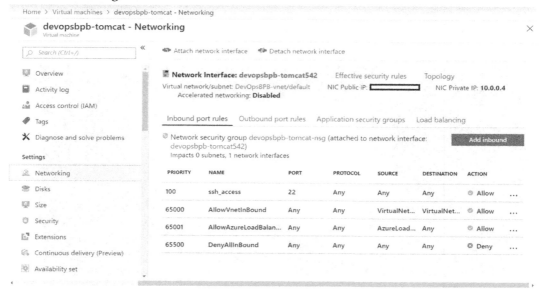

Figure 7.17: VMNetworking

18. Click on **Yes** in the **PuTTY Security Alert** window, as shown in the following screenshot:

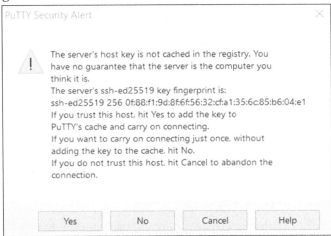

Figure 7.18: VMSecurity Alert

19. Login with the username and password created at the time of creation of the VM, as shown in the following screenshot:

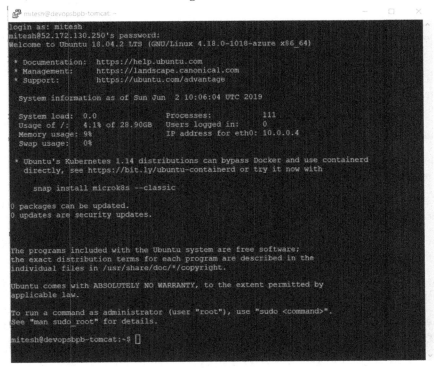

Figure 7.19: VMLogin

20. Let us update all the packages before installing and configuring Tomcat using the following command:

mitesh@devopsbpb-tomcat:~$ sudo apt-get update

Hit:1 http://azure.archive.ubuntu.com/ubuntu bionic InRelease

Get:2 http://azure.archive.ubuntu.com/ubuntu bionic-updates InRelease [88.7 kB]

Get:3 http://azure.archive.ubuntu.com/ubuntu bionic-backports InRelease [74.6 kB]

Get:4 http://azure.archive.ubuntu.com/ubuntu bionic-updates/main amd64 Packages [621 kB]

Get:5 http://azure.archive.ubuntu.com/ubuntu bionic-updates/main Translation-en [231 kB]

Get:6 http://azure.archive.ubuntu.com/ubuntu bionic-updates/ universe amd64 Packages [945 kB]

Get:7 http://azure.archive.ubuntu.com/ubuntu bionic-updates/ universe Translation-en [277 kB]

Get:8 http://security.ubuntu.com/ubuntu bionic-security InRelease [88.7 kB]

Get:9 http://azure.archive.ubuntu.com/ubuntu bionic-backports/ main amd64 Packages [2512 B]

Get:10 http://azure.archive.ubuntu.com/ubuntu bionic-backports/ main Translation-en [1644 B]

Get:11 http://azure.archive.ubuntu.com/ubuntu bionic-backports/ universe amd64 Packages [3716 B]

Get:12 http://azure.archive.ubuntu.com/ubuntu bionic-backports/ universe Translation-en [1696 B]

Get:13 http://security.ubuntu.com/ubuntu bionic-security/main amd64 Packages [361 kB]

Get:14 http://security.ubuntu.com/ubuntu bionic-security/main Translation-en [128 kB]

Get:15 http://security.ubuntu.com/ubuntu bionic-security/universe amd64 Packages [254 kB]

Get:16 http://security.ubuntu.com/ubuntu bionic-security/universe Translation-en [143 kB]

Fetched 3223 kB in 2s (1702 kB/s)

```
Reading package lists... Done
```

mitesh@devopsbpb-tomcat:~$

21. Now, let us download Tomcat 9 using the following command:

mitesh@devopsbpb-tomcat:~$ curl -O http://mirrors.estointernet. in/apache/tomcat/tomcat-9/v9.0.20/bin/apache-tomcat-9.0.20.tar.gz

```
% Total   % Received % Xferd  Average Speed   Time   Time   Time  Current
                Dload  Upload   Total   Spent    Left  Speed
100 10.3M  100 10.3M    0       0     9.8M      0  0:00:01  0:00:01
--:--:--   9.8M
```

22. Let us extract the Tomcat installation using the following command:

mitesh@devopsbpb-tomcat:~$ sudo tar xzvf apache-tomcat-9.0.20.tar. gz -C devopsBPB --strip-components=1

```
apache-tomcat-9.0.20/conf/

apache-tomcat-9.0.20/conf/catalina.policy

apache-tomcat-9.0.20/conf/catalina.properties

apache-tomcat-9.0.20/conf/context.xml

apache-tomcat-9.0.20/conf/jaspic-providers.xml

apache-tomcat-9.0.20/conf/jaspic-providers.xsd

apache-tomcat-9.0.20/conf/logging.properties

apache-tomcat-9.0.20/conf/server.xml

apache-tomcat-9.0.20/conf/tomcat-users.xml

apache-tomcat-9.0.20/conf/tomcat-users.xsd

apache-tomcat-9.0.20/conf/web.xml

apache-tomcat-9.0.20/bin/

apache-tomcat-9.0.20/lib/

apache-tomcat-9.0.20/logs/

apache-tomcat-9.0.20/temp/

apache-tomcat-9.0.20/webapps/

apache-tomcat-9.0.20/webapps/ROOT/

apache-tomcat-9.0.20/webapps/ROOT/WEB-INF/
```

.

.

```
apache-tomcat-9.0.20/bin/shutdown.sh

apache-tomcat-9.0.20/bin/startup.sh

apache-tomcat-9.0.20/bin/tool-wrapper.sh

apache-tomcat-9.0.20/bin/version.sh
```

23. Let us create a directory to extract Tomcat using the following command:

    mitesh@devopsbpb-tomcat:~$ mkdir devopsBPB

24. Let us try to run Tomcat using the following command:

    root@devopsbpb-tomcat:/home/mitesh/devopsBPB/bin# ./startup.sh

    Neither the JAVA_HOME nor the JRE_HOME environment variable is defined

    At least one of these environment variable is needed to run this program

25. Java is not installed on the newly created VM. Let us install Java using the following command:

    root@devopsbpb-tomcat:/home/mitesh/devopsBPB/bin# sudo apt-get install default-jdk

    Reading package lists... Done

    Building dependency tree

    Reading state information... Done

    The following additional packages will be installed:

    adwaita-icon-theme at-spi2-core ca-certificates-java default-jdk-headless default-jre

    default-jre-headless fontconfig fontconfig-config fonts-dejavu-core fonts-dejavu-extra

    gtk-update-icon-cache hicolor-icon-theme humanity-icon-theme java-common libasound2

    .

    openjdk-11-jre openjdk-11-jre-headless ubuntu-mono x11-common x11-utils

    x11proto-core-dev x11proto-dev xorg-sgml-doctools xtrans-dev

0 upgraded, 118 newly installed, 0 to remove and 4 not upgraded.

Need to get 267 MB of archives.

After this operation, 670 MB of additional disk space will be used.

Do you want to continue? [Y/n] Y

Get:1 http://azure.archive.ubuntu.com/ubuntu bionic/main amd64 fonts-dejavu-core all 2.37-1 [1041 kB]

Get:2 http://azure.archive.ubuntu.com/ubuntu bionic/main amd64 fontconfig-config all 2.12.6-0ubuntu2 [55.8 kB]

Get:3 http://azure.archive.ubuntu.com/ubuntu bionic/main amd64 libfontconfig1 amd64 2.12.6-0ubuntu2 [137 kB]

Get:4 http://azure.archive.ubuntu.com/ubuntu bionic/main amd64 fontconfig amd64 2.12.6-0ubuntu2 [169 kB]

.

Get:118 http://azure.archive.ubuntu.com/ubuntu bionic/main amd64 libxt-dev amd64 1:1.1.5-1 [395 kB]

Fetched 267 MB in 8s (32.3 MB/s)

Extracting templates from packages: 100%

Selecting previously unselected package fonts-dejavu-core.

(Reading database ... 55679 files and directories currently installed.)

Preparing to unpack .../000-fonts-dejavu-core_2.37-1_all.deb ...

Unpacking fonts-dejavu-core (2.37-1) ...

Selecting previously unselected package fontconfig-config.

.

Setting up libdrm-amdgpu1:amd64 (2.4.95-1~18.04.1) ...

Setting up liblcms2-2:amd64 (2.9-1ubuntu0.1) ...

Setting up libjbig0:amd64 (2.1-3.1build1) ...

.

update-alternatives: using /usr/lib/jvm/java-11-openjdk-amd64/bin/jhsdb to provide /usr/bin/jhsdb (jhsdb) in auto mode

Setting up humanity-icon-theme (0.6.15) ...

```
Setting up default-jre-headless (2:1.11-68ubuntu1~18.04.1) ...

Setting up default-jdk-headless (2:1.11-68ubuntu1~18.04.1) ...

Setting up openjdk-11-jre:amd64 (11.0.3+7-1ubuntu2~18.04.1) ...

Setting up libgtk2.0-bin (2.24.32-1ubuntu1) ...

Setting up ca-certificates-java (20180516ubuntu1~18.04.1) ...

head: cannot open '/etc/ssl/certs/java/cacerts' for reading: No
such file or directory

Adding debian:Starfield_Root_Certificate_Authority_-_G2.pem

Adding debian:Actalis_Authentication_Root_CA.pem

Adding debian:Trustis_FPS_Root_CA.pem


Setting up default-jdk (2:1.11-68ubuntu1~18.04.1) ...

Processing triggers for libc-bin (2.27-3ubuntu1) ...

Processing triggers for ureadahead (0.100.0-21) ...

Processing triggers for systemd (237-3ubuntu10.21) ...

Processing triggers for libgdk-pixbuf2.0-0:amd64 (2.36.11-2) ...

Processing triggers for ca-certificates (20180409) ...

Updating certificates in /etc/ssl/certs...

0 added, 0 removed; done.

Running hooks in /etc/ca-certificates/update.d...


done.
```

26. Let us check whether Java is installed properly or not using the following command:

root@devopsbpb-tomcat:/home/mitesh/devopsBPB/bin# java -version

```
openjdk version "11.0.3" 2019-04-16

OpenJDK Runtime Environment (build 11.0.3+7-Ubuntu-1ubuntu218.04.1)

OpenJDK 64-Bit Server VM (build 11.0.3+7-Ubuntu-1ubuntu218.04.1,
mixed mode, sharing)
```

27. Now, go to Tomcat Home Directory | bin directory and execute the **./startup.sh** command, as shown in the following code snippet:

root@devopsbpb-tomcat:/home/mitesh/devopsBPB/bin# ./startup.sh

```
Using CATALINA_BASE:    /home/mitesh/devopsBPB

Using CATALINA_HOME:    /home/mitesh/devopsBPB

Using CATALINA_TMPDIR: /home/mitesh/devopsBPB/temp

Using JRE_HOME:         /usr

Using CLASSPATH:        /home/mitesh/devopsBPB/bin/bootstrap.jar:/
                        home/mitesh/devopsBPB/bin/tomcat-juli.jar

Tomcat started.
```

root@devopsbpb-tomcat:/home/mitesh/devopsBPB/bin#

28. Let us try to access Tomcat in the browser using the public IP address of the VM and port number. You will get a network error. Create an inbound rule to allow access for the port configured in Tomcat (here **8080**).

29. Now, try again and you will get the Tomcat Home page, as shown in the following screenshot:

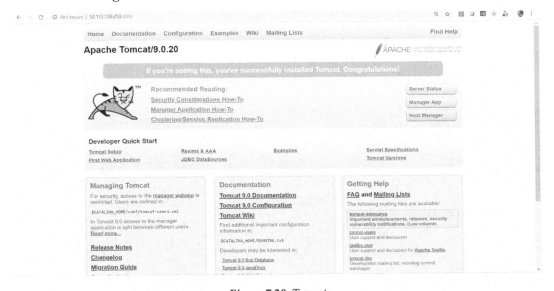

Figure 7.20: Tomcat

Let us summarize what we have done:

- Created a VM
- Configuredfirewall rules

- Installed updates
- Downloaded Tomcat
- Configured some permissions

It takes time. What if you need to create multiple virtual machines and configure load balancers? It takes some time to install and configure the runtime environment even if the templates are created or some other mechanism is provided by cloud service providers. It also requires skills in case of scripting to create the entire runtime stack.

How about having a platform that takes care of everything, and we only need to provide the application package. The rest of all the things are configuration based.

Platform as a Service - Azure App Services

Azure App Services help to host web applications or APIs or backends in a multi-tenant hosting environment. It supports a number of built in images, and ifthe runtime environment is not available, then built-in Docker images can be created for Linux platforms. It has support for Java, Node.js, PHP, Python, .NETCore, and Ruby. For Java, supported versions are Tomcat 8.5, 9.0, Java SE, and WildFly 14 (all running on JRE 8).Following are category of pricing for virtual machines.

- **Free and Shared tiers:** Worker processes on shared VMs
- **Standard and Premium tiers:** Dedicated VMs

Let us try to create the Azure App Service in a resource group named `DevOpsBPB` that we created earlierby performing the following steps:

1. Login to the Microsoft Azure Portal. Select the resource group `DevOpsBPB` and click on **Add**, as shown in the following screenshot:

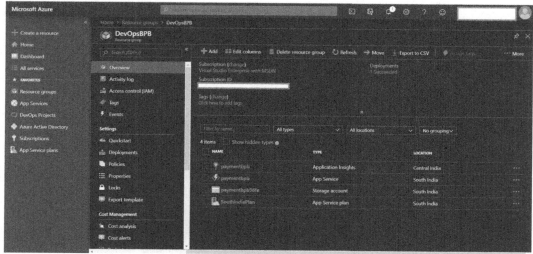

Figure 7.21: *App Services-Add to Resource Group*

2. Now, select the **Web App** option, as shown in the following screenshot:

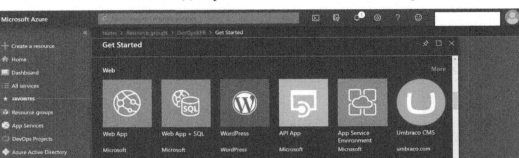

Figure 7.22: App Services-Web App

3. Select **Subscription** and keep the value in **Resource Group** as it is. Then, provide **Name** for the Web App / Azure App Service, as shown in the following screenshot:

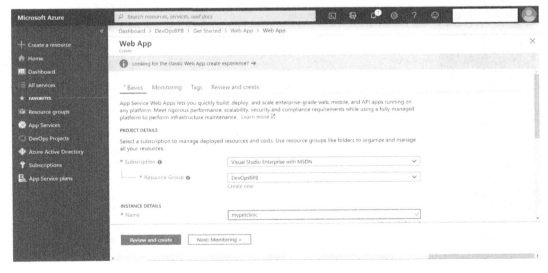

Figure 7.23: App Services-Configure Basics

4. Now, select **Runtime stack** based on the application. We have a lot of options, as shown in the following screenshot:

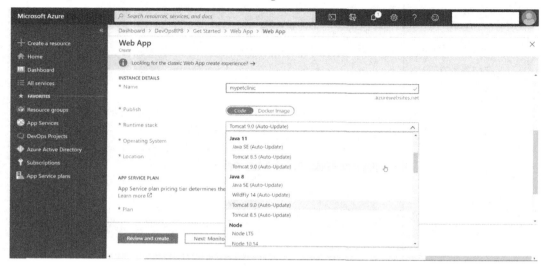

Figure 7.24: App Services-Runtime stack

5. Then, select **Location** accordingly, as shown in the following screenshot:

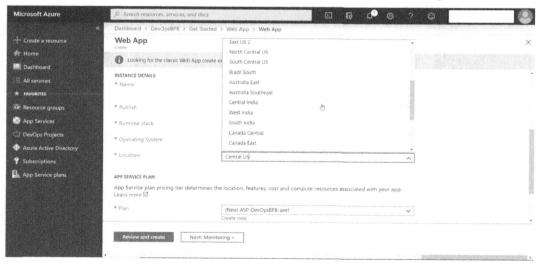

Figure 7.25: App Services-Location

6. Create a new App Service **Plan** or select from the existing list. Free and Shared workloads do not have the deployment slots feature, which allows you to create a slot such as **Dev/Test** in the same App Service Plan, but having complete isolation. Refer to the following screenshot:

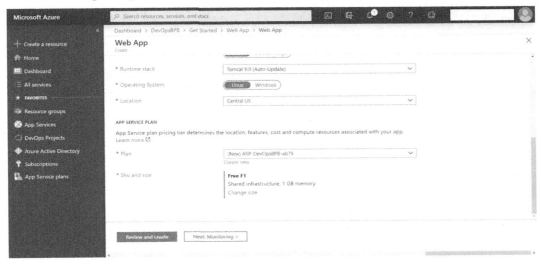

Figure 7.26: App Services-Pricing Tiers

7. We can change **Sku and size** available in the Service Plan by clicking on **Change size**, as shown in the following screenshot. Click on **Next : Monitoring>,** as shown in the following screenshot:

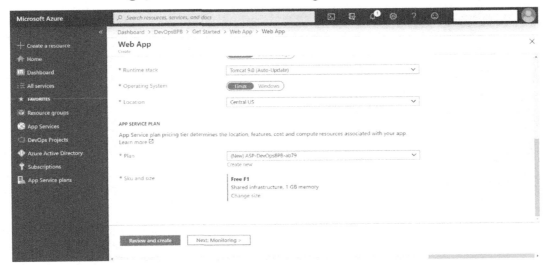

Figure 7.27: App Services-App Service Plan

8. Select the appropriate App Service Plan and click on **Apply**:

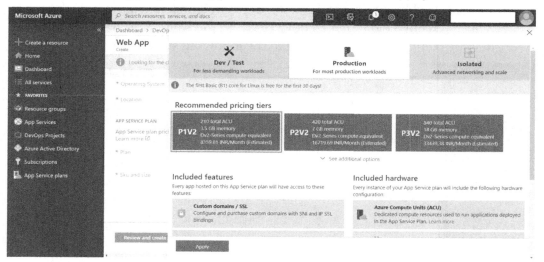

Figure 7.28: App Services-Recommended Pricing Tiers

9. Now, toggle **Enable Application Insights** to **Yes** to get/configure extensive monitoring details. Refer to the following screenshot:

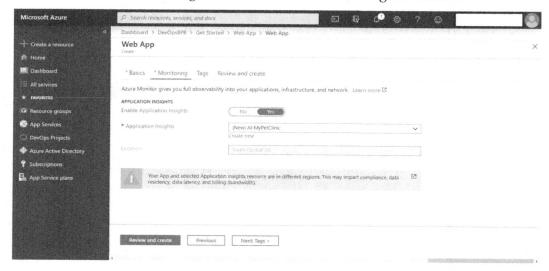

Figure 7.29: App Services-Monitoring

10. Click on **Next : Tags>**. Now, review the details and click on **Create**. You can also click on **Download a template for automation** if you want to see the template. Refer to the following screenshot:

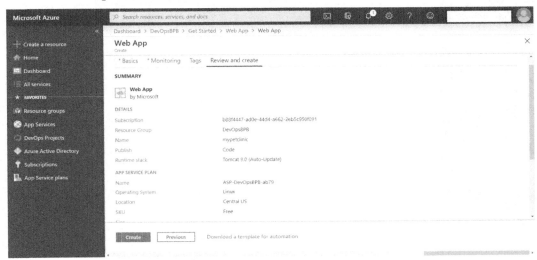

Figure 7.30: *App Services-Review and Create*

11. Verify the template and **Download** it, as shown in the following screenshot:

Figure 7.31: *App Services-template*

12. A screen will be displayed with the **Your deployment is underway** text and it will create multiple resources, as shown in the following screenshot:

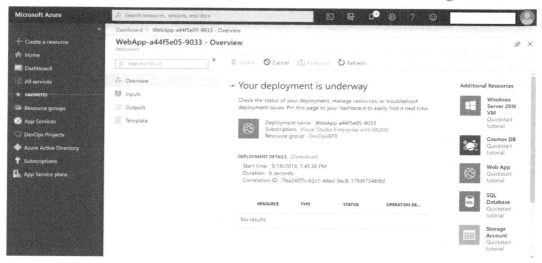

Figure 7.32: App Services-Deployment underway

13. Verify the **RESOURCES, TYPES,** and **STATUS** in the Azure Portal once the deployment is complete, as shown in the following screenshot:

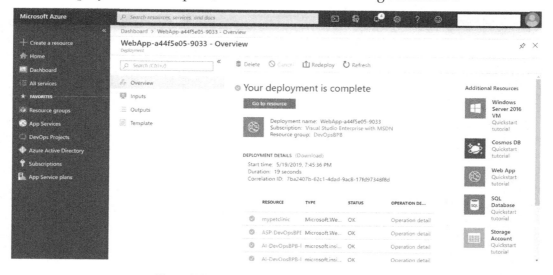

Figure 7.33: App Services-Deployment completed

14. Now, go to App Services in the Azure Portal and select the App Service that we created to get the details. You can refer to the following screenshot:

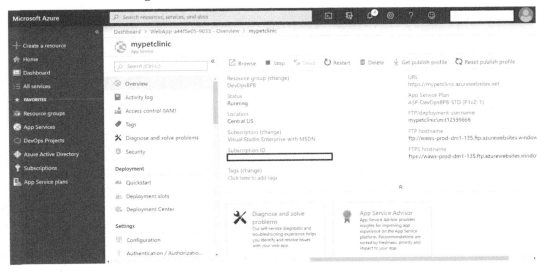

Figure 7.34: App Services-Overview

15. Now, click on App Service Plan and go to **Settings | Apps** to verify the number of apps hosted by that App Service Plan, as shown in the following screenshot:

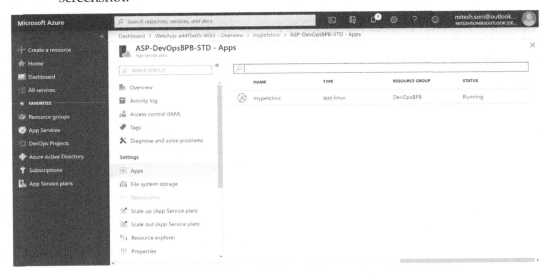

Figure 7.35: App Services-App Service Plan

16. Copy the URL from the Azure App Service **Overview** section and visit it. You will see a screen similar to the following screenshot:

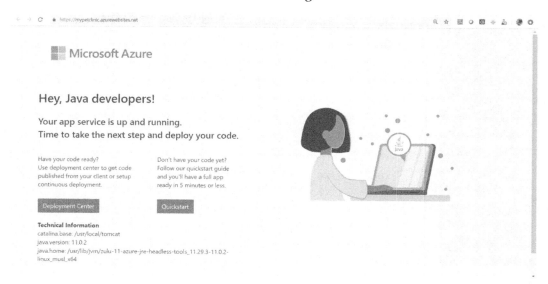

Figure 7.36: App Services-Web App

17. Just add SCM to the URL to go to the Kudu editor for Azure App Service, as shown in the following screenshot:

Figure 7.37: App Services-Kudu Editor

18. Now, go to the Azure Portal, select **App Services | mypetclinic | Deployment | Deployment slots.** With each deployment slot, you will get the following:

- Unique host name
- App content
- Configuration

Refer to the following screenshot:

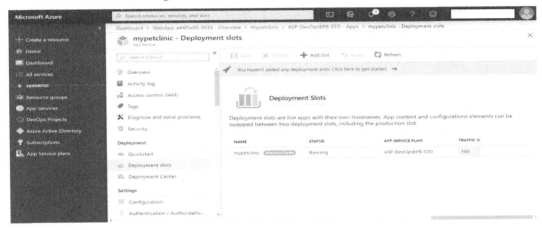

Figure 7.38: App Services-Deployment slots

19. Usually, Deployment slots are created for non-production environments. The Main app service is **PRODUCTION**. Click on **Add** to create a new deployment slot. Keep the other details as is and click on **Add**, as shown in the following screenshot:

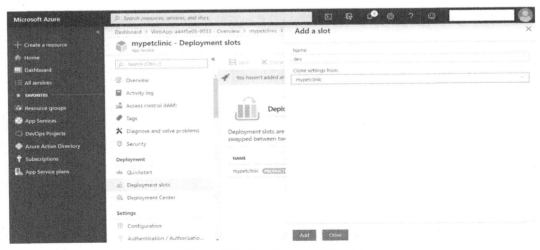

Figure 7.39: App Services-Add a slot

20. It will take a while to create your slot. It will display a screen similar to the following screenshot:

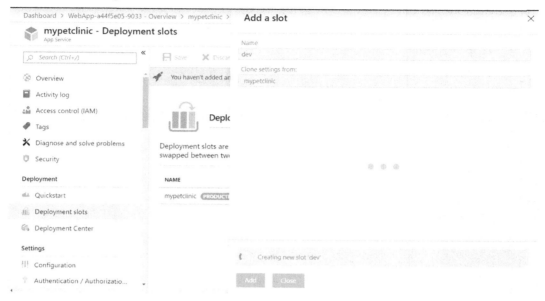

Figure 7.40: *App Services-Creating a new slot*

21. The Deployment slot is created successfully and you will get the following screen:

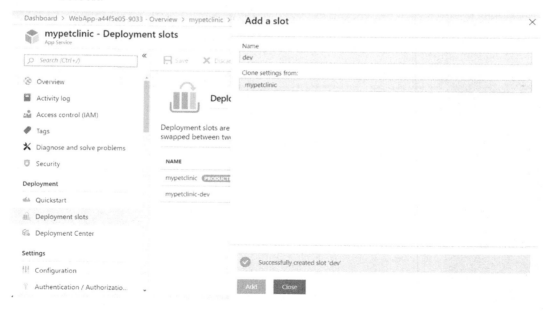

Figure 7.41: *App Services-Created a new slot*

22. Similarly, create other deployment slots, as shown in the following screenshot:

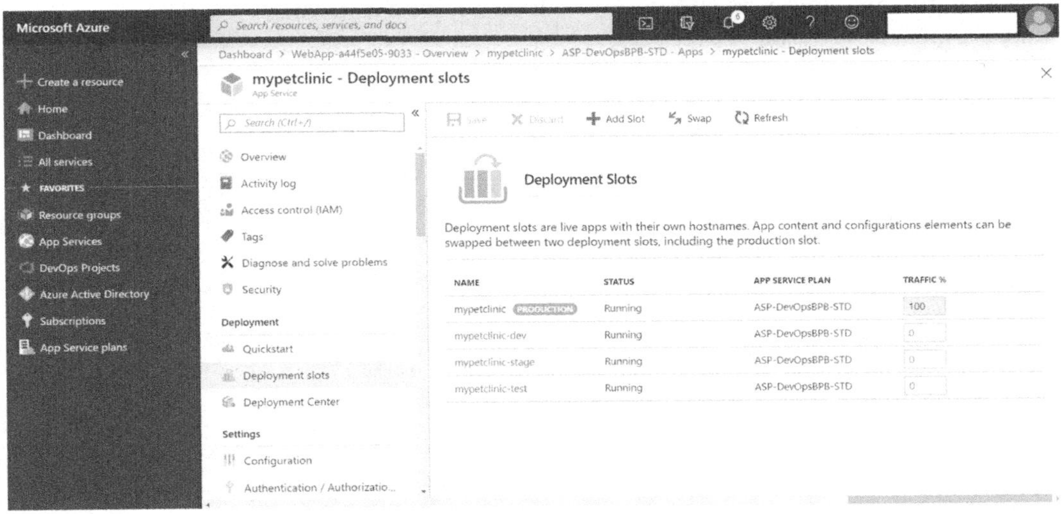

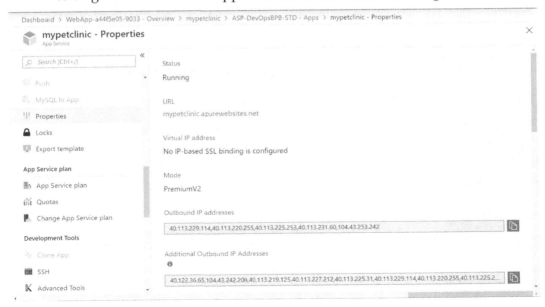

Figure 7.42: App Services-All deployment slots

23. We will deploy the application in the deployment slots using Azure DevOps. Let us go to **Properties** and verify **Outbound IP addresses**. These IP addresses are useful if any third-party API access is needed and access needs to be given to the Azure App Services. Refer to the following screenshot:

Figure 7.43: App Services-Properties

24. The Properties section contains details such as FTP user, FTP and FTPS host name and so on, as shown in the following screenshot:

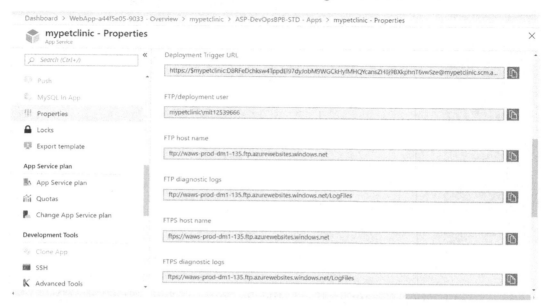

Figure 7.44: App Services-FTP details

25. Now, select **App Service | Configuration | Application settings.** Connection strings and the other key value pairs can be defined here so the application can access values from the environment directly. Refer to the following screenshot:

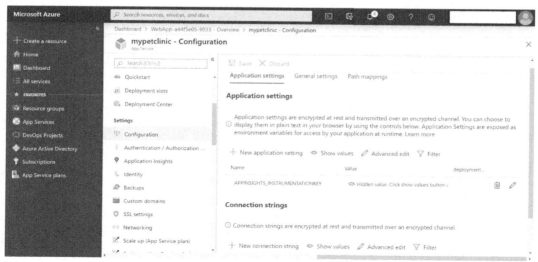

Figure 7.45: App Services-Application settings

26. Now, click on **General   settings**   on the same page. Here, you can configure the runtime stack and other platform settings easily, as shown in the following screenshot:

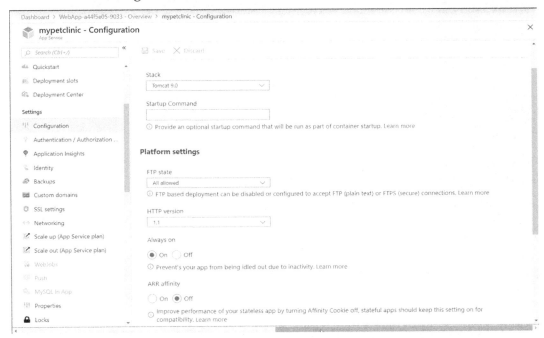

Figure7.46: *App Services-General settings*

In the next section, we will see basic monitoring available with Azure App Service.

Monitoring of resources

The Azure App Service overview section provides quick monitoring where you can get information related to a number of requests and average response time. It helps to detect issues based on unavailability of service due to high number of requests or issues related to slow response time. Refer to the following screenshot:

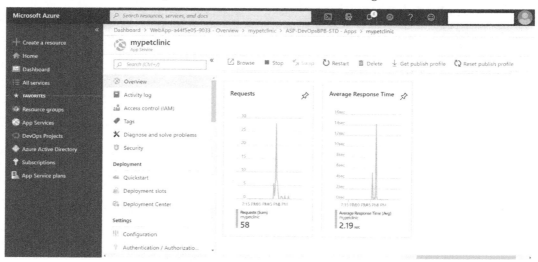

Figure 7.47: App Services-Monitoring

In the next section, we will discuss about high availability and fault tolerance.

High availability and fault tolerance

It is important to make the application available all the time in today's day and age. The App Service Plan has the configuration to scale up and scale out.

An App Service Plan is a combination of a region, number of VM instances, size of VM instances, pricing tier such as *Free, Shared, Basic, Standard, Premium, PremiumV2, Isolated, and Consumption*. Remember that based on pricing tiers, App Service features are different. To get more details on App Service Plan, visit **https://azure.microsoft.com/en-us/pricing/details/app-service/plans/**.

Based on requirements, the pricing tier can be selected. Refer to the following screenshot, which displays the scale up App Service Plan:

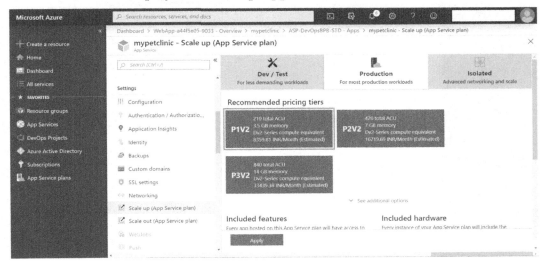

Figure 7.48: App Services-Scale up

In scale out, you can directly increase the instance counts to support the availability of an application, as shown in the following screenshot:

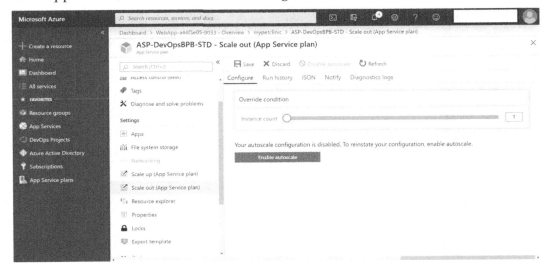

Figure 7.49: App Services-Scale out-Instance Count

Change **Instance count** and click on **Save**, as shown in the following screenshot:

Figure 7.50: App Services-Override condition

Click on **Enable autoscale**. It provides you to configure scale in and scale out configurations based on certain conditions. Select **Scale based on a metric** in **Scale mode**. Configure **Instance limits** and click on **Add a rule**, as shown in the following screenshot:

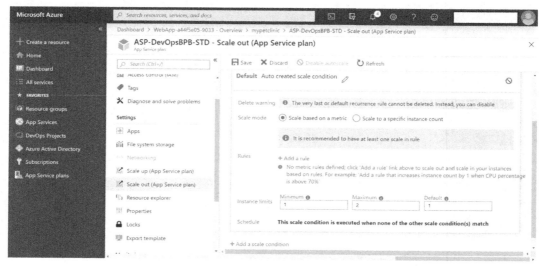

Figure 7.51: App Services-Rules

Select the metric name from the drop-down menu and configure the other required details and scroll down. Refer to the following screenshot:

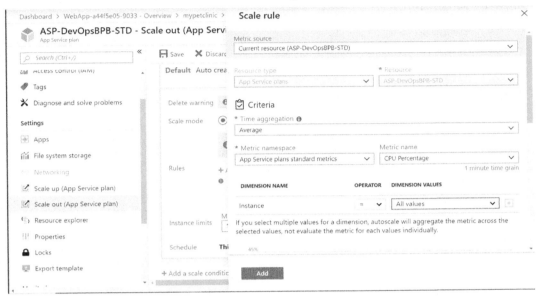

Figure 7.52: App Services-Scale Rule

It will show the existing monitoring numbers. Refer to the following screenshot:

Figure 7.53: App Services-Scale Rule-CPU Percentage

Select **Operator** and **Threshold** along with the duration. Configure the increase count by 1 instance in case the CPU percentage goes beyond 70%, as shown in the following screenshot:

Figure 7.54: *App Services-Scale Rule-Increase count by*

Next, click on the **Add** button, as shown in the following screenshot:

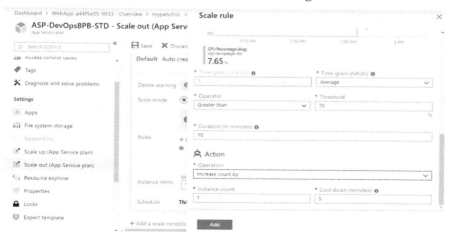

Figure 7.55: *App Services-Scale rule add*

Similarly, configure the action for decreasing the instance count. Configure the decrease count by 1 instance in case the CPU percentage goes lower than 30%. Refer to the following screenshot:

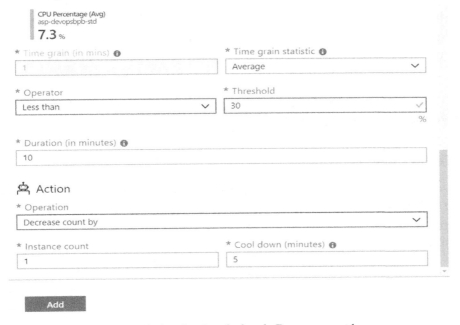

Figure 7.56: App Services-Scale rule-Decrease count by

Now, go to the Scale out (App Service plan) option for App Service Plan and verify both the actions configured for scale in and scale out, as shown in the following screenshot:

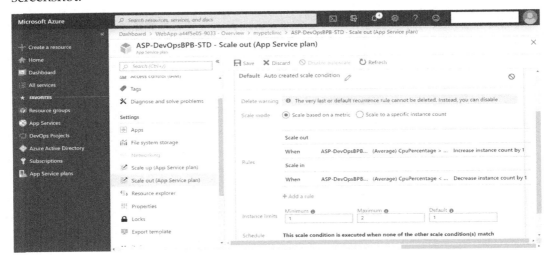

Figure 7.57: App Services - Scale and scale out rules

This is how the peak usage can be controlled or managed using the scale feature available in Azure App services.

How about load balancing? The Azure Traffic Manager helps to distribute requests to applications hosted in Azure App Services. These applications can be hosted in different geography and in different types of resources. Priority, weighted, performance, and geographic are four different routing methods used in the Azure Traffic Manager.

To get more details on the Azure Traffic Manager, visit **https://docs.microsoft.com/ en-us/azure/traffic-manager/traffic-manager-overview**.

Conclusion

We covered important topics available in Microsoft Azure Cloud, which are more related to hosting web applications, that is, VM and App Services, IaaS and PaaS, respectively. In the next chapter, we will have hands on activities for Azure DevOps for configuring CI.

## CHAPTER 8

Azure DevOps - Continuous Integration

Introduction

Continuous Integration(CI) is the base of the DevOps culture transformation. CI is often easier and faster to implement using open source and commercial tools. It helps to identify errors such as coding standards or code vulnerabilities or merging and integration issues in the beginning, and hence, it helps to limits defects or quality-related issues in the starting itself.

Azure DevOps has the CI configuration in the form of a build pipeline, that is,the YAML format earlier it was a build definition.

Structure

We will cover following topics in this chapter:

- Build pipeline implementation
- Java application - pipeline YAML
- Unit tests
- Hosted agent - Continuous Code Inspection

Objective

In this chapter, we will include an overview of build definitions available in Microsoft Azure DevOps. It will help us understand how CI is configured in Azure DevOps.

Azure Pipelines

Azure DevOps Pipelines is a **Continuous Integration and Continuous Delivery (CICD)** service. It helps users to configure automation and form CICD implementations tasks. We will see how we can create a build pipeline using the YAML syntax in the coming sections. The following are some supported version control systems, applications types, and deployment environments:

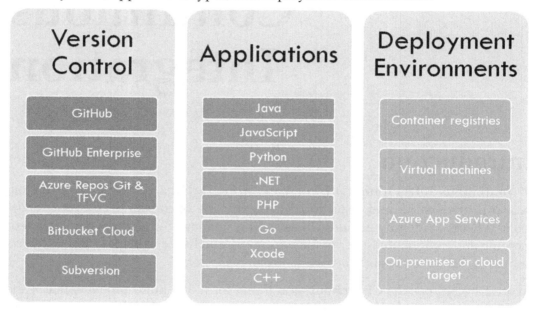

Figure 8.1: Supported version control systems, applications types, and deployment environments

Our main objective is to create an end-to-end automation pipeline that performs the following tasks that is all about CI:

- Compilation
- Unit test execution
- Package creation
- Archive package

Let us try to use the Azure DevOps build pipeline. This pipeline will help us to achieve the tasks mentioned above:

1. Login to the Azure DevOpsportal.Go to **Pipelines | Builds**.

2. If no build pipelines are available, then click on **New pipeline**, as shown in the following screenshot:

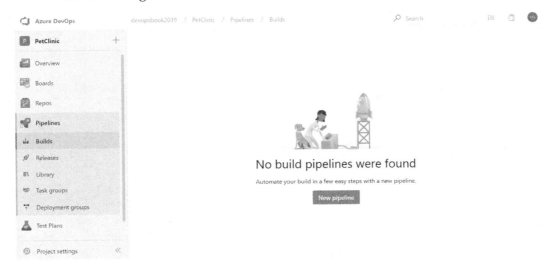

Figure 8.2: Build Pipelines

3. Click on Azure Repos Git. Refer to the following screenshot:

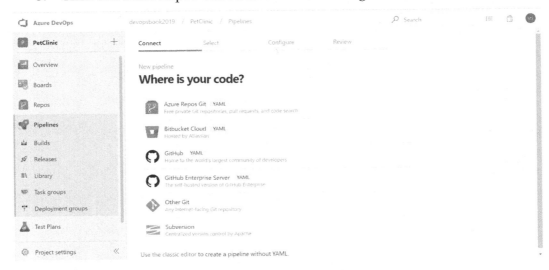

Figure 8.3: Connect to Code

4. Select the **PetClinic** repository that is already available in the Azure DevOps portal in the **Repos** section, as shown in the following screenshot:

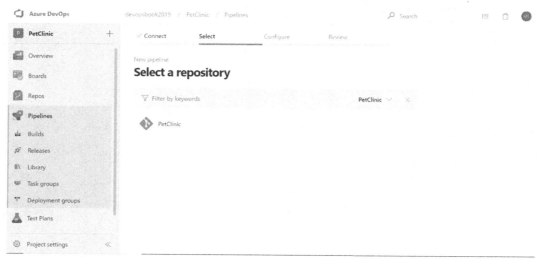

Figure 8.4: Select a repository

5. This is a Maven project so click on **Maven**, as shown in the following screenshot:

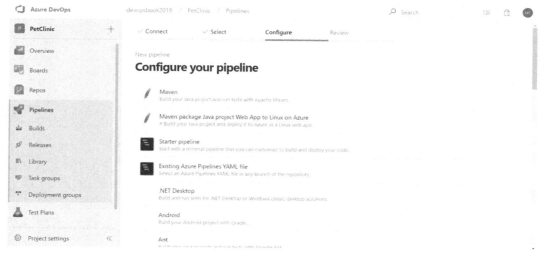

Figure 8.5: Configure Maven Pipeline

6. Review the pipeline for **Build**, as shown in the following screenshot:

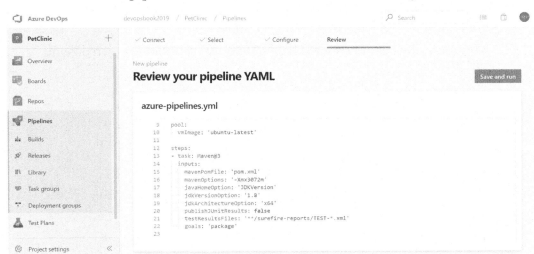

Figure 8.6: Default pipeline YAML

7. Click on **Save andrun**.

8. The `azure-pipelines.yml` file will be saved in the repository itself. It is a pipeline as a code is available in Azure DevOps.

9. Provide the commit message. Commit to a specific branch.

10. Click on **Save and run**, as shown in the following screenshot:

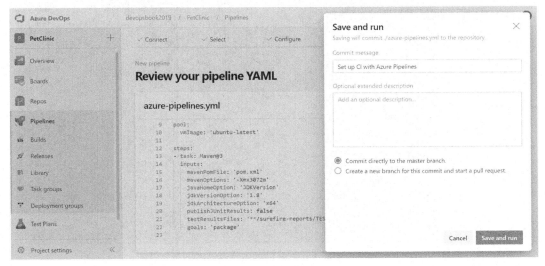

Figure 8.7: Save and run pipeline

11. We are executing this build pipeline on the hosted agent, which is already available in Azure DevOps, that already has all the packages available to build and package the Maven-based project.

12. Wait until the agent is not available. Refer to the following screenshot:

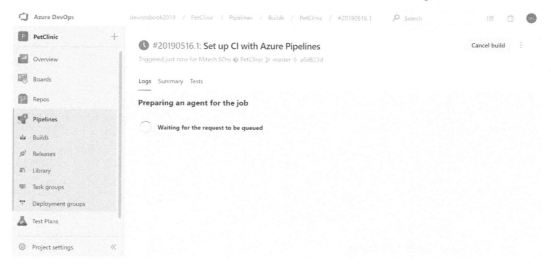

Figure 8.8: Run build pipeline

13. Once the hosted agent is available, the execution will start with the **Initialize job** task, as shown in the following screenshot:

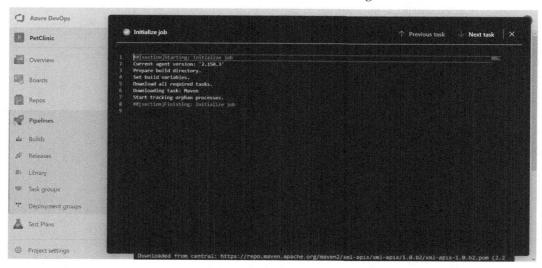

Figure 8.9: Initialize job

14. The Checkout task will checkout the code on the hosted agent for the execution of Maven goals. Refer to the following screenshot:

Figure 8.10: Checkout Code

15. Verify the execution of the **Builds** pipeline for the progress. The Maven goal will be executed, and for this, all Maven dependencies will be downloaded on the hosted agent. Refer to the following screenshot:

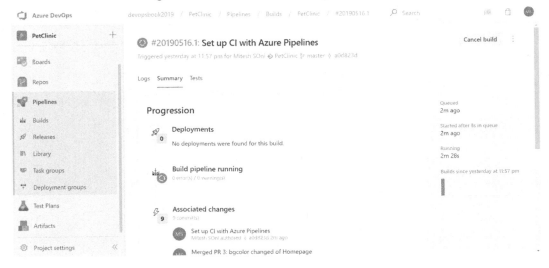

Figure 8.11: Pipeline execution summary

16. Once all the dependencies are available, the Maven goal will be executed, as shown in the following screenshot:

Figure 8.12: Successful build

17. In our case, a package goal will be executed. It will compile the code, execute unit tests, and create a WAR file for the deployment. It will look similar to the following screenshot:

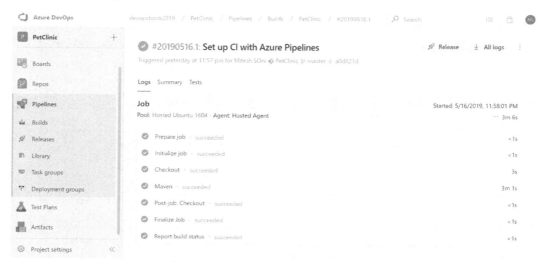

Figure 8.13: Pipeline execution logs

18. Verify the pipeline execution summary, as shown in the following screenshot:

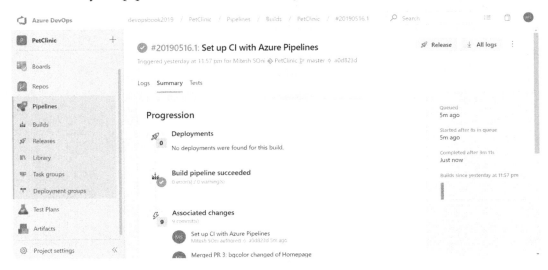

Figure 8.14: Verify associated changes

19. Verify the build result in the Azure DevOps portal.

20. Double click on the latest build execution log, as shown in the following screenshot:

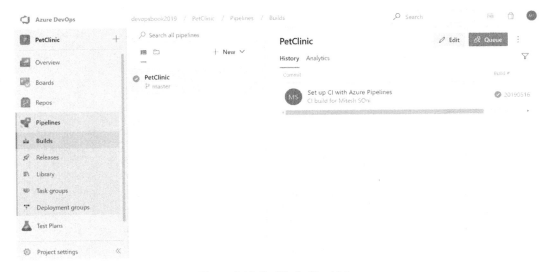

Figure 8.15: Build pipeline history

21. Click on the **Teststab**. There are no test results available even though we executed the package goal of Maven. Refer to the following screenshot:

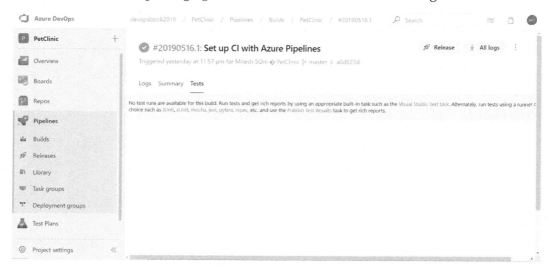

Figure 8.16: *No test results*

22. Let us revisit the Pipeline script, which is as follows:

```
steps:
- task: Maven@3
  inputs:
    mavenPomFile: 'pom.xml'
    mavenOptions: '-Xmx3072m'
    javaHomeOption: 'JDKVersion'
    jdkVersionOption: '1.8'
    jdkArchitectureOption: 'x64'
    publishJUnitResults: false
    testResultsFiles: '**/surefire-reports/TEST-*.xml'
    goals: 'package'
```

23. The **publishJUnitResults** parameter is set to false. We need to change it to true and commit in the repository, as shown in the following screenshot:

Figure 8.17: Default Azure-pipelines.yml with test settings

24. Execute the build pipeline again, and you will see a screen similar to the following screenshot:

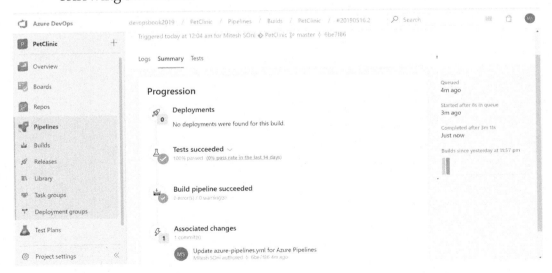

Figure 8.18: Successful test execution

25. Verify the build result in the Azure DevOps portal.

26. Double click on the latest build execution log.

27. Click on the **Tests** tab.We have test results available in the **Tests** tab. All the unit test execution results are available here. Refer to following screenshot:

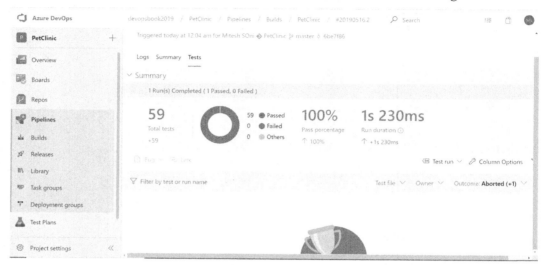

Figure 8.19: Test summary in the Azure DevOps portal

28. Verify **Test runs,** as shown in the following screenshot:

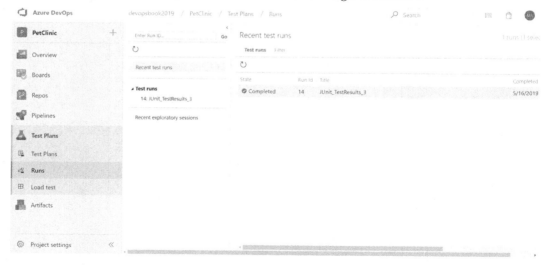

Figure 8.20: Test runs

29. Click on the Test run row to get more details on the unit test execution.

30. Verify **Summary** and **Outcome**, as shown in the following screenshot:

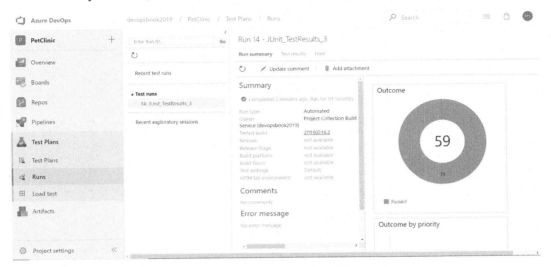

Figure 8.21: Run Summary and Outcome

31. Click on the **Test results** tab. Each test is mentioned with the outcome and duration of the test case execution.Click on the individual test case to get more details. Refer to the following screenshot:

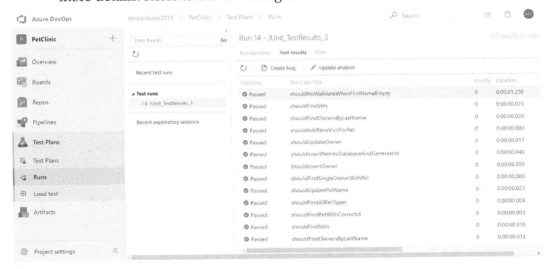

Figure 8.22: Test results

32. Verify details related to a specific unit test. Refer to the following screenshot:

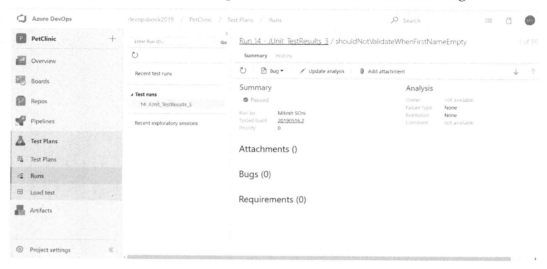

Figure 8.23: *Test results summary*

33. We can filter a specific test based on **Outcome**, as shown in the following screenshot:

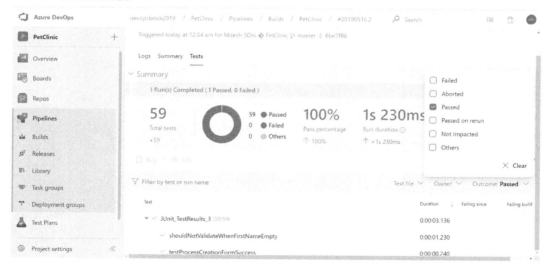

Figure 8.24: *Test results filter*

34. Go to the `azure-pipelines.yml` file to verify the changes. Go to **Repos** and select the repository, as shown in the following screenshot:

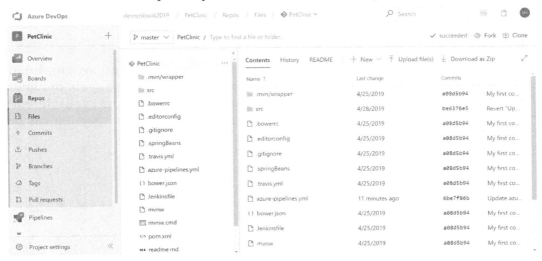

Figure 8.25: Azure-pipelines.yml in the repository

35. Select the `azure-pipelines.yml` file and verify the changes after the build definition is modified. The screen displayed should be similar to the following screenshot:

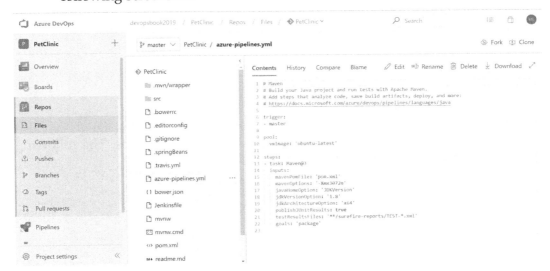

Figure 8.26: azure-pipelines.yml content

In the next section, we will see how the execution of a pipeline takes place on agents. Agents are physical or virtual machines where the runtime environment is available for build execution.

Agents

We still have not noticed one thing here. The place where the execution of the build pipeline takes place. The build execution takes place on agents. The agent provides the environment or runtime environment where all dependencies are available, and hence, with the use of the runtime environment and dependencies, a package can be created for deployment.

By default, the following agents are available:

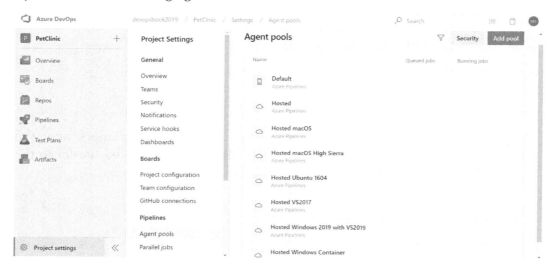

Figure 8.27: Agent pool

Agents are hosted that come with the Azure DevOps Service or the agents can also be the on-premise agents that are connected with Azure DevOps. The following diagram explains the different types of agents:

Figure 8.28: Types of agents

Let us understand both the types of agents in detail:

- **Microsoft-hosted agents:**
    - o Microsoft takes care of maintenance and upgrades
    - o A new VM is allocated, hence all packages are downloaded again and that takes time (for example, Maven dependencies)
    - o Execute jobs on the VM or in a container
    - o Less control to customize and download dependencies

- **Self-hosted agents:**
    - o User takes care of maintenance and upgrades
    - o The same VM is used, hence all packages are already available so time is saved (for example, Maven dependencies)
    - o Execute jobs on the VM or in a container
    - o More control to customize and download dependencies
    - o A self-hosted agent can be a Docker agent, Linux agent (x64, ARM, RHEL6), Windows agent (x64, x86), and macOS agent

The following screenshot displays the agent pool where no self-hosted agent is available as of now:

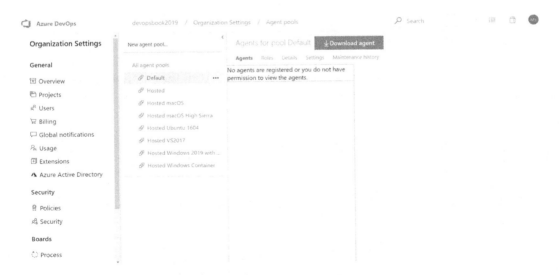

Figure 8.29: Default agent

Click on any agent to verify which **Jobs** or build pipelines have been executed on this specific agent, as shown in the following screenshot:

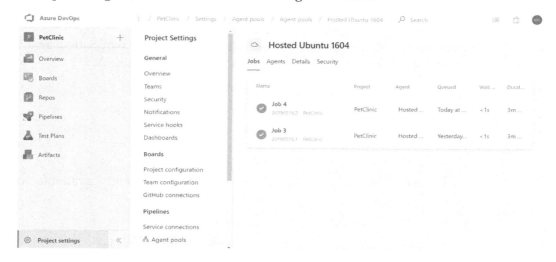

Figure 8.30: Hosted-agent Jobs

In the next section, we will create a self-hosted agent to perform the CI tasks.

Create a self-hosted agent

How to create an agent that is not hosted? Click on **Download agent** in the **Agents** tab, as shown in the *Figure 29*.

1. In my case, I have a Windows machine so I will **Download** the Windows agent and follow the instructions, as displayed in the following screenshot:

Figure 8.31: Download agent

2. To create an agent, we need **Personal Access Token**. To create a token, click on the username, and then click on `Security`, as shown in the following screenshot:

Figure 8.32: Security

3. There are no personal access tokens available here. Click on `New Token`, as shown in the following screenshot:

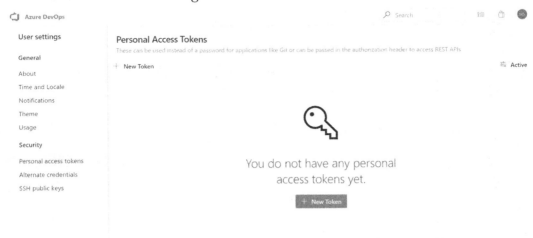

Figure 8.33: Personal access tokens

4. Provide the name and select the scope as well and click on **Create**, as shown in the following screenshot:

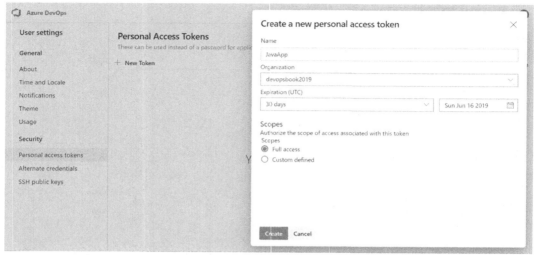

Figure 8.34: Create Personal Access Token

5. Copy the token. Note that token will not be available again for copy so this is the first and last chance. Refer to the following screenshot:

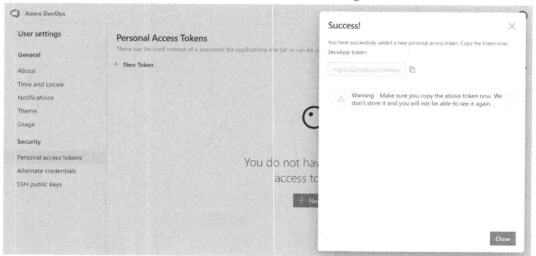

Figure 8.35: New Personal Access Token

6. Verify the newly created token in the Azure DevOps portal. It will look similar to the following screenshot:

Figure 8.36: Personal Access Token in the portal

7. Add a user as an administrator to the agent. We have created an agent for the default pool, as shown in the following screenshot:

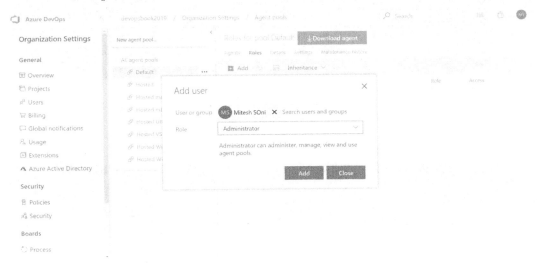

Figure 8.37: User Access

8. As per the instruction given above, run the configuration command.

9. Provide personal access token that we created in the Azure DevOps portal.

10. Keep this agent in the default pool. It will scan the agent for tools capabilities.

11. Keep the other default options and your configuration is complete. Refer to the following screenshot:

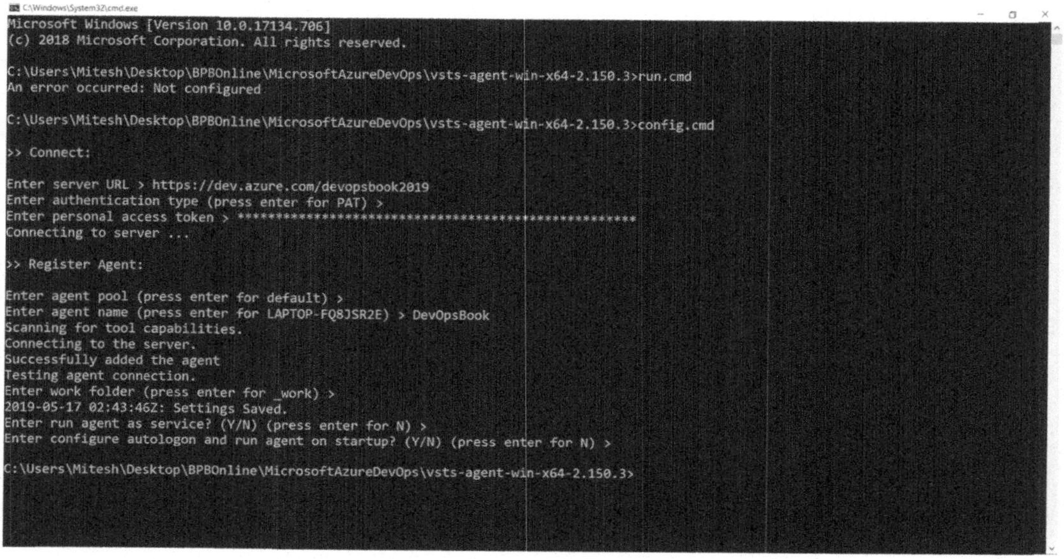

Figure 8.38: Configure a self-hosted agent

12. Execute the `run.cmd` command in the same directory, as shown in the following screenshot:

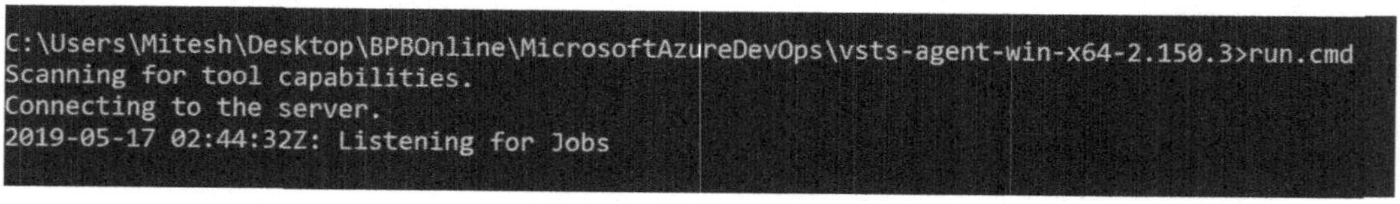

Figure 8.39: Make Agent available

13. Now, go to the Azure DevOps portal, navigate to **Organization settings | Agent pools | Default.** Check whether the newly created agent is availableand check SYSTEM CAPABILITIES in the Azure DevOps portal for the default agent. Refer to the following screenshot:

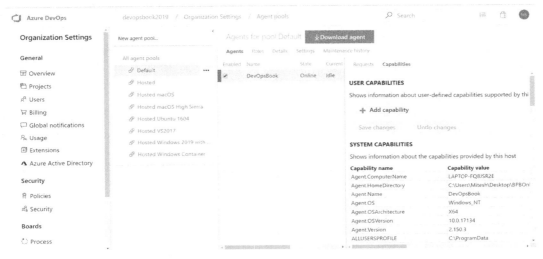

Figure 8.40: Default agent in the Azure DevOps portal

14. Now, we have an agent running with the following tools:
    - Maven
    - Java
    - SonarQube

15. We need to perform Continuous Code Inspection and CI on the default agent we created. We will perform the following things in the Azure DevOps build pipeline:

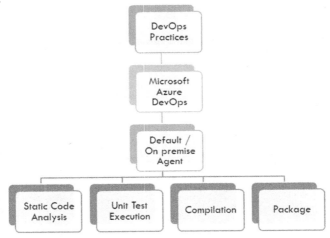

Figure 8.41: DevOps Practices

The following is the script that will perform the above jobs for us such as code analysis, unit tests execution, compilation, and package creation:

```
# Maven
# Build your Java project and run tests with Apache Maven.
# Add steps that analyze code, save build artifacts, deploy, and more:
# https://docs.microsoft.com/azure/devops/pipelines/languages/java
name: $(Date:yyyyMMdd)$(Rev:.r)

trigger:
- azure-pipelines

stages:
- stage: SCA
  jobs:
  - job: SCAonWindowsLocalAgent
    pool: Default
    steps:
    - script: echo SonarQube Analysis!
    - task: SonarQubePrepare@4
      inputs:
        SonarQube: 'SonarQube'
        scannerMode: 'CLI'
        configMode: 'manual'
        cliProjectKey: 'azuredevops-petclinic'
        cliProjectName: 'PetClinic'
        cliSources: '.'
- stage: Build
  jobs:
  - job: BuildJob
    pool: Default
    steps:
    - task: Maven@3
      inputs:
```

```
mavenPomFile: 'pom.xml'
mavenOptions: '-Xmx3072m'
javaHomeOption: 'JDKVersion'
jdkVersionOption: '1.8'
jdkArchitectureOption: 'x64'
sonarQubeRunAnalysis: true
publishJUnitResults: true
testResultsFiles: '**/surefire-reports/TEST-*.xml'
goals: 'package'
```

Let us understand why we created the default agent that is hosted on a laptop. We need to perform the static code analysis using **SoanrQube** that is available on the local environment/on-premise/laptop.

To make sure that the SonarQube Service connection in Azure DevOps is available to perform the SonarQube analysis, perform the following steps:

1. Go to **Project settings | Service connections.**

2. Then, click on **New service connection**. Select **SonarQube**, as shown in the following screenshot:

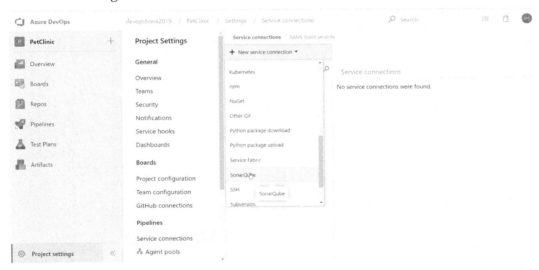

Figure 8.42: *SonarQube Service Connection*

3. Provide **Connection Name** and **Server URL** that SonarQube is running on the local system. Also, provide the user name and password forthe service connection and click on **OK**, as shown in the following screenshot:

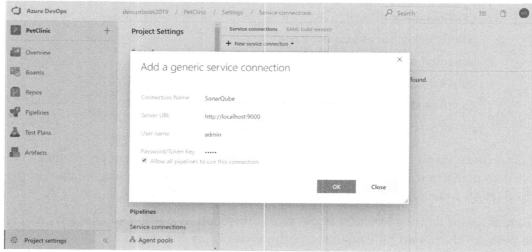

Figure 8.43: Add SonarQube service connection

4. Verify the newly created service connection in the Azure DevOps portal. It will look similar to the following screenshot:

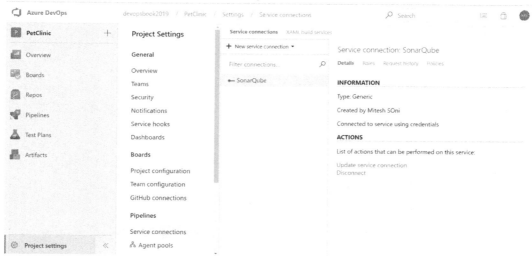

Figure 8.44: New SonarQube service connection

5. In SonarQube available in the local system, create a security token, as shown in the following screenshot:

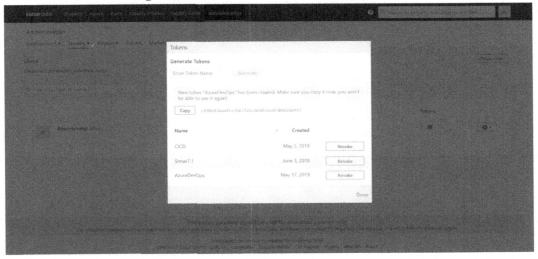

Figure 8.45: SonarQube Token

6. Once the **Service connections** is created, verify it with the logo of SonarQube, as shown in the following screenshot:

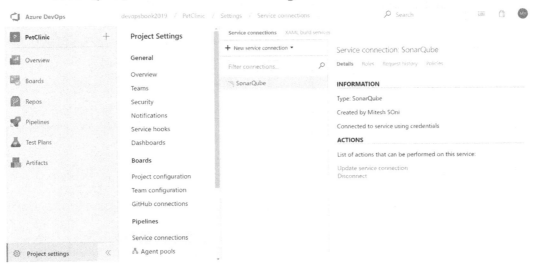

Figure 8.46: Available SonarQube service connection

7. The next step is to add the SonarQube task in the build pipeline that we created.

8. Edit the pipeline and select **Prepare Analysis Configuration**. Provide **SonarQube Server Endpoint** and select **Use standalone scanner**, as shown in the following screenshot:

Figure 8.47: SonarQube - Prepare Analysis Configuration

9. Select **Manually provide configuration** and click on **Add**, as shown in the following screenshot:

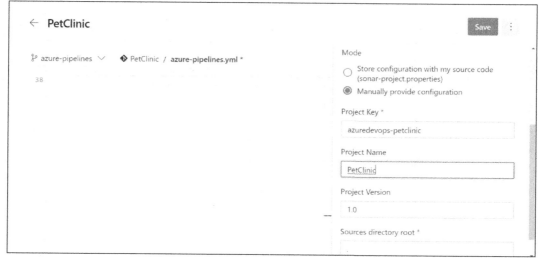

Figure 8.48: SonarQube configuration

10. The following code will be generated for YML:

```
- task: SonarQubePrepare@4
  inputs:
    SonarQube: 'SonarQube'
    scannerMode: 'CLI'
    configMode: 'manual'
    cliProjectKey: 'azuredevops-petclinic'
    cliProjectName: 'PetClinic'
    cliSources: '.'
```

Let us try to understand the `azure-pipelines.yml` file. Pipelines have one or more stages. Each stage has one or more jobs associated with it. Each job has one or more steps.

- **Stage:** A stage is a group of correlated jobs such as Code Analysis Job, Build Job, Test Job, or Deploy Job.
- **Job:** A job is a group of steps to be run by a hosted agent or custom agent.
- **Steps:** Steps are nothing but a sequence of operations that make up a job. Each step is a process itself on the hosted or custom agent. It has access to the workspace available on the hosted or custom agent.

The following diagram shows the Azure pipeline structure:

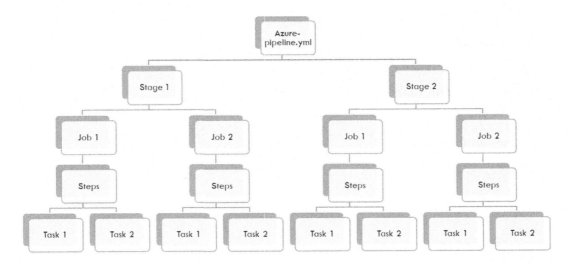

Figure 8.49: *Azure pipeline structure*

For a detailed discussion on the YAML schema, visit **https://docs.microsoft.com/en-us/azure/devops/pipelines/yaml-schema?view=azure-devops&tabs=schema.**

Trigger the build pipeline when there are any changes in the specific branch. In our case, it is an azure-pipelines branch. Therefore, any changes that are done in this specific branch will trigger the pipeline execution.The following is a trigger-based branch:

```
trigger:

- azure-pipelines
```

Prepare details for the SonarQube analysis or static code analysis:

```
stages:

- stage: SCA

  jobs:

  - job: SCAonWindowsLocalAgent

    pool: Default

    steps:

    - script: echo SonarQube Analysis!

    - task: SonarQubePrepare@4

      inputs:

        SonarQube: 'SonarQube'

        scannerMode: 'CLI'

        configMode: 'manual'

        cliProjectKey: 'azuredevops-petclinic'

        cliProjectName: 'PetClinic'

        cliSources: '.'
```

Let us execute the build:

```
- stage: Build

  jobs:

  - job: BuildJob

    pool: Default

    steps:
```

```
- task: Maven@3

  inputs:

    mavenPomFile: 'pom.xml'

    mavenOptions: '-Xmx3072m'

    javaHomeOption: 'JDKVersion'

    jdkVersionOption: '1.8'

    jdkArchitectureOption: 'x64'

    sonarQubeRunAnalysis: true

    publishJUnitResults: true

    testResultsFiles: '**/surefire-reports/TEST-*.xml'

    goals: 'package'
```

Once the pipeline is executed successfully, it looks like the following screenshot:

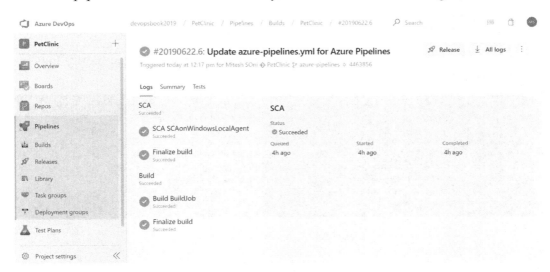

Figure 8.50: Azure Pipeline

Let us understand how it has been executed.

The SonarQube preparation task is executed here. Refer to the following screenshot:

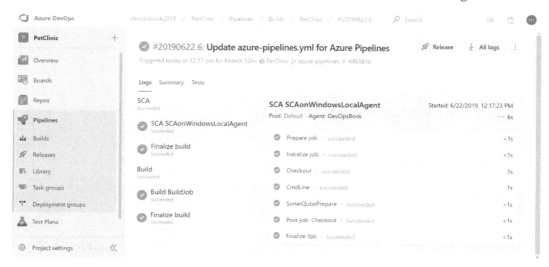

Figure 8.51: Stage SCA

When jobs are executing on the default agent that we created, we can verify logs on the console of agent using the following command:

```
C:\Users\Mitesh\Desktop\BPBOnline\MicrosoftAzureDevOps\vsts-agent-win-x64-2.150.3>run.cmd
Scanning for tool capabilities.
Connecting to the server.
2019-06-22 05:33:42Z: Listening for Jobs
2019-06-22 05:33:44Z: Running job: SCAonWindowsLocalAgent
2019-06-22 05:34:03Z: Job SCAonWindowsLocalAgent completed with result: Succeeded
2019-06-22 05:40:18Z: Running job: SCAonWindowsLocalAgent
2019-06-22 05:40:30Z: Job SCAonWindowsLocalAgent completed with result: Succeeded
2019-06-22 05:40:34Z: Running job: BuildJob
2019-06-22 05:44:18Z: Job BuildJob completed with result: Succeeded
```

Figure 8.52: A self-hosted agent log

Let us understand what happens with the build execution. Refer to the following screenshot:

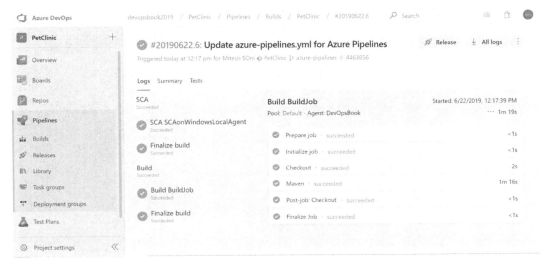

Figure 8.53: Build stage

Prepare job logs before the job execution starts, as shown in the following screenshot:

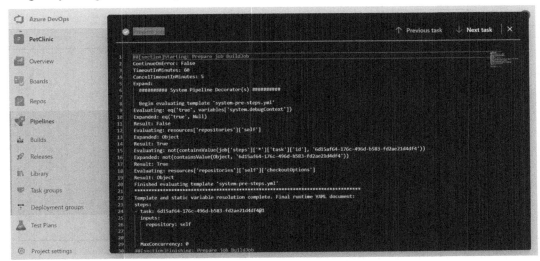

Figure 8.54: Prepare job logs

Verify the agent version in the **Initialize job** task, as shown in the following screenshot:

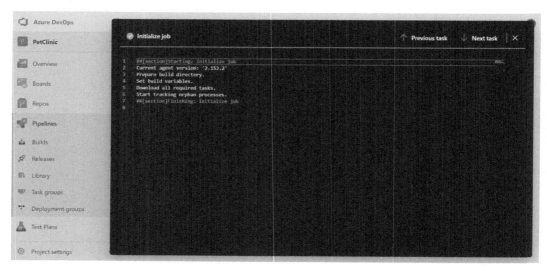

Figure 8.55: Initialize job logs

Check out the source code on the agent. Refer to the following screenshot:

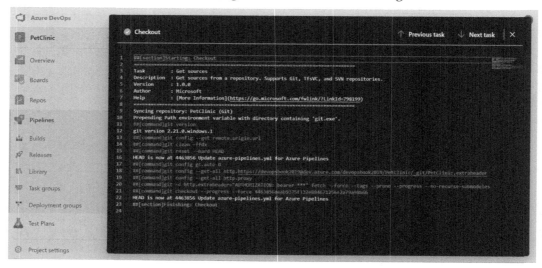

Figure 8.56: Checkout logs

Start executing the build job configured in the YML file, as shown in the following screenshot:

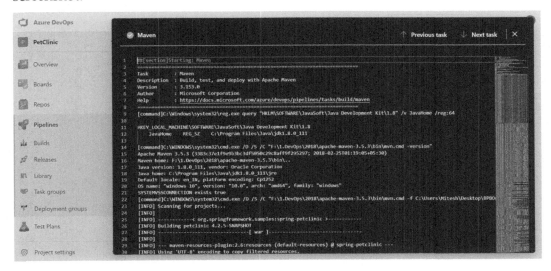

Figure 8.57: Maven logs

The test execution has started. The screen will look similar to the following screenshot:

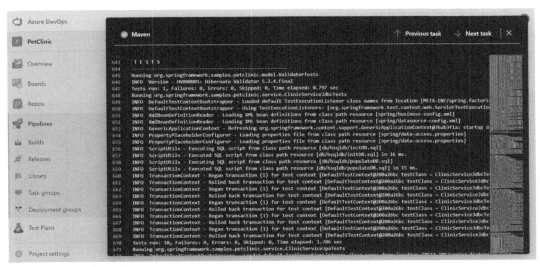

Figure 8.58: Maven Logs - Unit Tests

The SonarQube analysis has started on the agent machine. Refer to the following screenshot:

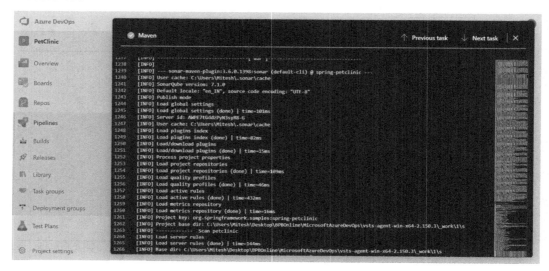

Figure 8.59: Maven Logs - SonarQube

Once all these are done, the following tasks will be completed successfully:

- Compilation of files
- Unit test execution
- Package creation
- Static code analysis

The build is successful, as shown in the following screenshot:

Figure 8.60: Maven logs - Build successful

Verify the local directory inside the agent. Refer to the following screenshot:

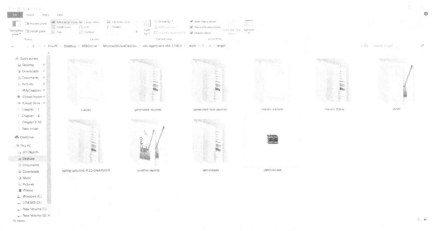

Figure 8.61: Artifacts on self-hosted agent

Once the package is available, we should copy it using Copy tasks. We need to provide relevant parameter values, as shown in the following code:

```
- task: CopyFiles@2
  inputs:
    SourceFolder: 'target'
    Contents: '*.war'
    TargetFolder: '$(Build.ArtifactStagingDirectory)'
```

A similar screen will be displayed as the output log:

Figure 8.62: Copy files logs

Publish the artifact so that the release pipeline can pickup the file and deploy it to Azure App Services. Refer to the following lines of code:

```
- task: PublishBuildArtifacts@1
  inputs:
    PathtoPublish: '$(Build.ArtifactStagingDirectory)'
    ArtifactName: 'drop'
    publishLocation: 'Container'
```

A similar screen will be displayed as the output log:

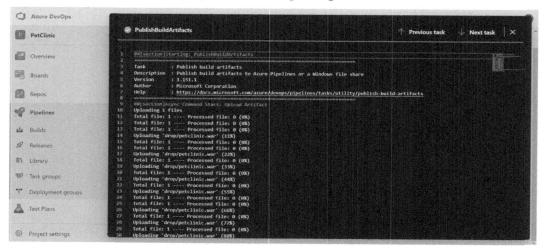

Figure 8.63: Publish build artifacts logs

The package is successfully published, as shown in the following screenshot:

Figure 8.64: Upload successful

The final `azure-pipelines.yml` file looks like the following code:

```
# Maven
# Build your Java project and run tests with Apache Maven.
# Add steps that analyze code, save build artifacts, deploy, and more:
# https://docs.microsoft.com/azure/devops/pipelines/languages/java
name: $(Date:yyyyMMdd)$(Rev:.r)


trigger:
- azure-pipelines


stages:
- stage: SCA
  jobs:
  - job: SCAonWindowsLocalAgent
    pool: Default
    steps:
    - script: echo SonarQube Analysis!
    - task: SonarQubePrepare@4
      inputs:
        SonarQube: 'SonarQube'
        scannerMode: 'CLI'
        configMode: 'manual'
        cliProjectKey: 'azuredevops-petclinic'
        cliProjectName: 'PetClinic'
        cliSources: '.'
- stage: Build
  jobs:
  - job: BuildJob
    pool: Default
```

```
steps:
- task: Maven@3
  inputs:
    mavenPomFile: 'pom.xml'
    mavenOptions: '-Xmx3072m'
    javaHomeOption: 'JDKVersion'
    jdkVersionOption: '1.8'
    jdkArchitectureOption: 'x64'
    sonarQubeRunAnalysis: true
    publishJUnitResults: true
    testResultsFiles: '**/surefire-reports/TEST-*.xml'
    goals: 'package'
- task: CopyFiles@2
  inputs:
    SourceFolder: 'target'
    Contents: '*.war'
    TargetFolder: '$(Build.ArtifactStagingDirectory)'
- task: PublishBuildArtifacts@1
  inputs:
    PathtoPublish: '$(Build.ArtifactStagingDirectory)'
    ArtifactName: 'drop'
    publishLocation: 'Container'
```

Verify the SonarQube portal for the results of SCA. SonarQube reports issues in three categories such as bugs, vulnerabilities, and code smells. Refer to the following the SonarQube portal:

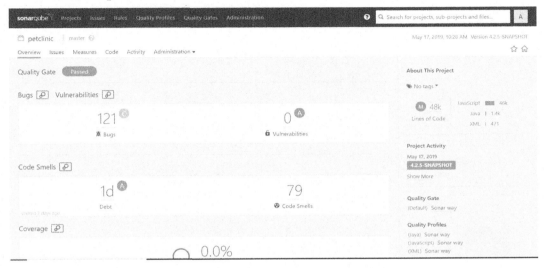

***Figure 8.65:** The SonarQube portal*

How do you fix the issues specified by SonarQube?

1. Fix all at once approach
2. Phase wise fixing issues

Considering the past experience of many projects and interacting with development teams, fixing all issues at once approach does not work effectively as it puts a lot of pressure on the development team.

We would suggest followingthe following approach:

Start from fixing high-priority issues first in each category and then slowly movedown to the hierarchy available in SonarQube. The big bang approach is a direction towards failure in the culture transformation for better code quality.

Refer to the following diagrammatic representation of a strategy to solve SonarQube issues

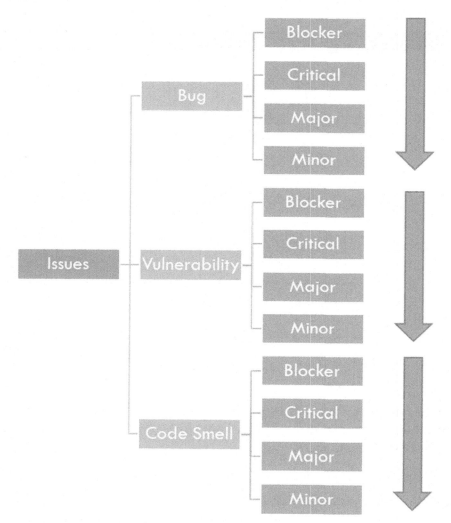

Figure 8.66: Strategy to solve SonarQube issues

Solve all **Blocker** and **Critical** issues first, and then approach the **Major** issues, and then the **Minor** issues, as shown in the following screenshot:

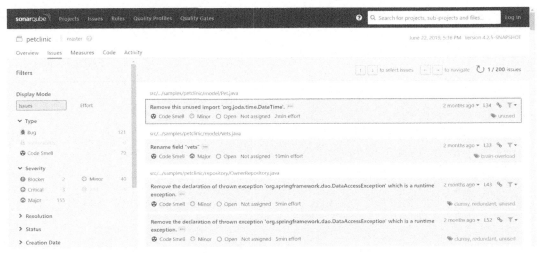

Figure 8.67: Issues in SonarQube

The development team needs to ensure that all issues highlighted by SonarQube are addressed and the culture is setup in the team to avoid those issues from happening itself rather than fixing them.

Over the time, developers identify the mistakes while coding itself and avoid those issues. Quality of code matters a lot and that can make the life of an organization easy in case of external audits from the customer side.

Conclusion

We covered important topics available in Microsoft Azure DevOps – Build (CI). We provided an example of azure-pipelines.yml. The Azure pipeline executes tasks such as compilation of source files, unit test execution and publishing results of unit tests, package (WAR) file creation, **Static Code Analysis (SCA),** and publish artifacts for deployment.

In the next chapter, we will cover deployment of artifacts in Azure App Services.

## CHAPTER 9

Azure DevOps – Continuous Delivery

Continuous Delivery (CD) is an extension or continuation of CI. CD deals with deploying packages into different environments. Multiple environments can be created for different types of testing with the invent of cloud computing. All the environments can be the same, created, and destroyed within a few minutes. The objective of CD is to make the product increment ready to deploy into production with faster time to market and high quality. In addition, it brings the culture of discipline and standardization in the deployment process. Releases in Azure DevOps provide us the facility to deploy artifacts or packages into multiple environments.

Structure

We will cover following topics in this chapter:

- Azure DevOps releases
- Azure Resource Manager Service Connection
- Continuous Delivery - release pipeline

Objective

In this chapter, we will include an overview of release definitions available in Microsoft Azure DevOps.

Azure DevOps releases

Continuous Delivery (CD) is an extension or continuation of **Continuous Integration (CI).** Azure DevOps Release pipelines helps to deliver applications to end users or to non-production environments with proper governances in places such as approval processes and so on. The following diagram displays CD:

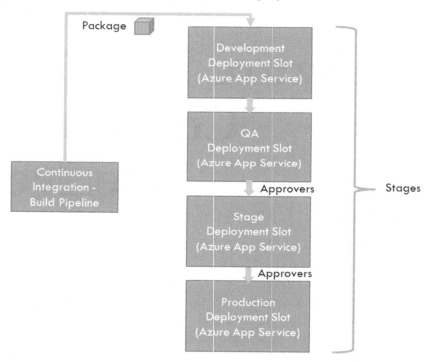

Figure 9.1: Continuous integration and Continuous delivery (CI and CD)

We will perform deployment in multiple environments. In our case, the following environments are available:

- Dev
- QA
- Stage
- Production

In *Chapter 6: Microsoft Azure Cloud,* we used Azure App Services that is PaaS to create different environments.

Azure App Services has a feature called deployment slots that can be utilized to create or clone different environments in a cost effective manner if they share the App Service Plan.

To make an application accessible in different environments or to production environments, we will try to deploy a WAR file into Azure App Service or deployment slots that we created earlier.

Go to the Azure DevOps portal and click on **Releases** to check whether any existing release pipelines are available or not. Refer to the following screenshot:

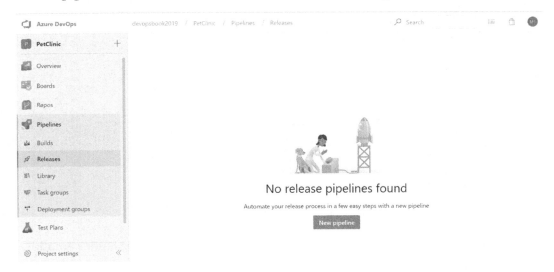

Figure 9.2: Release pipelines in Azure DevOps

Before we a create release pipeline, we need to get access to the Microsoft Azure Servicesby performing the following steps:

1. Go to project.
2. Navigate to **Settings | Service connection**.
3. Add **Azure Resource Manager service connection.**
4. Provide **Connection name** and service **Scope level**.

5. Select **Subscription** if you have multiple subscriptions available and then click on **OK**, as shown in the following screenshot:

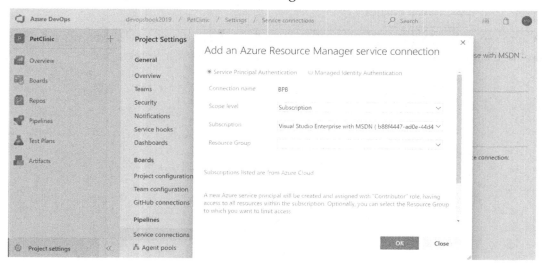

Figure 9.3: *Add Azure Resource Manager service connection*

6. It will open the **Sign in** dialogue box. Provide a valid user name/email ID, as shown in the following screenshot:

Figure 9.4: *Sign in for Azure Resource Manager service connection*

7. Provide a valid password and click on **Sign in**, as shown in the following screenshot:

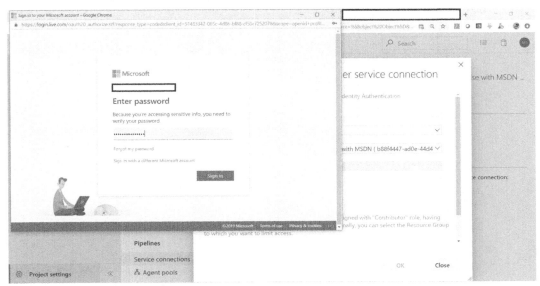

Figure 9.5: *Password for Azure Resource Manager service connection*

8. Verify the newly created service connection in the **Service connections** tab, as shown in the following screenshot:

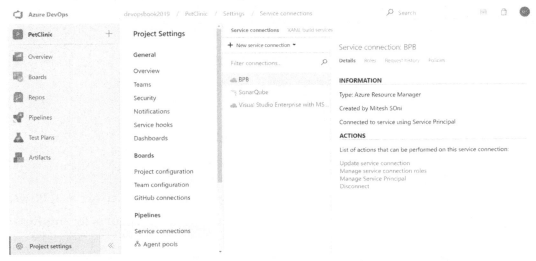

Figure 9.6: *Azure Resource Manager service connection in Azure DevOps portal*

9. Before we get createthe release pipeline and its execution, let us try to understand how the release execution works with the help of the following flow diagram:

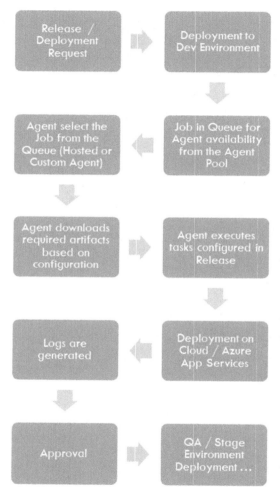

Figure 9.7: *Release execution process*

Let us understand a few concepts related to a release pipeline, which are as follows:

- **Stages:** A stage helps us to organize deployment jobs for multiple environments. A stage consists of tasks.
- **Tasks:** With the use of combination of tasks, we can define or orchestrate automation for a stage.

10. Click on **Releases** in sidebar and Click on **New release pipeline**.

11. In the existing **Stages** section, click on the available stage.

12. Provide a new stage name and click on **Tasks** on the Azure DevOps portal, as shown in the following screenshot:

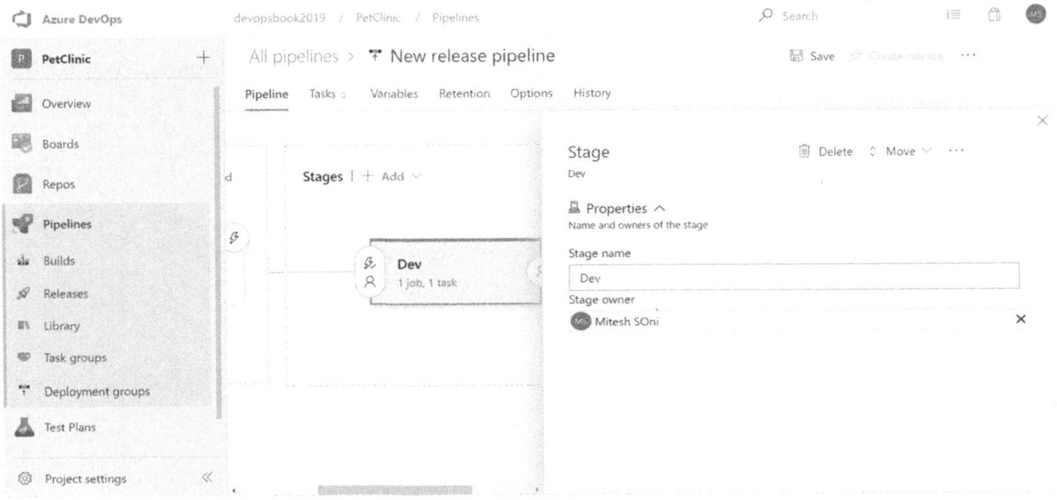

Figure 9.8: Dev Stage in a release pipeline

13. Select the **Azure App Service Deploy** task.

14. Provide a proper **Display name**, select **Connection type** as **Azure Resource Manager**.

15. Select the **Service connection** that we created.

16. Our Azure App Service was **Web App on Linux**. Hence, select that **App Service type**, as shown in the following screenshot:

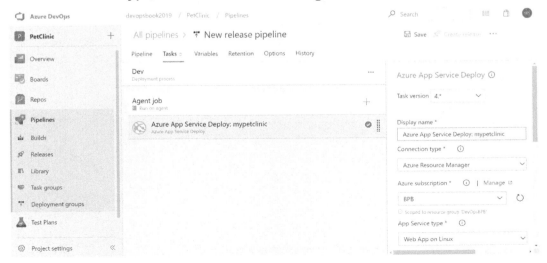

Figure 9.9: Azure App Service Deploy Task

17. We created multiple slots in Azure App Services. Our objective is to deploy on a slot.

18. Select **Deploy to Slot or App Service Environment** checkbox.

19. Select the appropriate **Resource group** and **Slot** name, as shown in the following screenshot:

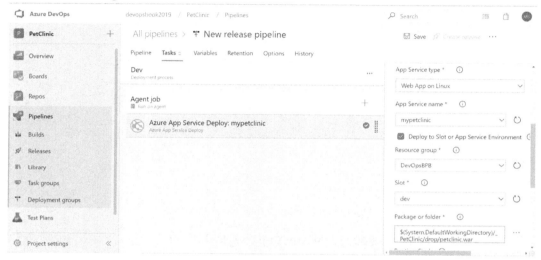

Figure 9.10: Azure App Service Deploy - Deployment slot configuration

20. Before we execute our deployment, let us try to create a new stage. Go to **Add | New stage**, as shown in the following screenshot:

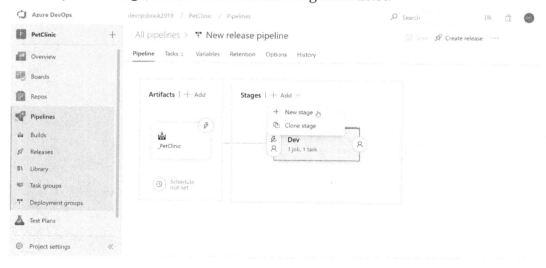

Figure 9.11: Azure DevOps Release - New stage

21. Provide a new stage name.Now, we have the **QA** stage with 1 job but no tasks, as shown in the following screenshot:

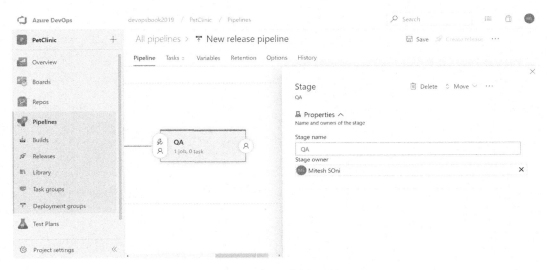

Figure 9.12: QA stage

22. Click on the link available in the **QA** stage. Refer to the following screenshot:

Figure 9.13: Release pipeline with multiple stages

23. Now, click on **Add tasks** in the **Tasks** tab, as shown in the following screenshot:

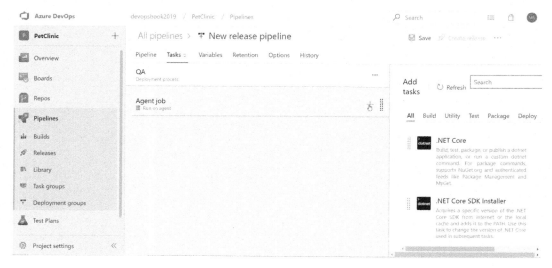

Figure 9.14: QA stage configuration

24. Search for the **Azure App Service Deploy** task in the search box.

25. Select it and click on **Add**, as shown in the following screenshot:

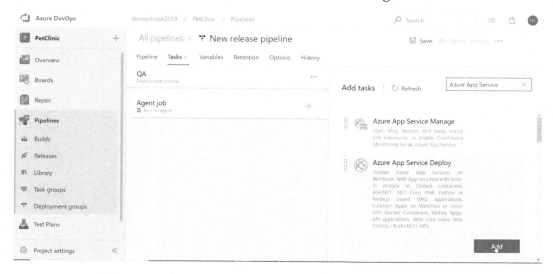

Figure 9.15: Azure App Service Deploy task configuration for the QA stage

26. Then, provide the **Azure subscription** name, as shown in the following screenshot:

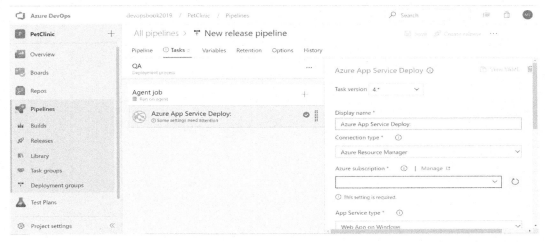

Figure 9.16: *Azure App Service Deploy - Azure subscription*

27. The following **App Service type** are available:

- **Web App on Windows**
- **Web App on Linux**
- **Web App for Containers (Linux)**
- **Function App on Windows**
- **Function App on Linux**
- **Function App for Containers (Linux)**
- **API App**
- **Mobile App**

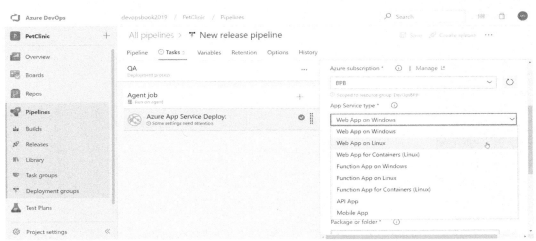

Figure 9.17: *Azure App Service Deploy - App Service Configuration*

28. Select **Deploy to Slot or App Service Environment** checkbox.

29. Select **test** as **slot**, as shown in the following screenshot:

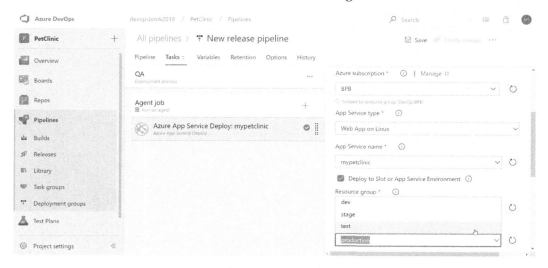

Figure 9.18: Azure App Service Deploy - Deploy to slot for QA stage

Before executing the release pipeline, let us verify the configuration of App Service in Azure App Services.

30. Verify the runtime stack, major and minor version in the Azure App Service configuration to check whether the existing application supports it or not. Refer to the following screenshot:

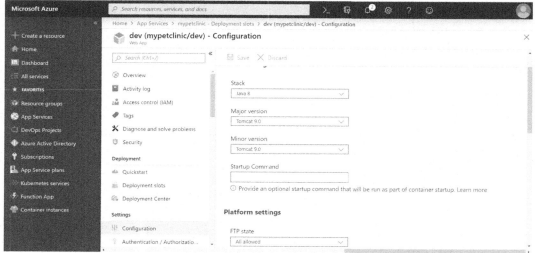

Figure 9.19: Azure App Service - Deployment slot configuration

We are now all set to go for deployment into two different deployment slots. Remember, we have two stages available in our release pipeline.

31. Click on **Create release**, as shown in the following screenshot:

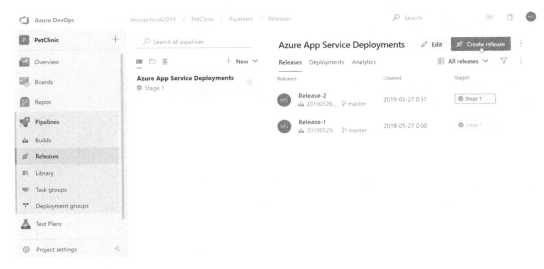

Figure 9.20: Create release

32. Select the number of stages where you want to deploy. Refer to the following screenshot:

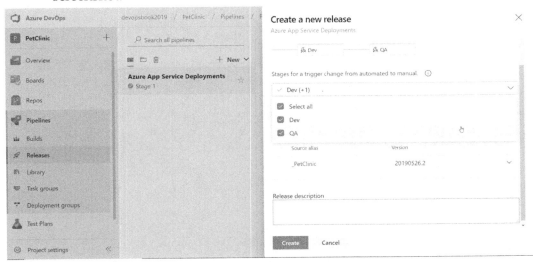

Figure 9.21: Create a new release

An artifact is already available.

33. Provide **Release description** and click on **Create**, as shown in the following screenshot:

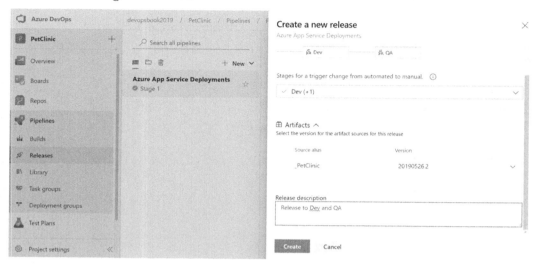

Figure 9.22: *Release description*

34. This will result in a newly created release to be queued for the execution, as shown in the following screenshot:

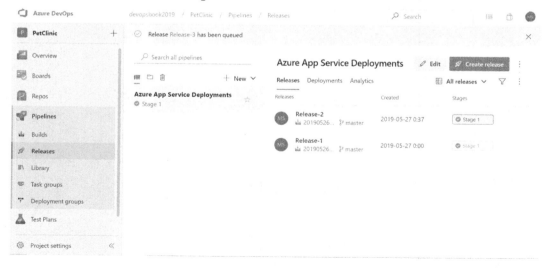

Figure 9.23: *Release queue*

35. Verify the new release with the two stages that we created. Refer to the following screenshot:

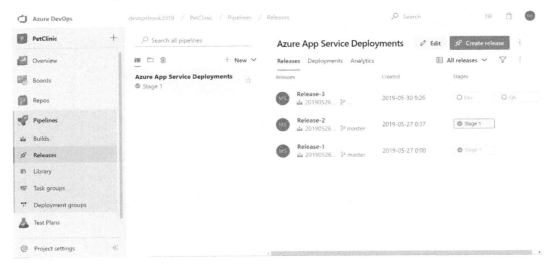

Figure 9.24: *Release history*

36. Click on the new release available in the Azure DevOps portal.

37. Verify the trigger, artifact, and stages in the **Pipeline** section, as shown in the following screenshot:

Figure 9.25: *Azure App Service Deployment Release Pipeline*

38. Click on **Deploy** and select **Deploy multiple**, as shown in the following screenshot:

Figure 9.26: Azure App Service Deployment Release Pipeline - Deploy multiple

39. Select all the stages and provide comments for deployment and click on **Deploy**, as shown in the following screenshot:

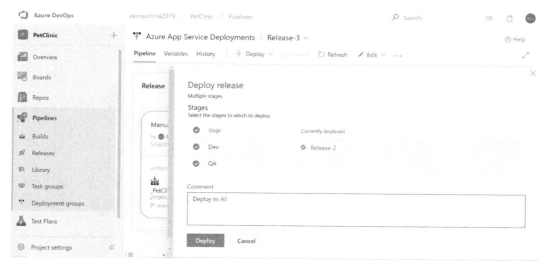

Figure 9.27: Azure App Service Deployment Release Pipeline - Deploy release

40. The deployment to the **Dev** slot will start based on the availability of the agent.

41. Click on the stage progress icon, as shown in the following screenshot:

Figure 9.28: Azure App Service Deployment Release Pipeline - Dev stage

42. Verify the pool and agent utilized for deployment to the **Dev** slot of Microsoft Azure App Services using the **Dev** stage created in Azure DevOps. Refer to the following screenshot:

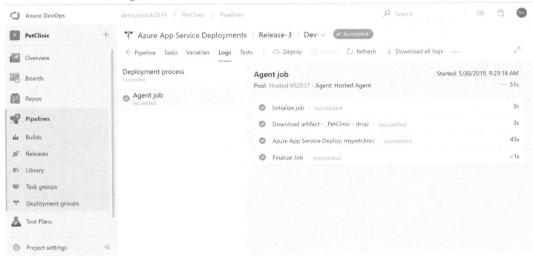

Figure 9.29: Azure App Service Deployment Release Pipeline logs

43. Verify the log of the successful deployment into the **Dev** slot, as shown in the following screenshot:

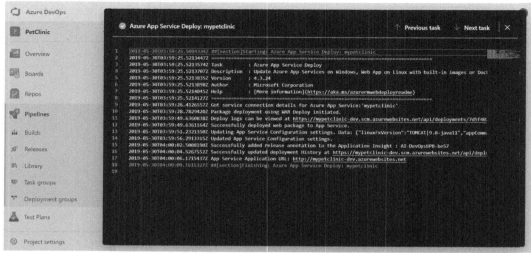

Figure 9.30: Azure App Service Deployment Release Pipeline - Successful

44. The **Dev** stage is in the green state while the **QA** stage started and failed so that is in the red state. Refer to the following screenshot:

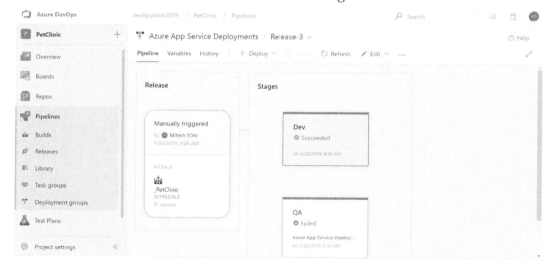

Figure 9.31: Azure App Service Deployment Release Pipeline - failure

45. Click on the **Logs** tab to verify the failed deployment. The error displayed will be **Error is "No package found with the specified pattern"** for deployment.

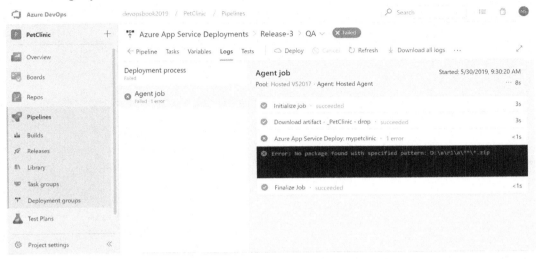

Figure 9.32: No package found with the available pattern for deployment

46. Now, go to the **QA** stage and **Edit**.

47. Click on the **...** icon near the package or folder box. Select the artifact and click on **OK**, as shown in the following screenshot:

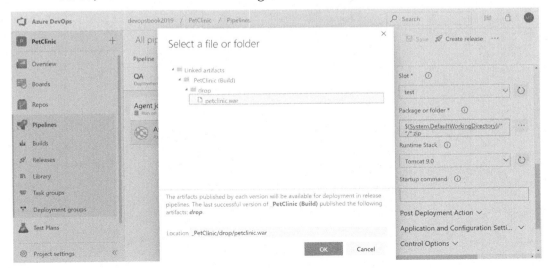

Figure 9.33: Select package

48. Once the changes are done, click on **Save** to release definition, as shown in the following screenshot:

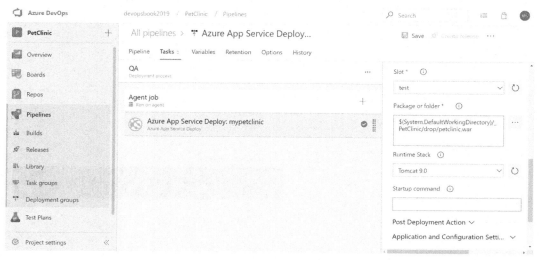

Figure 9.34: QA stage configuration

49. Create a new release for deployment, as shown in the following screenshot:

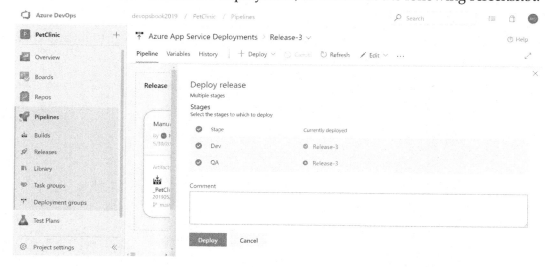

Figure 9.35: Deploy multiple releases

50. Now, you will see that deployment to both the slots are successful, as shown in the following screenshot:

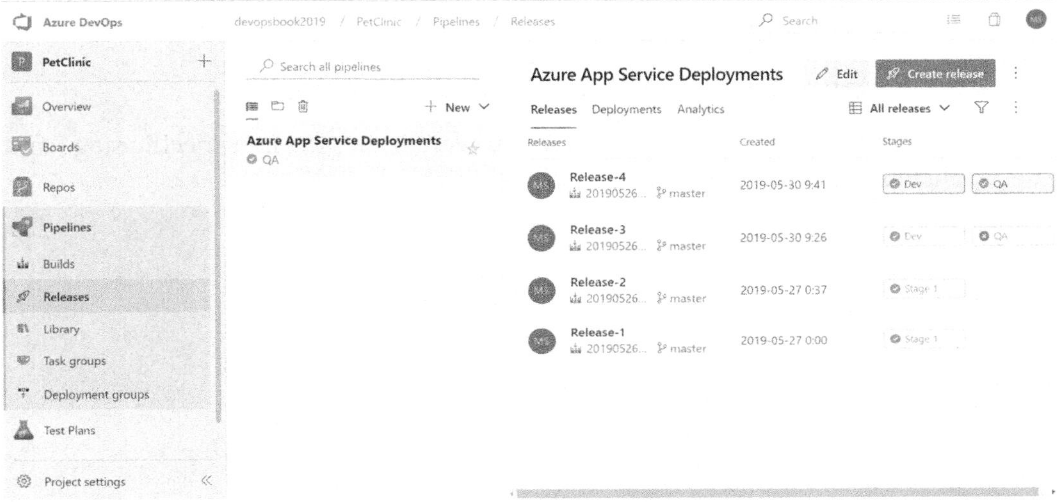

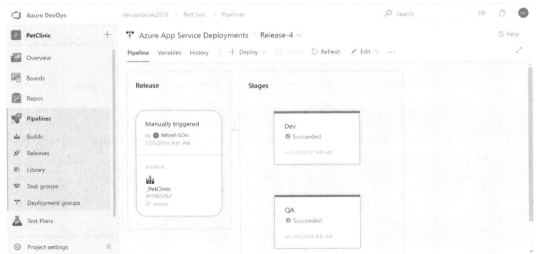

Figure 9.36: Release pipeline results

51. Go to the **Dev** slot URL and check whether the application is deployed successfully or not.

52. Go to the test slot URL and check whether the application is deployed successfully or not.

53. Verify the stage status in the Azure DevOps portal for successful deployment, as shown in the following screenshot:

Figure 9.37: Successful Pipeline execution for release

What if you want to configure the trigger for a stage?

For example, start the **QA** deployment after the **Dev** deployment is completed.

54. Click on the trigger icon before the stage.

55. A `Trigger` screen popsup.Select the `After Stage` option.

56. Select the stage name after which you want to deploy in a specific stage and click on **Save**, as shown in the following screenshot:

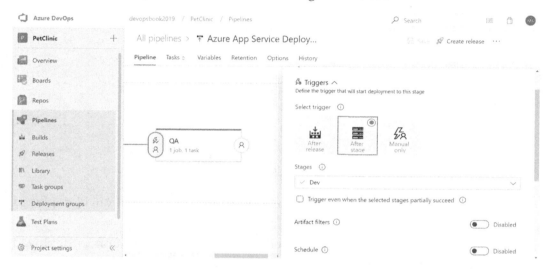

Figure 9.38: Configuration of a trigger

How to configure approvals?

For example, use the pre-deployment approvals. Before deployment takes place, someone should approve this deployment to check whether everything is perfect or not.

57. Click on the approval icon. A `Pre-deployment approvals` screens popsup.

58. Select the `Approver` available in the team.

59. Configure the `Timeout` for the approval from the approver and keep the rest of the default options.

60. Click on **Save**, as shown in the following screenshot:

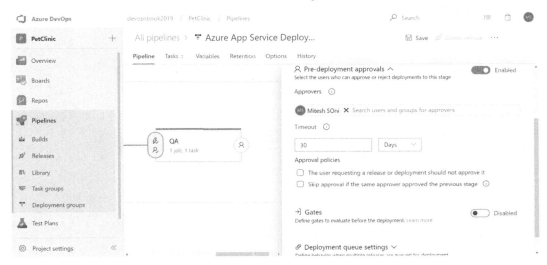

Figure 9.39 Pre-deployment approvals

61. Now, let us configure or create a release.The **Dev** stage will be completed successfully. The **QA** stage will be in the state with **Pending approval.**

62. Click on the **Approve** button, as shown in the following screenshot:

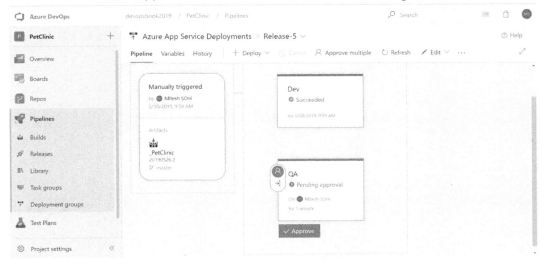

Figure 9.40: Pending pre-deployment approval

63. Add a comment and click on **Approve**, as shown in the following screenshot:

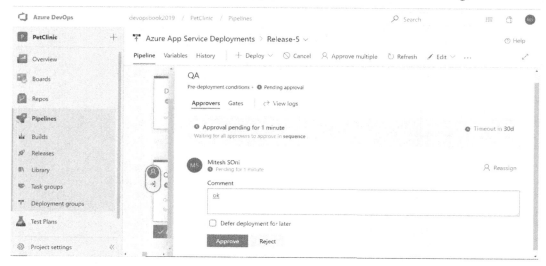

Figure 9.41: Approvals

64. Verify the status of pre-deployment approvals. Refer to the following screenshot:

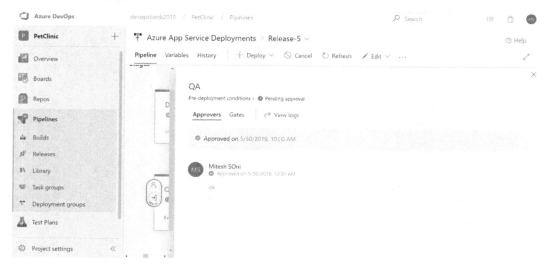

Figure 9.42: Approval status

65. We can also define gates to evaluate before deployment.We can configure delay before evaluation, as shown in the following screenshot:

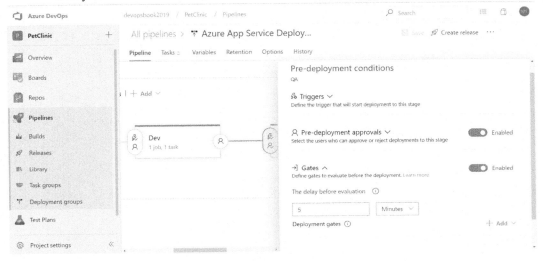

Figure 9.43: Pre-deployment conditions

66. When the release is in progress, deployment will take place after pre-deployment gates. Refer to the following screenshot:

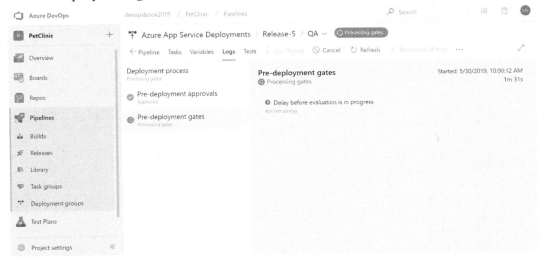

Figure 9.44: Pre-deployment gates

67. Check whether the **QA** stage is completed after pre-deployment approvals and pre-deployment gates. It will look similar to the following screenshot:

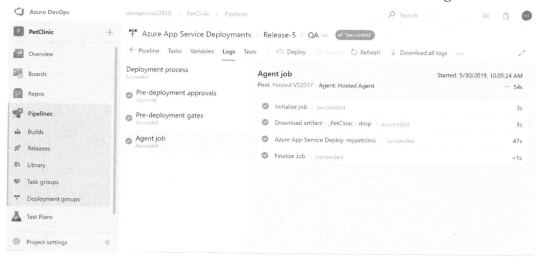

Figure 9.45: *Logs with approvals and gates*

68. Verify the release state, and check whether both the **Dev** and **QA** stages are in the green state, as shown in the following screenshot:

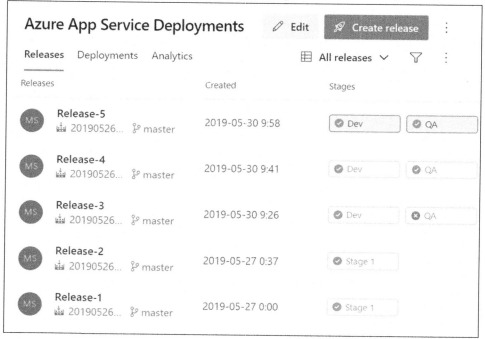

Figure 9.46: *Release history*

69. Many preview features are available. Go to `User | Preview features`, as shown in the following screenshot:

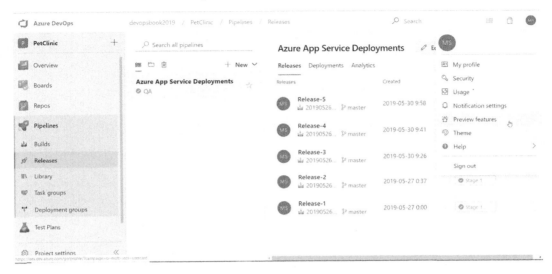

Figure 9.47: *Azure DevOps preview features*

70. Toggle to enable `Multi-stage pipelines`, as shown in the following screenshot:

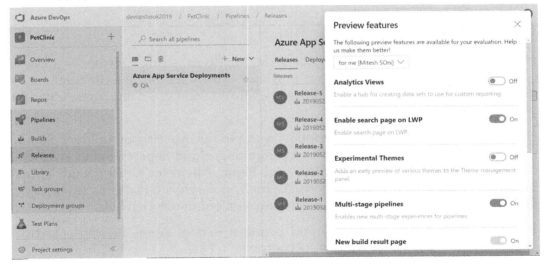

Figure 9.48: *Multi-stage pipeline preview feature*

71. The sidebar options will change. Click on the **Pipelines** option. Now, you can see the visualization of all the stages in one section at a one go. As of now, this feature is in preview. Refer to the following screenshot:

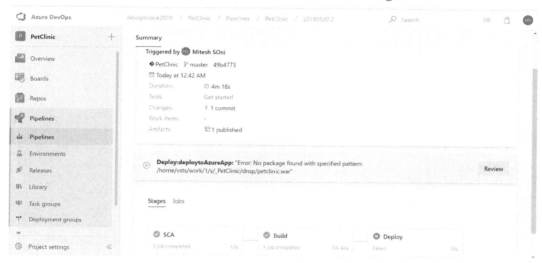

Figure 9.49: Multi-stage pipeline

Thus, we have completed build and release pipelines in the previous and this chapter.

Conclusion

We covered important topics available in Microsoft Azure DevOps – Release (Continuous Delivery). With release pipelines, we configured the different stages for different deployments. We configured approvals and pre-deployment gates for better governance in releases.

Hence, in this book, we covered the following topics: an overview of Agile and Scrum, DevOps with DevOps practices, cloud computing, cloud deployment models, and cloud service models, Azure Boards, Azure Repos, Microsoft Azure Cloud, Virtual Machine – Infrastructure as a Service, Azure App Services – Platform as a Service, Builds – Continuous Integration, and Releases – Continuous Delivery.

We tried to cover the theoretical and practical part of Agile, DevOps practices implementation and cloud computing concepts.

CHAPTER 10

Multi-stage Pipelines in Azure DevOps

In hands-on labs, you will learn how to configure **Continuous Integration (CI)** and **Continuous Delivery (CD)** for your applications using multi-stagepipelines in Azure pipelines. We will use the same Java web application to configure multi-stagepipelines.

Structure

We will cover the following topics in this chapter:

- Multi-stage pipelines
    - o Continuous Integration
        - ▪ Static Code Analysis
        - ▪ Maven package
- Unit test execution
- Code coverage
- Build quality checks on minimum coverage of code
- Package – War file creation
- Publish artifacts
    - o Continuous delivery

- Download artifacts
- Deploy the WAR file to Azure App Service (Platform as a Service)
- Templates

Objective

This chapter includesan overview of the CICD pipeline using the multi-stage pipeline feature that is in preview in Microsoft Azure DevOps.

In this chapter, we will use multi-stage pipelines available in Azure DevOps to implement DevOps practices or Continuous practices such as CI and CD.

Let's enable the multi-stage pipeline preview feature in the Azure DevOps dashboard. Click on the User icon in top right-hand corner, as shown in the following screenshot:

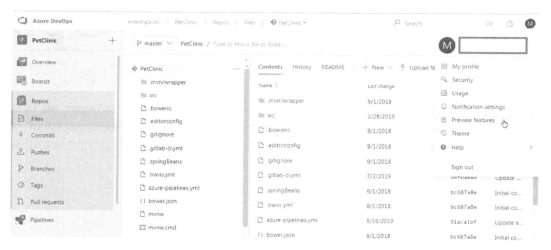

Fig 10.1: *Preview Features in Azure DevOps*

Enable the multi-stage pipelines feature in the pop-up menu, as shown in the following screenshot:

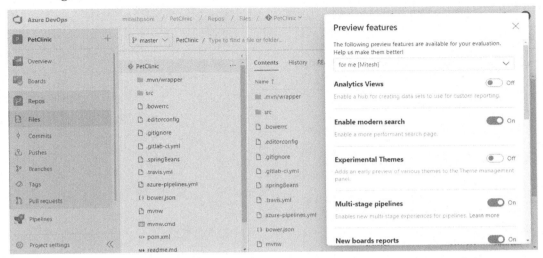

Fig 10.2: Multi-stage pipelines

Create two stages; each one with a Job that prints the statement to see how the multi-stage pipeline looks like:

Fig 10.3: Sample Pipeline to display messages with two stages

The following is the YAML script for printing messages for different Stages and Jobs. We have covered Stages, Jobs, and Tasks concepts in *Chapter 8: Azure DevOps - Continuous Integration* and *Chapter 9: Azure DevOps - Continuous Delivery:*

```yaml
stages:
- stage: Continuous Integration
  jobs:
  - job: CI
    pool:
      vmImage: 'ubuntu-latest'
    steps:
    - task: Bash@3
      inputs:
        targetType: 'inline'
        script: |
          # Write your commands here
          echo 'Configure Static Code Analysis, Unit Tests, Code Coverage,
          Package creation'
- stage: Continuous_Delivery
  jobs:
  - job: CD
    pool:
      vmImage: 'ubuntu-latest'
    steps:
    - task: Bash@3
      inputs:
        targetType: 'inline'
        script: |
          # Write your commands here
          echo 'Download Artifacts, and Deploy it in Azure DevOps'
```

Save the pipeline. Refer to the following screenshot:

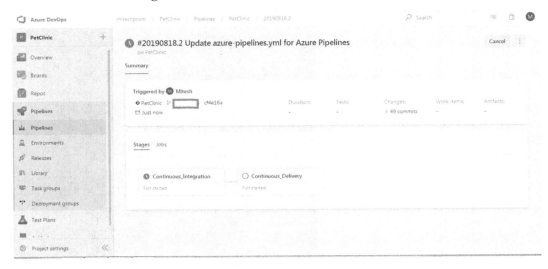

Fig 10.4: Save pipeline

Go to **Pipelines | Pipelines | Run** to execute the pipeline. Click on the latest pipeline in the **Runs** tab. Then, click on the **Continuous Integration** stage, as shown in the following screenshot:

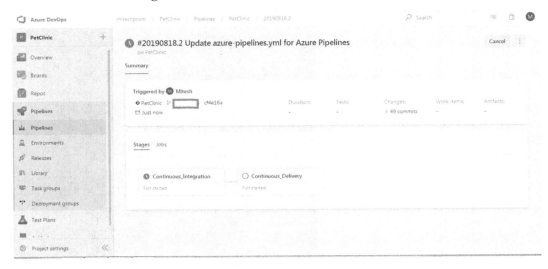

Fig 10.5: Pipeline summary

Verify the message output according to the pipeline. These are logs specific to Stages and Jobs. Tasks logs are in the console directly. Refer to the following screenshot:

Fig 10.6: CI stage logs

Verify the logs for the **Continuous_Delivery** stage, as shown in the following screenshot:

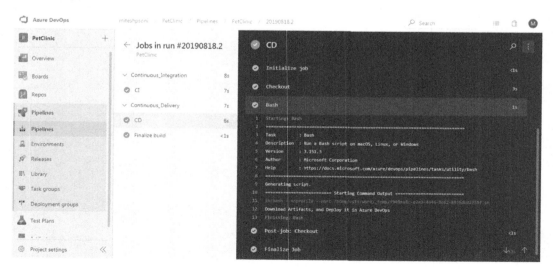

Fig 10.7: CD stage logs

Let's configure automation of different practices in a step-by-step manner. Register on **https://sonarcloud.io** to create a token. Install the **SonarCloud** extension from the marketplace.

Go to **Project settings | Service connections | New service connection | SonarCloud**. Provide **Connection name** and **SonarCloud Token**. Click on **Verify connection** to verify the authenticity, as shown in the following screenshot:

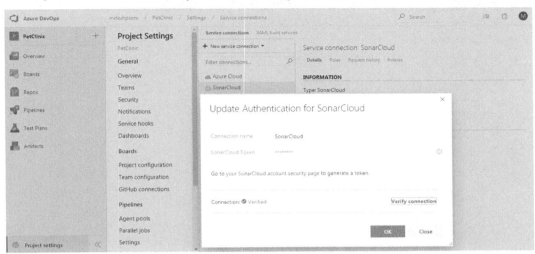

Fig 10.8: SonarCloud service connection

Create a new organization.Click on the plus sign and select **Create new organization**. Click on **Create manually**. You will get the following screen:

Fig 10.9: Create organization

Provide the name of an organization. Click on **Continue**, as shown in the following screenshot:

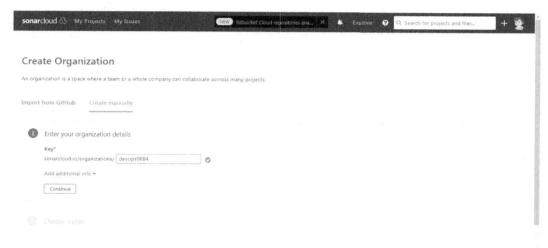

Fig 10.10: Create an organization manually

Select a plan and click on **Create Organization**, as shown in the following screenshot:

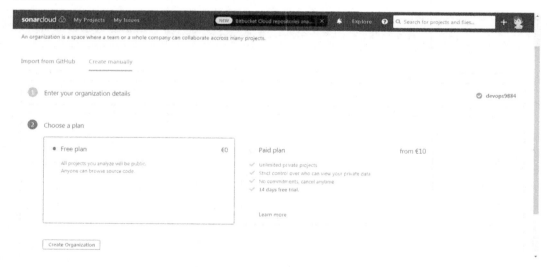

Fig 10.11: Choose a plan in SonarCloud

Observe the organization dashboard in SonarCloud. It will look similar to the following screenshot:

Fig 10.12: Organization dashboard in SonarCloud

Let's configure the SonarCloud task. It is similar to SonarQube tasks we configured in *Chapter 8: Azure DevOps - Continuous Integration*:

Fig 10.13: SonarCloud configuration

Select and configure **Prepare Analysis Configuration**, as shown in the following screenshot:

Fig 10.14: *SonarCloud Prepare Analysis Configuration*

Let's verify the script for SonarCloud:

```
stages:
- stage: Continuous_Integration
  jobs:
  - job: CI
    pool:
      vmImage: 'ubuntu-latest'
    steps:
    - task: Bash@3
      inputs:
        targetType: 'inline'
        script: |
          # Write your commands here
          echo 'Configure Static Code Analysis, Unit Tests, Code Coverage,
Package creation'
    - task: SonarCloudPrepare@1
```

```
    inputs:
      SonarCloud: 'SonarCloud'
      organization: 'devops9884'
      scannerMode: 'Other'
      extraProperties: |
      # Required metadata
            sonar.projectKey=petclinic9883
            sonar.projectName=Simple Java project analyzed with the
SonarQube Runner
            sonar.projectVersion=1.0

            # Comma-separated paths to directories with sources (required)
            sonar.sources=src
            sonar.test.inclusions=**/*Test*/**
            sonar.exclusions=**/*Test*/**
            sonar.java.binaries=.
            # Language
            sonar.language=java

            # Encoding of the source files
            sonar.sourceEncoding=UTF-8


- stage: Continuous_Delivery
  jobs:
  - job: CD
    pool:
      vmImage: 'ubuntu-latest'
    steps:
    - task: Bash@3
      inputs:
```

```
targetType: 'inline'
script: |
# Write your commands here
echo 'Download Artifacts, and Deploy it in Azure DevOps'
```

Edit the pipeline and select the Maven task. Configure the Maven goal and Unit test-related details. Refer to the following screenshot:

Fig 10.15: Maven Task with Goal

Configure **Code Coverage** and **Code Analysis** and then click on the **Add** button, as shown in the following screenshot:

Fig 10.16: Maven task with Code Coverage

Configure the **Publish Quality Gate Result** task, as shown in the following screenshot:

Fig 10.17: SonarCloud-Publish Quality Gate Result

Configure the task for publishing code coverage results, as shown in the following screenshot:

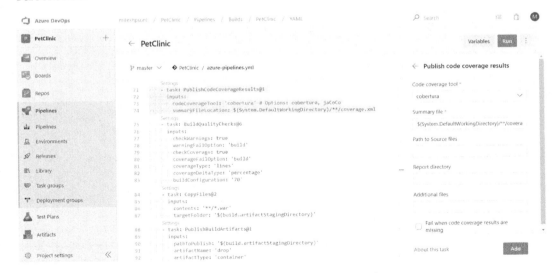

Fig 10.18: Publishingcode coverage results

Install the **Build Quality Checks** extension from the marketplace so that we can keep a check on code coverage based on percentage. Refer to the following screenshot:

Fig 10.19: Build Quality Check plugin

Configure the copy and publish artifacts that arethe WAR file in this case. Refer to the following screenshot:

Fig 10.20: Publish artifacts

Here, we have configured CI for our sample application. The next step is to configure automated deployment.

We are considering that Azure App Service is already available and we can deploy our Microsoft Azure Cloud PaaS application.

Go to **Project settings | Service connections | New service connection | Azure Resource Manager**. Now, provide the subscription ID, name, principle client ID, principle key, and tenant ID based on the Microsoft Azure subscription. Refer to the following screenshot:

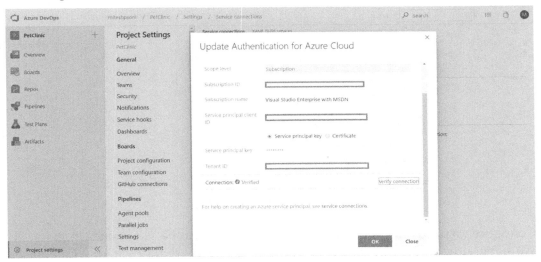

Fig 10.21: Service Connection - Azure Resource Manager

Now, Azure Cloud Service Connection is available for usage. Refer to the following screenshot:

Fig 10.22: Azure Service Connection

Configure the download task to download the latest WAR file, as shown in the following screenshot:

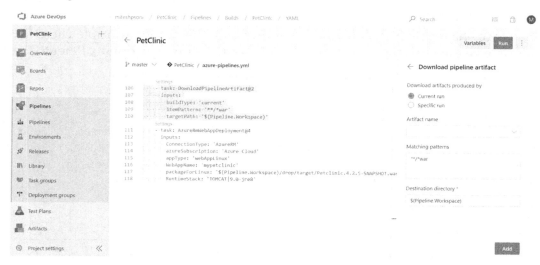

Fig 10.23: Download Pipeline Artifact

Configure Azure App Services using the connection type we created previously. We have already accomplished this in the *Chapter 9: Azure DevOps - Continuous Delivery*:

Fig 10.24: Azure App Service Deploy Task

Let's verify the available YML file after we have done the new configuration:

```
stages:
- stage: Continuous_Integration
  jobs:
  - job: CI
    pool:
      vmImage: 'ubuntu-latest'
    steps:
    - task: Bash@3
      inputs:
        targetType: 'inline'
        script: |
          # Write your commands here
          echo 'Configure Static Code Analysis, Unit Tests, Code Coverage,
Package creation'
      - task: SonarCloudPrepare@1
        inputs:
          SonarCloud: 'SonarCloud'
          organization: devops9883
          scannerMode: 'Other'
          extraProperties: |
            # Required metadata
            sonar.projectKey=petclinic9883
                sonar.projectName='Simple Java project analyzed with the
SonarQube Runner 1'
                sonar.projectVersion=1.0

            # Comma-separated paths to directories with sources (required)
            sonar.sources=src
            sonar.test.inclusions=**/*Test*/**
```

```yaml
        sonar.exclusions=**/*Test*/**
        sonar.java.binaries=.
        # Language
        sonar.language=java


        # Encoding of the source files
        sonar.sourceEncoding=UTF-8
  - task: Maven@3
    inputs:
      mavenPomFile: 'pom.xml'
      mavenOptions: '-Xmx3072m'
      javaHomeOption: 'JDKVersion'
      jdkVersionOption: '1.8'
      jdkArchitectureOption: 'x64'
      publishJUnitResults: true
      sonarQubeRunAnalysis: true
      testResultsFiles: '**/surefire-reports/TEST-*.xml'
      codeCoverageToolOption: cobertura
      goals: 'package'
  - task: SonarCloudPublish@1
    inputs:
      pollingTimeoutSec: '300'


  - task: PublishCodeCoverageResults@1
    inputs:
      codeCoverageTool: 'cobertura' # Options: cobertura, jaCoCo
          summaryFileLocation: $(System.DefaultWorkingDirectory)/**/
coverage.xml
    - task: BuildQualityChecks@6
    inputs:
```

```
        checkWarnings: true
        warningFailOption: 'build'
        checkCoverage: true
        coverageFailOption: 'build'
        coverageType: 'lines'
        coverageDeltaType: 'percentage'
        buildConfiguration: '70'
    - task: CopyFiles@2
      inputs:
        contents: '**/*.war'
        targetFolder: '$(build.artifactStagingDirectory)'
    - task: PublishBuildArtifacts@1
      inputs:
        pathToPublish: '$(build.artifactStagingDirectory)'
        artifactName: 'drop'
        artifactType: 'container'


- stage: Continuous_Delivery
  jobs:
  - job: CD
    pool:
      vmImage: 'ubuntu-latest'
    steps:
    - task: Bash@3
      inputs:
        targetType: 'inline'
        script: |
          # Write your commands here
          echo 'Hello world'
```

```
  - task: DownloadPipelineArtifact@2
    inputs:
      buildType: 'current'
      itemPattern: '**/*war'
      targetPath: '$(Pipeline.Workspace)'
  - task: AzureRmWebAppDeployment@4
    inputs:
      ConnectionType: 'AzureRM'
      azureSubscription: 'Azure Cloud'
      appType: 'webAppLinux'
      WebAppName: 'mypetclinic'
    packageForLinux: '$(Pipeline.Workspace)/drop/target/Petclinic.4.2.5-
SNAPSHOT.war'
      RuntimeStack: 'TOMCAT|9.0-jre8'
```

Go to the **Pipelines** section and click on the **PetClinic** pipeline. Refer to the following screenshot:

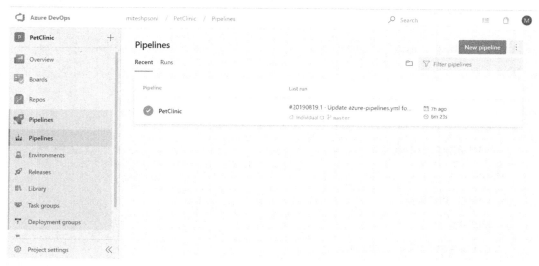

Fig 10.25: *Azure DevOps Pipelines*

Verify the earlier **Runs** and click on the **Run pipeline** button, which is in the right-hand side corner of the screen. Refer to the following screenshot:

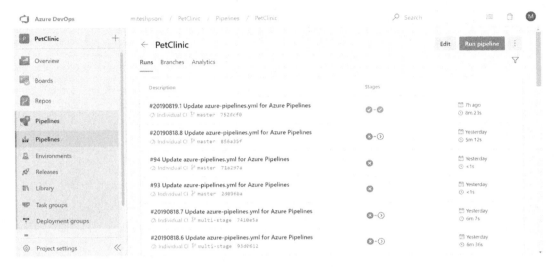

Fig 10.26: *Pipeline Runs*

Select a **Branch/tag** and click on **Run** as shown in the following screenshot:

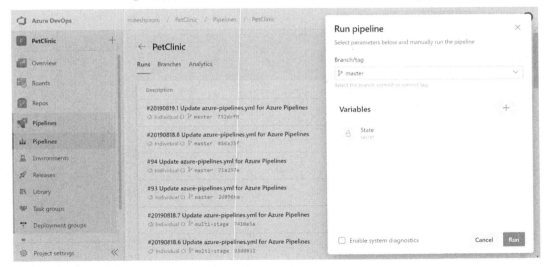

Fig 10.27: *Run Pipeline*

Verify the pipeline **Summary** and click on the **Continuous Integration** stage, as shown in the following screenshot:

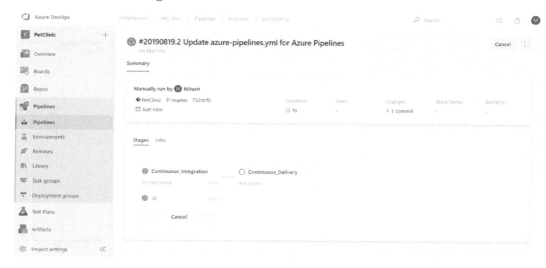

Fig 10.28: Pipeline Summary

Verify the logs in CI Job, as shown in the following screenshot:

Fig 10.29: CI Logs

All the tasks available in the CI stage are successful. Refer to the following screenshot:

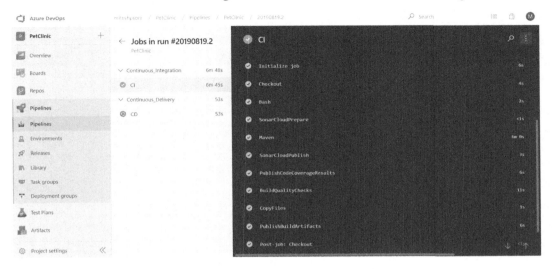

Fig 10.30: *Tasks in Continuous Integration Stage*

Verify logs in the CD stage. Refer to the following screenshot:

Fig 10.31: *Deployment to Azure App Service*

Go to the **Summary** page to verify the execution of the Azure DevOps pipeline, as shown in the following screenshot:

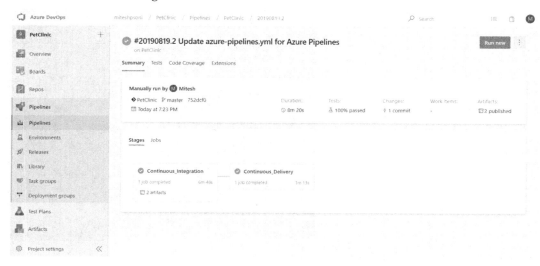

Fig 10.32: Summary page of the Azure DevOps Pipeline

The **Tests** tab contains results of Unit test execution. Refer to the following screenshot:

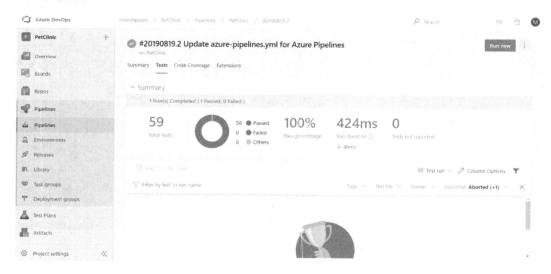

Fig 10.33: Unit Test Results

The **Code Coverage** tab contains results of all code coverage by Unit tests, as shown in the following screenshot:

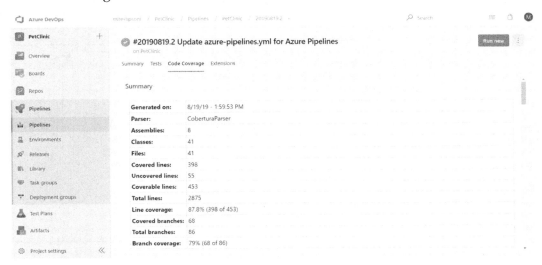

Fig 10.34: *Code Coverage Summary*

Verify the file-specific coverage with the line and branch coverage. Refer to the following screenshot:

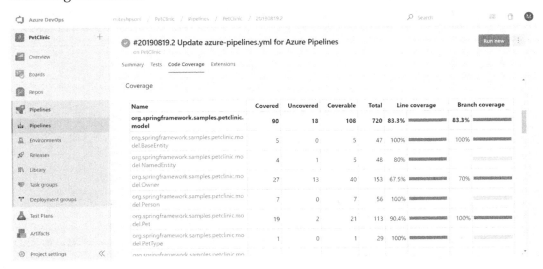

Fig 10.35: *File-specific Code coverage*

The **Extension** tab provides all results related to **SonarCloud** and **Build Quality Checks**. Click on the **Details SonarCloud report>** link, as shown in the following screenshot:

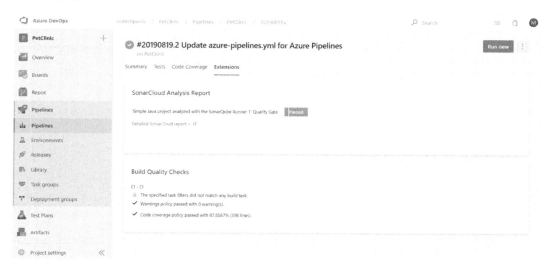

Fig 10.36: Extensions

Verify the SonarCloud report, as shown in the following screenshot:

Fig 10.37: SonarCloud Report

The pipeline has a CI Stage that has created artifacts in the form of coverage files and packages. Click on the artifact link, as shown in the following screenshot:

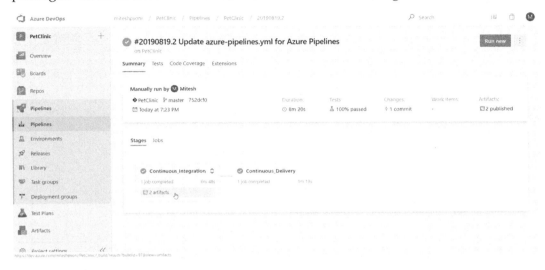

Fig 10.38: Artifacts

Verify the artifacts available for the pipeline. Refer to the following screenshot:

Fig 10.39: Published Artifacts

After the recent execution of the pipeline, verify the **History** or **Runs** tab. Refer to the following screenshot:

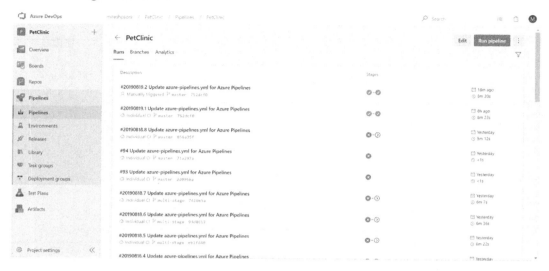

Fig 10.40: Runs tab

Click on the **Branches** tab to get reports of the pipeline execution based on branches, as shown in the following screenshot:

Fig 10.41: Pipeline results as per Branches

Click on the **Analytics** tab to verify the **Pipeline pass rate, Test pass rate,** and **Pipeline duration** report. Refer to the following screenshot:

Fig 10.42 Pipeline Analytics

Click on the pipeline failure chart to get more insights. Refer to the following screenshot:

Fig 10.43: Pipeline failure report

Now, what if you want to reuse a section or Job in multiple pipelines?

Yes, you can do it using the Templates feature. Let's see the Template usage in the next section.

Templates

You can utilize Template to reuse the YAML blocks of Jobs or Steps. Parameterized Templates are helpful to create flexible templates. It is a good practice to keep a repository of Templates and use them across other repos. Let's understand how to configure a template in Azure repos.

Create another repository for Templates in Azure DevOps. Let's create an YML file that we can use in another project and shift the entire CI Job of the earlier pipeline to this template. Refer to the following screenshot:

Fig 10.44: Template Repository

Add parameters so that we can use customizable templates as well. Refer to the following code snippet:

```
# Maven
# Build your Java project and run tests with Apache Maven.
# Add steps that analyze code, save build artifacts, deploy, and more:
# https://docs.microsoft.com/azure/devops/pipelines/languages/java
parameters:
  vmImage: 'ubuntu 16.04'
  organization: ''
  sonarProjectKey: ''
  sonarProjectName: ''
jobs:
```

```yaml
- job: CI
  pool:
    vmImage: ${{ parameters.vmImage }}
  steps:
  - task: SonarCloudPrepare@1
    inputs:
      SonarCloud: 'SonarCloud'
      organization: ${{ parameters.organization }}
      scannerMode: 'Other'
      extraProperties: |
        # Required metadata
        sonar.projectKey=${{ parameters.sonarProjectKey }}
        sonar.projectName=${{ parameters.sonarProjectName }}
        sonar.projectVersion=1.0

        # Comma-separated paths to directories with sources (required)
        sonar.sources=src
        sonar.test.inclusions=**/*Test*/**
        sonar.exclusions=**/*Test*/**
        sonar.java.binaries=.
        # Language
        sonar.language=java

        # Encoding of the source files
        sonar.sourceEncoding=UTF-8
  - task: Maven@3
    inputs:
      mavenPomFile: 'pom.xml'
      mavenOptions: '-Xmx3072m'
      javaHomeOption: 'JDKVersion'
      jdkVersionOption: '1.8'
      jdkArchitectureOption: 'x64'
      publishJUnitResults: true
```

```yaml
      sonarQubeRunAnalysis: true
      testResultsFiles: '**/surefire-reports/TEST-*.xml'
      codeCoverageToolOption: cobertura
      goals: 'package'
  - task: SonarCloudPublish@1
    inputs:
      pollingTimeoutSec: '300'

  - task: PublishCodeCoverageResults@1
    inputs:
      codeCoverageTool: 'cobertura' # Options: cobertura, jaCoCo
      summaryFileLocation: $(System.DefaultWorkingDirectory)/**/coverage.
xml
  - task: BuildQualityChecks@6
    inputs:
      checkWarnings: true
      warningFailOption: 'build'
      checkCoverage: true
      coverageFailOption: 'build'
      coverageType: 'lines'
      coverageDeltaType: 'percentage'
      buildConfiguration: '70'
  - task: CopyFiles@2
    inputs:
      contents: '**/*.war'
      targetFolder: '$(build.artifactStagingDirectory)'
  - task: PublishBuildArtifacts@1
    inputs:
      pathToPublish: '$(build.artifactStagingDirectory)'
      artifactName: 'drop'
      artifactType: 'container'
```

Go to our project's YML file and provide the reference to the YML file that we created in the Template Repository and provide the resources block for reference. Also, provide the Template name in the Job section along with parameters. Following is the script that uses template created earlier to perform Job with different tasks:

```
# File: azure-pipelines.yml

resources:

  repositories:

    - repository: Template

      type: git

      name: Template/Template

stages:

- stage: Continuous_Integration

#  condition: and(succeeded(), eq(variables['State'], 'Production'))

  jobs:

  - template: java-maven-CI.yml@Template  # Template reference

    parameters:

      vmImage: 'ubuntu-latest'

      organization: 'devops9883'

      sonarProjectKey: 'petclinic9883'

      sonarProjectName: 'Simple Java project analyzed with the SonarQube
Runner 1'

- stage: Continuous_Delivery

  jobs:

  - job: CD

    pool:

      vmImage: 'ubuntu-latest'

    steps:

    - task: Bash@3

      inputs:

        targetType: 'inline'

        script: |

          # Write your commands here
```

```
      echo 'Hello world'
- task: DownloadPipelineArtifact@2
  inputs:
    buildType: 'current'
    itemPattern: '**/*war'
    targetPath: '$(Pipeline.Workspace)'
- task: AzureRmWebAppDeployment@4
  inputs:
    ConnectionType: 'AzureRM'
    azureSubscription: 'Azure Cloud'
    appType: 'webAppLinux'
    WebAppName: 'mypetclinic'
  packageForLinux: '$(Pipeline.Workspace)/drop/target/Petclinic.4.2.5-
SNAPSHOT.war'
    RuntimeStack: 'TOMCAT|9.0-jre8'
```

It's done and now, we can use the same template in multiple projects. It will give a centralized control and utilize the same script in multiple projects.

For more details on Templates, visit **https://docs.microsoft.com/en-us/azure/devops/ pipelines/process/templates?view=azure-devops# using-other-repositories.**

Conclusion

We covered one of the important topics available in Microsoft Azure DevOps – multi-stage pipelines and Templates. We configured SonarCloud for Static Code Analysis, Code Coverage using Cobertura, Build Quality Checks using the Marketplace extension and deployment to Azure App Services using multi-stage pipelines.

Index